The 4A's of Marketing

In this book, the authors present a powerful and tested approach that helps managers see a business's every action through the eyes of its customers. This approach is organized around the values that matter most to customers: Acceptability, Affordability, Accessibility, and Awareness. Taken together, these attributes are called the "4A's." The 4A framework derives from a customer-value perspective based on the four distinct roles that customers play in the market: seekers, buyers, payers, and users. For a marketing campaign to succeed, it must achieve high marks on all four A's, using a blend of marketing and non-marketing resources.

Jagdish N. Sheth is a Charles H. Kellstadt Professor of Marketing at Emory University.

Rajendra S. Sisodia is Professor of Marketing at Bentley University and cofounder and Chairman of the Conscious Capitalism Institute.

"The 4P's can thankfully be retired as the 4A's provide a much superior roadmap to delivering great offerings and marketing programs and a framework that will help screen out both strategic and tactical disasters."

David A. Aaker
E.T. Grether Professor Emeritus of Marketing and Public Policy, UC Berkeley
Vice-Chairman, Prophet

"This is a splendid book for the neophyte and accomplished manager alike. Sheth and Sisodia combine razor-sharp analyses with useful action plans and in the process teach us how to think better about market opportunities and how to apply the 4As framework to advantage. A model of exposition, this book brings to life principles and policy guidelines with new diagnoses of both market successes, from the Aflac Duck to buying shoes on the web with Zappos, and market failures, from Apple's, yes Apple's, Newton to Ford's Edsel. The focus is on learning how to be a better analyst, manager, innovation implementer, and sustainer. Meticulously argued and illustrated, this book will make the reader better able to succeed in the knowledge economy and beyond. Two thumbs up!"

Richard P. Bagozzi
Dwight F. Benton Professor of Behavioral Science in Management
Stephen M. Ross School of Business, University of Michigan

"Move over marketing mix. The 4A framework wins on every dimension that matters. It is dynamic rather than static, active rather than passive, and requires decision makers to look at marketing activities and investments from the outside in, by putting the customer value proposition at the center of the strategy dialogue. Best of all, it engages the entire organization in key marketing decisions."

George Day
Geoffrey T. Boisi Professor of Marketing
The Wharton School, University of Pennsylvania

"A 'must-read' for any business that wants to be customer-oriented! It offers a simple and powerful way for businesses to keep from falling prey to navel gazing."

Ajay Kohli
Gary T. and Elizabeth R. Jones Professor of Marketing, Georgia Tech
Editor, *Journal of Marketing*

"As a long time practitioner of the 4P's seller-oriented toolbox of marketing, I welcome the more customer-oriented 4A's toolbox to be employed before undertaking to set the 4Ps. Sheth and Sisodia are to be complimented for their insightful development, application, and illustration of 4A thinking. I believe that the 4A's will rank as an important contribution to marketing theory and practice."

Philip Kotler
S.C. Johnson & Son Distinguished Professor of International Marketing
Kellogg School of Management, Northwestern University

"*The 4A's of Marketing* represents a long overdue, truly novel framework for thinking about marketing decision-making. Despite decades of exhortations that companies adopt a more customer-centric stance, the decidedly company-centric 4P's paradigm has endured. In *The 4A's of Marketing*, Professors Sheth and Sisodia creatively convert the 4P's to the desired customer perspective. Think benefits rather than features: Price becomes Affordability; Place becomes Accessibility; and so forth. The shift in perspective is deceptively simple but profound in its implications for how marketers anticipate the impact of their decisions on the consumer. *The 4A's of Marketing* offers a game-changing perspective for the any manager or organization striving to become market-driven and customer-centric."

Richard J. Lutz
JC Penney Professor of Marketing
University of Florida

"Jagdish Sheth and Rajendra Sisodia have teamed up to develop a powerful treatment of customer-centric marketing. Built around the notion that the customer is the dominant actor in most markets, *The 4A's of Marketing* identifies four roles of customers to which marketers must respond if they are to be successful. Written in an engaging and highly accessible style, this book is filled with real world examples that illustrate the concepts and ideas it offers. It is 'must' reading for every marketer and contains especially sage advice for marketers who want to return the marketing function to a central role in the strategic planning of firms."

David W. Stewart
Professor of Marketing and former Dean, University of California, Riverside
Past Editor, *Journal of Marketing* and *Journal of the Academy of Marketing Science*

The 4A's of Marketing

Creating Value for Customers, Companies and Society

Jagdish N. Sheth, Emory University

Rajendra S. Sisodia, Bentley University

Routledge
Taylor & Francis Group

NEW YORK AND LONDON

First published 2012
by Routledge
711 Third Avenue, New York, NY 10017
Simultaneously published in the UK
by Routledge
2 Park Square, Milton Park, Abingdon, Oxon OX14 4RN

Routledge is an imprint of the Taylor & Francis Group, an informa business

Library of Congress Cataloging in Publication Data
Sheth, Jagdish N.
The 4A's of marketing: creating value for customer, company and society/Jagdish Sheth, Rajendra Sisodia.
    p. cm.
Includes index.
1. Relationship marketing. 2. Customer relations—Management.
3. Marketing. I. Sisodia, Rajendra. II. Title. III. Title: Four A's of marketing.
HF5415.55.S54 2011
658.8—dc23   2011022801

ISBN: 978-0-415-89835-5

Typeset in Berling Roman and Futura by
Book Now Ltd, London

Printed and bound   Nutech Photolithographers

Dedication

We dedicate this book to Philip Kotler, who has been a towering figure in the world of marketing for more than five decades. Phil's pioneering work on the marketing concept laid the foundations of the marketing discipline and brought it worldwide relevance and respectability. Millions of marketing practitioners and scholars were first exposed to the field through Phil's *Marketing Management* textbook, a magisterial and encyclopedic work from its inception in 1967 to the present day. Phil continues to explore and expand the frontiers of marketing thinking. We are deeply grateful for his guidance and friendship, which has been a constant in our lives for decades.

Contents

Contents

Notes on the Authors

Jagdish N. Sheth is the Charles H. Kellstadt Professor of Marketing at Emory University. He has been an educator, thought leader and advisor to governments and industries for more than forty years. He has published more than thirty books and over 200 academic papers in all top marketing journals. His book, *The Theory of Buyer Behavior* (with John A. Howard) published in 1969 is a classic in marketing.

Dr. Rajendra S. Sisodia is Professor of Marketing at Bentley University and cofounder and Chairman of the Conscious Capitalism Institute. He has published seven books and over 100 academic articles and writes frequently for the *Wall Street Journal*. His work has been featured in *The New York Times, Fortune, Financial Times, The Washington Post, The Boston Globe*, CNBC, and numerous other media outlets. Previous books include *The Rule of Three, Firms of Endearment, Tectonic Shift*, and *Does Marketing Need Reform?*

Acknowledgements

We gratefully acknowledge the work of hundreds of our students at Emory University, George Mason University and Bentley University over the past 15 years. They have helped us to think more deeply about this framework and develop it further. They have also helped us greatly through their case studies of product successes and failures. This book is our gift to them. We would also like to acknowledge the contributions of The Coca Cola Company, where a precursor to our framework, The 3A's of Marketing, was developed. We were inspired by that framework to develop a richer and more comprehensive version.

Introduction
How to Succeed in Marketing

Among all the business disciplines, marketing routinely experiences and accepts the highest rates of failure. Consider the results of a study conducted by Copernicus Marketing Consulting[1] that paints a grim picture of marketing performance:

- 84 percent of 500 marketing programs studied resulted in declining brand equity and market share.
- Most customer acquisition efforts fail to break even.
- Fewer than 10 percent of new products succeed.
- Most sales promotions are unprofitable.
- Advertising ROI is below 4 percent.

Why do otherwise highly efficient free markets continue to experience high rates of new product failures, despite heavy annual expenditures on market research? Why do so many advertising campaigns flop, even when the managers who stand behind them are talented, experienced, and hard working? Is it because of environmental uncertainty, unpredictable customers, or tough competition? Is it due to poor measurement systems? Or is it because of the way marketing managers plan and implement product launch strategies?

We have found that marketing failures can almost always be attributed to management decisions that reflect a poor understanding of what really drives customers. Marketing failures are often chalked up to fate (reflected in the statement "most new products fail anyway") or poor timing ("the market wasn't ready for this product"). Other convenient fall guys for failure: manufacturing, the advertising agency, and retail partners. While some of these excuses may be valid, more often than not they're simply lame.

Of all the business functions, marketing is subject to the highest degree of uncertainty. Desirable customer behavior cannot be mandated; it can only be hoped for. The link between marketing actions and marketplace effects is often unclear and tenuous. Marketing managers too often operate in the dark, tinkering with marketing tactics and inventing new gimmicks to improve the odds of success. Examples of such gimmicks include "employee pricing for all" and "0 percent financing."

Not surprisingly, CEOs and corporate boards are growing increasingly skeptical of the marketing function's ability to deliver reasonable returns on resources invested. Scholars have suggested that marketing has lost its seat at the table when it comes to making strategic decisions at many companies, because of its failure to perform.[2]

Marketing has failed to deliver because it has become too selling oriented and too obsessed with inventing tactics to get customers to buy. Too many marketers do not clearly understand the factors that fulfill marketing's purpose, which is to acquire and retain satisfied customers at a profit. The principal drivers usually under marketing's control or influence—the product's attributes, price levels, distribution methods, and promotional messages and approaches—do not readily map to performance indicators such as customer satisfaction, loyalty, market share, profit contribution, and growth.

When marketing is done right, customers are happier, the business grows faster, and profits accumulate. To achieve this, *everyone* in the company must stand in the customer's shoes, not just the marketing department. Marketing managers must ensure that the voice of the customer is heard throughout a company's operations. Regardless of who "owns" R&D, logistics, finance, and all the other functions that define an enterprise's activities, marketing must take responsibility for the final outcome as seen by customers. Managers must use marketing's tools—the arts of understanding, informing, influencing, and persuading—to align all aspects of the organization around a set of common customer-centered goals.

A NEW TOOL FOR FOCUSING ON THE CUSTOMER

It's not that most marketers don't want to organize around the customer; it's that they lack a tool that enables them to do so effectively. To understand the *true* causes of marketing success and failure, marketing managers must have a way to see the *effects* of their company's myriad actions on the customer. They must look through the "other end of the lens" to view the marketing effort "coming" rather than "going." From that vantage point, things look very different. The bottlenecks that lead to product underperformance or outright failure often become quite clear—and are not always found at the top of the bottle. Rather, they are spread throughout, especially in areas outside the traditional marketing department's domain. For example, logistics and customer service loom far larger on the radar screens of existing customers than do sales and advertising.

In this book, we present a powerful and tested approach that helps managers see a business's every action through the eyes of its customers. This approach is organized around the values that matter most to customers: Acceptability, Affordability, Accessibility, and Awareness. Taken together, these attributes are called the "4A's." The 4A framework derives from a customer-value perspective based on the four distinct roles that customers play in the market: seekers, buyers, payers, and users.[3] For a marketing campaign to succeed, it must achieve high marks on all four A's, using a blend of marketing and non-marketing resources.

The 4A framework helps companies create value for customers by identifying exactly what they want and need, as well as by uncovering new wants and needs. (For example, none of us knew we "needed" an iPad until Apple created it.) That means not only ensuring that customers are aware of the product, but also ensuring that the product is affordable, accessible, and acceptable to them.

This book is based on over a dozen years of research on hundreds of products and services. We have used the 4A framework to study approximately 400 marketing successes and failures. Products evaluated include such major marketing hits as the Apple iPod, DirecTV, Gatorade, Swatch, Quicken, America Online, Starbucks, Blockbuster, Chrysler Neon, Ford Mustang, Gillette Sensor, and cellular telephony. We've also used the framework to dissect marketing disasters such as APS cameras and film, Crystal Pepsi, Crosspad, Sony's Betamax, the XFL football league, Webvan, and GTE Airfone. Throughout the book, we draw on these and many other cases to illustrate our discussion of the framework and elaborate on the individual elements within it. By analyzing these case histories in detail, we have arrived at many of the book's recommendations.

OUR PURPOSE IN WRITING THIS BOOK

Throughout this book, we will show how looking at the world through the 4A lens helps companies avoid marketing myopia (an excessive focus on the product) as well as managerial myopia (an excessive focus on process). In fact, it is a powerful way to operationalize the marketing concept; it enables managers to look at the world through the customer's eyes. This ability has become an absolute necessity for success in today's hyper-competitive marketplace.

Importantly, the 4A's define the requirements for overall *business* success, not just marketing success. First of all, business success and marketing success cannot occur in isolation from one another. Second, managers must use all of the tools and resources at their disposal—internal as well as external—to enhance each of the A's in the most cost-effective manner possible.

Though the 4A's drive overall business success, the marketing department must take the lead in achieving high levels on each of them. Most companies today understand that a strong customer orientation is a necessary requirement for sustained success. This proposition is widely supported at the board and executive levels, and is even acknowledged by other business functions such as finance and operations. The problem, as we have seen first-hand in many organizations, is that marketing has done a poor job of helping companies *become* truly customer oriented. Our analysis of marketing failures shows that too many marketers are preoccupied with relative trivialities such as cents-off coupons, media impressions, and creative executions. As a result, they have gradually lost credibility and influence within many companies. A major reason for marketing's credibility problem is that marketers have lacked a tool that can help them communicate and spread the gospel of customer orientation throughout the corporation. We believe the 4A framework is the tool that managers have been looking for.

We will show how the 4A framework provides managers with an intuitively appealing yet conceptually rich way to examine and measure the results of their marketing efforts. By monitoring those results along four clearly defined criteria, managers can dynamically reallocate marketing resources to the various action levers at their command, until they achieve the desired results. In some cases, they may quickly discover that the resource implications are so severe that they must consider a drastically different marketing strategy, change their target market, or abandon the project altogether. Either way, the 4A's can help prevent the company from investing resources unwisely.

As the required sophistication level of modern marketing grows, the value of simple, conceptually elegant frameworks also increases. The legendary Supreme Court justice Oliver Wendell Holmes, Jr. once said, "I would not give a fig for the simplicity this side of complexity, but I would give my life for the simplicity on the other side of complexity." The 4A framework provides such simplicity.

Part of the value of any business framework resides in its capacity to be seamlessly transferred from one industry to another, where different types of customers are involved and different market forces are at work. We will demonstrate how the highly versatile 4A tool can be readily applied to any marketing context. It is structured and concise, an easy leap for managers who are already familiar with marketing's popular 4P framework.

What's more, the 4A's (with appropriately modified definitions) can be readily applied to most exchange situations: goods versus services, business-to-business versus consumer. It applies to customer acquisition as well as retention. It is our hope that the 4A framework will also serve an important societal objective, by helping to deliver life-enhancing technologies and services across a much broader spectrum of the world's population. By using the 4A's to identify the bottlenecks and craft creative ways to address them, companies, developmental agencies, and governments can work together to raise the quality of life of millions of people.

HOW THE BOOK IS ORGANIZED

In the book's first chapter, we argue that the traditional approaches to marketing no longer work. We trace the long decline in marketing's productivity and credibility and highlight the forces that are contributing to marketing's problems. We then propose the 4A's as a solution to marketing's malaise, and show how the framework has grown out of two widely accepted business concepts: marketing's widely known 4P's formula and Peter Drucker's Management by Objectives theory. At every step, we draw on real-world case studies of marketing missteps and breakthroughs.

In the second chapter, we present the 4A framework in more detail. We start by discussing the four roles of a customer, and how those roles dovetail nicely with the 4A framework. We then discuss the various ways in which managers can use the framework to create value for companies and customers. We also discuss the composite 4A score (known as Market Value Coverage) and its relationship with the market share that the firm can expect to capture. The chapter also shows how managers can leverage other functional areas within the company, as well as a variety of external resources to achieve the desired impacts at the lowest net cost.

Starting with Chapter 3, we take a deeper look at each of the four elements in turn. Chapter 3 deals with Acceptability, Chapter 4 with Affordability, Chapter 5 with Accessibility, and Chapter 6 with Awareness. In each chapter, we discuss issues relating to the definition, dimensions, and measurement of that particular value driver. We also demonstrate how to create high levels of each value component for new offerings, as well as how to diagnose and correct problems relative to each component for existing offerings.

Chapter 7 focuses on how the framework can be used in day-to-day marketing. We discuss in more detail how the 4A's can be used as a planning tool for new products, diagnosing and troubleshooting existing marketing programs, and evaluating potential partners. We also discuss how companies can lower marketing costs while simultaneously improving market performance. We conclude the book by showing how companies should implement this approach, including what kinds of organizational changes may be warranted.

In Appendix A, we provide guidelines for conducting a 4A audit. This includes a generalized measurement instrument, along with recommendations on how it should be customized for different contexts. The book concludes with Appendix B that contains a number of mini cases of 4A analyses of well-known marketing successes and failures.

It is our hope and expectation that this book will lead to a closer alignment between what businesses do and what customers truly need. By doing so, we will be able to save precious financial resources that can better be invested elsewhere.

We will also reduce the tremendous amount of waste that is generated through poorly focused marketing activities. Ultimately, the widespread adoption of the 4A framework will result, we believe, in a better quality of life for customers, more satisfied and fulfilled employees, healthier and more profitable corporations, and more thriving societies worldwide.

Chapter 1

Marketing Remix
Introducing the 4A's

WHY MARKETING NEEDS A MAKEOVER

Seeing a growing need for convenience, Kellogg launched Breakfast Mates, a product that combined cereal, milk, a bowl, and a spoon in one package, in August 1998. Breakfast Mates was originally targeted at working parents with small children. It was positioned as a product that children could use themselves without parental help, and something that parents themselves could take from the fridge and eat on the go. However, the packaging was too difficult for children to open by themselves. The product had many parts and required considerable effort to eat; you had to open the package, open the cereal, open the milk, pour the cereal in, and then sit down and eat it with a spoon. While promising greater convenience, the product was anything but convenient, especially compared to the portable breakfast bars that could be eaten with one hand on the road. Psychologically, the product's high level of packaging was unacceptable to consumers concerned about the packaging's impact on the environment. Americans believed that vacuum sealed milk was artificial and not nutritious, and most found the taste of warm milk disgusting. In response, Kellogg started selling the product in the refrigerator section, which caused the cereal to be cold. So customers had two unappetizing choices: warm milk and warm cereal or cold cereal and cold milk. Kellogg only offered four cereal options and customers could not choose the type of milk to be included in the package (e.g. 1 percent, 2 percent or skim). The product achieved a low level of Accessibility, since it was found in the refrigerated section, which is not where most customers look for breakfast options. In terms of Affordability, the cost per serving for 4 ounces of cereal and 4 ounces of milk was $1.39 with the Breakfast Mate and only $0.21 out of a regular box of cereal. Not surprisingly, Breakfast Mates was a big failure. One year and $30 million later, Kellogg discontinued the offering.[1]

After its initial release in 1954, the Ford Thunderbird quickly became an icon: the epitome of a classic American automobile. Ford discontinued the line in the

1990s, but decided to bring it back in 2001 as a retro vehicle that harkened back to the T-Bird's 1950s and 1960s glory days. The car's launch was highly anticipated by customers as well as the automotive press. However, Ford sold only 19,000 T-Birds in the first year, well below its sales target, and sales declined rapidly after that. The reasons for the Thunderbird's failure become clear when looked at through the 4A lens. While Ford was very successful in drumming up hype around the car, it failed to deliver in terms of the vehicle's design and function, availability and price. The re-launch was described as "one of the most hyped rollouts in history," with two years of appearances in auto shows, on magazine covers, and in TV shows. Initial demand was very high, but Ford ran into production issues and delayed shipments to dealerships, frustrating potential customers. Because of the shortage of cars, initial customers paid $8,000 to $10,000 above its $35,495 base MSRP. At nearly $50,000, the car was competing with luxury models from Mercedes, BMW, and Audi. Initially, the Thunderbird enjoyed a high level of psychological acceptability. Ford went to great lengths to ensure the new T-Bird was true to the spirit of its famous predecessors, even studying recordings of the 1957 Thunderbird to ensure the new exhaust growl produced the same roar. The *Wall Street Journal* reported that the car literally "stopped traffic" during a road test. Functional acceptability soon emerged as a fail point, eventually taking psychological acceptability down with it. The car used molded plastic-chrome, and its grille, wheels, instrument panel, interior trim, and switches all looked and felt cheap. Approximately 65 percent of the car's parts, including body structure, transmission, instrument panel, seats, and even keys were borrowed from other cheaper Ford vehicles such as the Taurus. The T-Bird was ultimately psychologically and functionally unacceptable because it was a contradiction in terms: a "luxury" car constructed of common parts; an expensive car, but still a Ford; a sports car not strong or sporty enough to fit that bill, but not practical enough to serve as anything else. As production picked up and quality problems started to surface, the car went from commanding a $10,000 premium to being sold for $10,000 below sticker price. The car was discontinued in 2005.[2]

"Marketing as usual" simply doesn't work anymore. Fundamentally new thinking is needed to revive and rejuvenate this vital business function and to overcome growing skepticism and distrust among its stakeholders within and outside the company. Marketing executives need a new way of looking at the world because of two interrelated reasons: poor marketing productivity and the marginalization of the marketing function within the organization.

Marketing's Productivity Crisis

Marketing budgets have been rising steadily over the past several decades, as companies in many industries have stepped up their marketing spending in order to survive in increasingly competitive markets where customers have a wealth of choices. The proportion of corporate spending attributable to marketing activities has grown from approximately 25 percent in 1950 to approximately 50 percent in 2006. Spending on manufacturing/operations has declined from approximately 50 percent to approximately 25 percent, while spending on management went through a period of increase in the 1960s and 1970s before declining again back to approximately 25 percent.[3] The increased spending on marketing did not result in higher levels of performance. In fact, a study of Fortune 1000 firms found that companies that increased their marketing spending the most over a 20-year period (1985–2004) grew at a lower rate than those that increased their spending the least.[4] The explanation for these rather stunning results is that marketing spending is often aimed at trying to make up for fundamental weaknesses in products and overall strategy.

Nevertheless, marketers are for the most part responsible for marketing's malaise. Too few marketing campaigns capture the imagination or generate any excitement among customers. Customer satisfaction and loyalty are unacceptably low and customer trust is almost non-existent.[5] The majority of new products fail. Tactics such as advertising, sales promotions, direct marketing, and telemarketing drain millions of dollars from corporate coffers, but usually fail to deliver sufficient value to the company or to customers. Customers typically view marketing efforts as irritants or entitlements. For example, too many "loyalty" programs elicit more gluttony than fidelity, by conditioning customers to always expect more rewards. The ironic result: Companies must fund ever fatter inducements to get customers to stick with the brand.

Marketing's productivity crisis is reflected in some startling numbers. Here are some lowlights:

- In the US, companies collectively spend $11,000 every year per family of five on advertising and sales promotion alone—an amount that exceeds the per-capita income of 85 percent of the world's population![6]
- Research shows that many large companies waste billions of dollars on unnecessary and poorly conceived advertising.[7] For example, one study found that doubling advertising expenditures for established brands raises sales by only 1 percent.[8] Numerous companies with well established and universally recognized brands nonetheless spend hundreds of millions of dollars every year on advertising, much of it with nothing new to say.
- Yankelovich estimates that city dwellers now see up to 5,000 advertising messages a day! Obviously, only a tiny fraction of those messages actually impact people's attitudes and behavior.[9]
- Studies have found that 84–90 percent of sales promotions for packaged goods result in lowered profits.[10] This is because many sales promotions are very effective at moving large volumes of products but at very low or even

negative net profit margins. The frequency with which they are used also diminishes their effectiveness over time in attracting and retaining new customers.

Most sales promotions are so poorly designed and targeted, they achieve redemption rates of 1 percent or less, and most of those who redeem are not the consumers the company needs to target; they are just the most "deal prone" and thus inherently less brand loyal customers in the market. For example, in 2005, companies sent out six billion pre-approved credit card applications to 120 million consumers in the US alone. The response rate fell from 2.8 percent in 1992 to 0.3 percent in 2005—that is, just three out of every 1000 offers generated a response. Yet most companies blithely ignore the implications of a 99.7 percent rejection rate, and continue to assail unwilling consumers with unwanted sales pitches. What a colossal misuse of society's resources!

Three primary forces account for marketing's troubles:

- Misguided resource allocation: Few companies allocate marketing resources in a way that maximizes profits. More typically, they respond reflexively to disappointing sales by increasing advertising and promotions and/or lowering prices.
- Faulty metrics: Lacking reliable metrics for measuring the factors and variables that matter most, companies track weak proxies instead. "What gets measured gets managed" is not necessarily an effective marketing strategy!
- Lack of customer focus: Despite decades of paying lip service to the concept, very few companies are truly customer-driven. Most remain product and profit driven, focusing their measurement and management efforts on financial reporting and numbers. Ironically, such short-term, bottom-line thinking is usually detrimental to the company's well-being and that of its customers.

The Marginalization of Marketing

Given the growing consensus around the need for companies to become more customer-centric, it was once believed that marketing would assume ultimate influence and control over the corporation and become the dominant business function. As Fred Webster wrote in 1992, "Marketing can no longer be the sole responsibility of a few specialists. Rather, everyone in the firm must be charged with responsibility for understanding customers and contributing to developing and delivering value for them. It must be part of everyone's job description and part of the organization culture."[11] However, this is not the case at the vast majority of companies today.

Marketing used to have a seat at the table for senior management meetings, even at the board level. In many start-up companies, marketing is still highly valued. But as industries have matured, the traditional approach to marketing is becoming less effective and thus devalued. Marketing departments have become largely reactive and tactical rather than proactive and strategic; they have failed to take the lead in conceiving or implementing initiatives that have a significant impact on customers. For example, the customer satisfaction movement originated in operations rather than marketing. Likewise, the Total Quality Movement and "Six Sigma" had little to do with marketing. Even the recent emphasis on brand equity did not originate in marketing; it's an offshoot of the thinking around intangible assets, a concept that grew out of the finance function.

Despite marketing's demotion in the organizational hierarchy, few commentators question its value. Researchers have amply demonstrated that companies that can objectively be classified as "market oriented" deliver superior financial performance.[12] However, many companies have marginalized their marketing departments, letting other parts of the organization control such important functions as pricing and decisions about new products. Often, the finance department sets the budget for advertising, not the marketing group.

MARKETING BY OBJECTIVES

Anyone who's worked on a faltering marketing campaign knows the fruitless feeling that's captured in this widely circulated, anonymous quotation: "We didn't know where we were going so we redoubled our efforts." The 4A's framework seeks to eliminate much of the guesswork that goes with marketing, because it lets managers work toward a set of objectives, rather than count on their intuition.

Fans of the late Peter Drucker will note that this notion of "marketing by objectives" owes a debt to "Management by Objectives" (MBO), which Drucker first described in his 1954 book, *The Practice of Management*. Company leaders who utilize the MBO framework establish a detailed set of goals, communicate them throughout the organization, and work to achieve them in a resource-efficient manner. This ensures that managers and employees have a clear understanding of their own roles and responsibilities in achieving those aims. MBO lets companies focus on the essential drivers of business success, rather than fritter away organizational energy and resources on activities that don't help it achieve key objectives.

Drucker suggested that objectives should be focused on results (not activities), and that they be consistent, specific, measurable, related to time, and attainable. Corporate objectives are typically set at the board level; these then "trickle down" to specific objectives at the business unit, functional, and individual levels. Andy Grove, the former CEO of Intel and an ardent user of the MBO approach, emphasizes the need for focus: having a small number of precisely articulated objectives, and giving managers throughout the organization significant leeway in determining the best way to achieve the objectives.

Marketing departments often do not operate with clearly articulated objectives. Instead they rely on such fuzzy goals as "improve customer satisfaction" or "increase market share." Since the factors that contribute to the attainment of such objectives are many and are diffused across the corporation, marketing has historically suffered from a lack of accountability and a poor ability to trace a problem back to its root causes and implement effective solutions.

This is where the 4A's come in. The framework represents a powerful "marketing by objectives" approach to the management of this increasingly vital business function. The 4A's deliver a clear and compelling set of goals; they can be easily communicated throughout the organization; and managers can be given far greater leeway in determining the most effective and efficient ways to achieve them.

Equally important, the 4A's framework allows managers to predict the success of products and services *before* they are launched. Indeed, that is this book's primary focus—to show managers how to use this framework to fine-tune their marketing plans so as to maximize their chances for success. Just consider the very different experiences of two widely heralded high-tech services, Airfone and DirecTV.

A key problem is that most marketing managers are not financially literate and therefore have difficulty demonstrating the return on marketing investments. Conversely, other managers are usually not marketing literate. Too often, they fail to understand how loyal customers and the power of the brand positively impact the balance sheet. Many companies view marketing expenditures as discretionary rather than committed costs, so the marketing budget is considered "soft money" that can readily be cut. Marketers, except in consumer packaged goods (CPG) industries, are hard-pressed to justify their budget requests, since they command little trust and credibility within many organizations. And yet, anyone who doubts marketing's capacity to make—or break—a promising product would do well to consider the very different fortunes of two technological marvels, the Roomba robotic vacuum cleaner and the Segway Human Transporter.

HITS AND MISSES, PART I: ROOMBA VS. SEGWAY

Two of the more intriguing and unusual products to come along in recent years are the Segway Human Transporter and the Roomba robotic vacuum cleaner. Both products represent significant technological breakthroughs and attempts to create new markets. But their track records have been very different.

The Segway HT, unveiled in December 2001, is a two-wheeled, battery-powered mobile device that looks like an old-style push mower. The Segway can transport a rider for an entire day using a battery charged with household electricity. Its gyroscopic sensors detect subtle shifts in the operator's body and respond by moving the device in the appropriate direction. Most people who try the Segway HT are amazed at its stability, uncanny responsiveness, and ease of use.

The Roomba from iRobot (a company previously known for its successful military robots) is about the size of a home bathroom scale. It allows busy parents, pet owners and physically handicapped people to keep their floors impeccably clean with minimal effort. The Roomba uses intelligent algorithms and advanced sweeping and vacuuming mechanisms to cover 90 percent of a room with just a touch of a button. Employing a three-stage cleaning system, it brushes, sweeps, and vacuums, all in one collaborative motion. With its low profile, it can reach under sofas and other objects.

Owners love to demonstrate their robotic helper to families and friends. Watching a Roomba navigate through the house, turning in seemingly random directions, staying within the virtual walls' limits, stopping just a few inches short of falling down stairs, and returning dutifully to its charging station once its work is done can be quite entertaining. Users are amazed to see the amount of dirt in its garbage bin after it completes its rounds. The product just keeps getting better; based on customer suggestions, the company has added features such as bigger bins, brush cleaning, dirt detection, rapid charging, and automatic return to the charging station. There are now eight members in the Roomba family, each with its own functionality, price, and personality.

Two years after it was launched in October 2002, iRobot sold its 1 millionth Roomba, making the product a bona fide hit. By contrast, only 6000 Segways were sold in the first two years after its launch, a far cry from the company's expectations of selling 30,000–50,000.[13] Both products are marvels of cutting-edge technology, and are easy to use, rugged, and reliable. So why is one floundering while the other soars? The answer lies largely in how each technological wonder has been marketed.

Although both companies spent a minimal amount of money on advertising, their products were greeted with much fanfare, thanks to extensive media publicity. The Roomba benefited from a flurry of glowing write-ups in publications such as *Time*, as well as prominent appearances on hit TV shows including *Oprah*, *Friends*, and *Arrested Development*. The Segway was the subject of enormous pre-release hype, attracting a "Who's Who" of famous investors and boosters. Many declared that the Segway would revolutionize personal transportation in the same way that the automobile had rendered the horse and buggy obsolete. Not many products can live up to such sky-high expectations. In contrast, the Roomba debuted with modest expectations (given the poor performance of previous robotic appliances) and was easily able to exceed them.

The Segway has run into some major challenges. From a customer perspective, using the product runs counter to the cultural trend of walking for exercise. Some people experience back pain with prolonged use. In terms of infrastructure, most cities and towns don't allow motorized vehicles on their sidewalks. The Segway was literally a product with nowhere to go. A savvy marketing group might have anticipated these issues and devised a better launch strategy.

For a long time, the only place where consumers could buy a Segway was Amazon.com, which meant that people couldn't experience the product before the purchase. Later, the company started selling the product at Brookstone. However, by July 2004, there were still only 35 Segway dealerships in the US. Soon after the Roomba's launch, however, the product was widely available at many retailers, including Home Depot, Sears, Target, and Brookstone, as well as Amazon.com, Hammecher Schlemmer.com, and many other websites.

The lowest priced Segway sold for $3995, way above the price of other motorized scooters. The Roomba launched with a price of $199, comparable to the prices of "regular" vacuum cleaners and far lower than the $1500–$1800 price for other robotic vacuums.

The Roomba's stellar performance is largely the result of its ability to fully leverage the prime drivers of marketplace success, that is, the 4A's of marketing. These are: Acceptability, Affordability, Accessibility, and Awareness. Each is a rich, multidimensional construct measured strictly from the customer's perspective; each is equally vital to the success of an enterprise. In other words, a poor performance in even one of the 4A's will almost certainly derail a project.

The 4A framework is a tool that helps marketers align their actions with the four essential values sought by customers. These values can be summarized as:

- *Acceptability:* The extent to which the firm's total product offering meets and exceeds customer expectations. It has two dimensions: functional acceptability and psychological acceptability.
- *Affordability:* The extent to which customers in the target market are able and willing to pay the product's price. It has two dimensions: economic affordability (ability to pay) and psychological affordability (willingness to pay).
- *Accessibility:* The extent to which customers are able to readily acquire and use the product. It has two dimensions: availability and convenience.
- *Awareness:* The extent to which customers are informed regarding product characteristics, persuaded to try it, and, if applicable, reminded to repurchase it. It has two dimensions: brand awareness and product knowledge.

Looked at through the lens of the A's, it becomes relatively easy to understand why products succeed or fail. Let's reconsider the Roomba and Segway.

- *Acceptability:* The Roomba clearly meets a customer need for clean floors in an innovative, even fun way. The Segway addresses the need for individual transportation, but in a way that is not very compelling. To put it another way, who needs the Segway? Is it meant to replace motorized scooters, walking, or bicycling? The fact that most towns do not allow motorized vehicles on sidewalks further dampens the product's Acceptability to potential customers.

- *Affordability:* At $3995, the Segway is priced beyond the reach of most; it is priced more like a used car than a motorized scooter, which it resembles. On the other hand, the Roomba's $199 price tag is affordable to most customers and is in line with what they expect to spend for an innovative home appliance.
- *Accessibility:* The Roomba is readily available in numerous stores, while the Segway has very few outlets. Moreover, customers are required to undergo several days of training, often in inconvenient locations, before they can start using the Segway.
- *Awareness:* Both products achieved high levels of brand awareness, primarily through extensive free publicity. However, product knowledge for the Segway is difficult to create without first-hand usage experience.

Put it all together, and it becomes clear why the Roomba is cleaning up but the Segway has stumbled. More importantly, this type of analysis immediately starts to suggest specific actions that companies with a struggling product can take to improve their odds of success. Indeed, Segway has done just that; it has been reimagined as a niche device (for mall/airport police, etc.) and now largely complies with the 4A's—for operators of malls, airports, etc., the much ballyhooed Segway is far more Acceptable, Affordable, and Accessible, and increasing numbers are becoming aware of it as well.

HITS AND MISSES, PART II: AIRFONE VS. DIRECTV

In 1984, a number of airlines began installing a revolutionary new air-to-ground telephony service called Airfone, which was launched by GTE and later acquired by Verizon. Despite impressive technological achievements and great expectations all around, the service's business performance ultimately proved an abject failure. In the ten years before Verizon finally pulled the plug, Airfone generated only 50 million total calls—a fraction of the calls carried daily by cellular companies. While the Airfone service was heavily used when bad weather caused significant delays, the system's utilization at other times was extremely low. A typical plane was equipped with as many as 60 phones. From these, the average large jet generated fewer than 100 calls per day in about 16 hours of flying time. As a result, the expensive system, with its heavy load of fixed costs, remained idle well over 99 percent of the time.

On the other hand, few new product introductions in the past 30 years have been as successful as Hughes Network Systems' DirecTV, a Direct Broadcast Satellite service that uses a pizza-sized dish to beam hundreds of television and music channels directly into subscribers' homes. The service attracted over 1 million customers in its first 13 months, reaching that plateau faster than any other consumer electronics product—including color TVs, VCRs, and CD players. In fact, DirecTV was so successful that Hughes was hard pressed to keep up with the demand.

How did Hughes succeed so dramatically while Airfone delivered such dismal results? The 4A's dashboard helps us understand.

Acceptability: In the first years following the system's deployment (before the advent of digital systems), calls were noisy and barely audible. Second, passengers complained of a lack of privacy—a problem that ironically worsened when airlines installed phones in passenger seats instead of restricting them to a calling booth. These drawbacks made the service largely *unacceptable* to most customers, except in emergencies.

Affordability: Airfone's princely price tag—calls cost $4 to set up, $5 for the first minute and $2.50 a minute thereafter—made it impractical for routine calls, even for individuals with deep enough pockets to pay. In other words, while many travelers were *able* to pay the high price, most were not *willing* to pay it, since they did not see a commensurate value in the offering.

Unfortunately, the company failed to anticipate Airfone's Affordability problem. In 1994, Mark Schneider, Airfone's vice president of marketing, suggested that the price of in-flight telephony services was not unreasonable. "If you compare costs with ground cellular, it's not all that much more, especially when you consider the technology hurdles." Trouble was, customers *don't care* about technological hurdles—that's the company's problem. They care only about the value they receive from a service relative to the price they are being asked to pay.

Verizon, which inherited Airfone in the merger of Bell Atlantic and GTE however, seemed to focus on only the ultra high-end business traveler. "If it's a million-dollar deal," argued a company spokeswoman, "what's $10 (on a phone call)?" Since million-dollar deals are few and far between, most travelers opted to delay their calling until they arrived at their destination airports. While Airfone claimed that some customers' monthly bills topped out at $4000, there were not nearly enough of them to sustain the service's sky-high fixed costs.

Awareness and *Accessibility:* Given that it garnered maximum media exposure— and the fact that the handset itself was literally in your face—the Airfone scored highly in terms of customers' Awareness and the service's Accessibility. But that was far from sufficient. Because customers decided that the Airfone was neither acceptable nor affordable, this technological *tour de force* failed to deliver adequate profits for the investment.

Within a few years of the service's launch, airlines started to remove the expensive phone infrastructure from their cabins, since the Airfone cost them more in increased fuel consumption (because of the system's weight) than it generated revenues through their revenue sharing arrangement with Verizon. In June 2006, Verizon announced plans to terminate the service altogether, closing the book on a service that should have been a slam-dunk success. The 4A's framework would have predicted that the Airfone would never fly with its planned marketing approach and would have thus saved GTE/Verizon millions. If it had been used to diagnose the problem early on, it would have enabled Verizon to make mid-flight corrections that may have saved the service.

In contrast, DirecTV did almost everything right. First, Hughes' outstanding technological capabilities and good relationships with content providers enabled the company to offer a service that provided 175 channels (now over 250) of sharp digital pictures and CD quality sound, making the offering highly *Acceptable* to the target market.

Second, Hughes picked Thompson Consumer Electronics of France as the sole manufacturer of the receiving units. As a result, DirecTV achieved widespread customer *Awareness*, since Thompson used its well-known RCA brand name, which it had acquired from General Electric some years earlier.

Third, the brand also helped Hughes win widespread *Accessibility*, since RCA had a well-established, 11,000-dealer network in the US, bringing the product to market on a massive scale.

Finally, Hughes ensured that DirecTV was *Affordable*. Hughes, by giving Thompson exclusive rights to manufacture the first million units, was able to negotiate a reasonable price of $699. Wisely, Hughes abandoned its original plan to manufacture the units itself. Had it done so, the cost would have been in the thousands, killing the venture or relegating it to a small niche.

Hughes' satellite technology was also instrumental in ensuring that DirecTV was accessible as well as affordable, since it was able to provide coverage for 93 percent of the US market using just two satellites. After meeting the initial surge of demand, Hughes licensed additional manufacturers to produce the units, driving prices down further and making the service affordable to even more customers. By 2008, the company had 17 million subscribers in the US and another 1.6 million in Latin America.

As we can see from these two examples, the 4A framework readily allows us to determine whether a marketing plan is likely to succeed, and if not, what needs to be done to correct it. Though neither of these companies consciously used the framework, DirecTV had an intuitive understanding of what needed to be done to make the product a success. GTE/Verizon did not, and would have benefited greatly from it had they been able to use it.

HITS AND MISSES, PART III: IRIDIUM VS. CELL PHONES

To further underscore the value of the 4A's as a planning and predictive tool, let's take a look at some more examples. Let's start with two technologies that (like the Airfone) were designed to enhance human communications.

Like the Airfone, Motorola's Iridium venture, with its 66 satellites orbiting the earth at 17,000 miles per hour (34 times faster than commercial jetliners), was an extraordinary technological, logistical, and regulatory triumph. And like the Airfone, it was a colossal business failure.

The 66 satellites were launched and deployed in the span of less than one year (in 1998). The resulting wireless-communications network spanned the globe, providing voice and paging connectivity from the deepest forests to the highest mountains to the remotest oceans. Prior to launch, agreements were reached with 140 countries. Dozens of partners—companies as well as governments—were involved in managing and marketing the service.

Iridium targeted business executives who frequently traveled internationally. The expectation was that these executives could easily afford a premium service that would allow them to communicate from anywhere in the world. In the nine years between Iridium's conceptualization and launch, however, the communications world had changed dramatically. Cellular communications exploded worldwide, making a speedy transition to higher quality digital systems in the late 1990s. By 2000, when Iridium was fully deployed, the GSM system already allowed seamless roaming in 62 countries—and more countries were rapidly coming online. Airtime charges crashed as usage soared; customers could make unlimited calls domestically for 10–15 cents per minute.

Here is how Iridium stacked up on the 4A's:

Acceptability: Iridium fared poorly on all facets of Acceptability. The one-pound handset, roughly the size of a shoe, was huge by contemporary standards and service reliability and call clarity were poor. The phone could not be used inside buildings or cars, since it required a line-of-sight connection to satellites. Iridium's coverage was advertised as global, but in fact excluded many countries in Europe, Asia, and Africa. Overall, Acceptability could be judged less than 5 percent for business travelers, though it was substantially higher for miners, oil and gas explorers, and other specialized markets (segments that were targeted later).

Affordability: In an era of $100 miniature cell phone wonders, the Iridium handset cost $3000, and airtime prices ranged from $4–9 per minute (before later price cuts). As with the Airfone, even most of those who could afford such prices were not willing to pay them. Affordability could be rated at 10 percent at best.

Accessibility: Not only was the service unavailable in many countries, it could serve only 25,000 simultaneous users. With an inadequate sales force and poor phone-based customer service, Accessibility could be rated 50 percent at most.

Awareness: This is the one area where Iridium truly excelled. In addition to garnering huge amounts of free publicity, the company orchestrated an intense $180 million media blitz, running ads in the *Wall Street Journal, Fortune,* and 37 airline magazines. In addition, it launched a major direct mail campaign in 20 markets and in 20 languages. It is safe to say that virtually everyone in Iridium's target market was quickly made aware of the service. Awareness could easily be rated at 90 percent, if not higher.

Iridium's conversion rate from prospects to customers was especially reflective of its problems. In the advertising and direct-mail campaign's first quarter, Iridium received 1.5 million inquiries from potential customers, of whom only a few thousand signed up—a conversion rate well below 1 percent! Given the problems outlined above, the reasons behind such a pathetic rate are not hard to gauge. What's more, the company's executives could have readily anticipated Iridium's pitfalls, had they looked at the market through the 4A lens.

Not surprisingly, Iridium went bankrupt a short time after its launch. And yet, satellite telephony lives on, in part through Iridium Satellite LLC, which bought the company (whose satellites and other assets had cost an estimated $6 billion) for $25 million in 2001. Like the Segway, Iridium, while far smaller than originally envisioned, has found viable niche markets with maritime, aeronautical, government/defense, public safety, utilities, oil/gas, mining, forestry, heavy equipment, and transportation. A 4A analysis would clearly indicate Iridium's suitability for these markets, where users often operate out of the reach of terrestrial cellular networks and are not highly price sensitive.

In contrast to Iridium, the cellular telephony business has been one of the biggest business winners of the past quarter century. Nevertheless, it was by no means an overnight success. In the industry's early years, most observers were highly skeptical. In the late 1970s, a leading management consulting firm retained by AT&T to assess the future of cellular telephony, concluded there would be fewer than 1 million cellular phone users—*ever*—since there simply were not that many people who wanted to use a phone while driving their cars!

In cellular telephony's early years, it appeared that such pessimism was justified, especially since cell phones fared poorly on each of the 4A's. Just consider:

Affordability: Because phone companies targeted only an elite market of business executives, airtime was expensive and handsets cost thousands of dollars.

Acceptability: Service was very unreliable and only available for cars; installation was cumbersome and the handset choice was limited.

Accessibility: Phones and service could only be obtained from a few authorized resellers, and the networks only covered limited areas.

Awareness: Little advertising or other promotional activity was done. The resulting low volumes of calling did little to offset the huge upfront infrastructure costs; cellular companies lost large amounts of money while delivering minimal value to a small number of customers. The industry was essentially irrelevant.

All of that changed when the industry adopted some marketing innovations. First, the target market was broadened to include many more segments, including sales people, professional service people, and women concerned primarily with safety. Second, the industry started to subsidize handsets by bundling them with service contracts, thereby removing upfront barriers to adoption and improving customer retention. Airtime prices were lowered and multiple pricing packages were created to appeal to different segments, vastly increasing cellular telephony's Affordability.

The industry also took great strides in making the service universally accessible. Distribution was expanded to include electronics retailers, mass merchandisers, and even kiosks, and the geographic reach of networks was expanded.

Finally, the industry rapidly accelerated its promotional efforts, which greatly increased Awareness and changed consumers' negative perceptions about the service. The service's Acceptability improved as handsets grew smaller and yet more fully featured, and voice quality and network coverage both improved. With the transition to digital technology, an even richer feature set became available.

With all cylinders firing on the 4A's front, the industry took off and experienced explosive growth rates of 40–50 percent per year. As a result, there were an estimated 100 million subscribers by the year 2001 in the US alone, 100 times more than originally predicted. In 2005, an estimated 119 million handsets were sold in the US, generating revenues for handset vendors of more than $17 billion. The number of worldwide cellular subscribers hit an astounding 5.3 billion by the end of 2010, and continues to grow healthily.[14] With handset prices starting at $30 and airtime charges as low as 1 cent per minute, much of the growth now comes from the emerging economies of India and China, which had a billion subscribers between them by the end of 2008.

While the human need for communication is universal, the dramatically different paths followed by the cellular and satellite telephony industries indicate the extraordinary potential that can be unleashed when an industry operates with an explicit or implicit understanding of the factors that lead customers to embrace new products. The 4A's enables this to happen on a far more consistent basis than we have become accustomed to.

BENEFITS OF USING THE FRAMEWORK

As we have seen with the examples above, getting each of the A's right can unlock the full market potential for any offering. Before we conclude this chapter, we would like to summarize how the framework benefits marketing managers:

- Enables true customer centricity.
- Helps improve marketing productivity and accountability.
- Enables more effective resource allocation.
- Takes a holistic view of business success.
- Provides clear managerial prescriptions.

Enabling Customer Centricity

The 4A framework helps transform the marketing process from an un-measurable "blind push" effort based on traditional product marketing techniques into a measurable and optimized effort that is driven from the customer's perspective. Instead of answering how, where, and when products can be sold, the framework focuses on *why* products are desired and the factors that can impede their success. Had Motorola used the 4A's lens to find and focus on Iridium's true market—the defense, oil, and other front-line industries—the original business might still be in orbit. By focusing on customers in a clear and direct way, the framework facilitates the creation of profitable long-term relationships. By enabling the ready implementation of a customer-oriented philosophy, it eliminates the need for "hard selling" and helps reduce customer churn.

A key point to remember when considering the 4A's is that each variable generates value. Creating affordable products and services, for example, does more than recover costs; it drives sales. Ensuring that products are widely accessible not only clears the way for customers to take possession of the product; it increases market share.

Helping Improve Marketing Productivity and Accountability

The 4A framework improves the marketing function's productivity and accountability, which, of course, is especially important in today's cost conscious environment. The reason for this is clear: measurability. Any marketing action that fails to measurably raise the level of at least one "A" should be questioned and probably rejected (unless it offers a lower cost way of maintaining the level of the "A"). If the product or service fails to garner high marks on all 4A's, it too should be rejected. As we saw with the Airfone, which did well on Accessibility and Awareness but fared poorly on Affordability and Acceptability, scoring two out of four will result in a loss—a very, very big loss.

Enabling More Effective Resource Allocation

Allocating marketing resources effectively is a major challenge for all companies. The 4A's enable managers to take a focused look at the strengths and weaknesses of marketing programs and base their allocation decisions on clear objectives rather than gut intuition.

Moreover, the framework helps managers allocate resources to the marketing program's weakest link. For example, if Awareness is the area that is hurting the success of a product the most, then more resources (both people and money) can be made available to make adjustments to a myriad of factors that contribute to raising Awareness. After all, when the cell phone industry accelerated its promotional efforts and began to convince consumers to give the gadgets a second look, breathtaking sales soon followed. Of course, the issue may not be the quantity of resources dedicated to raising Awareness, but the manner in which they are deployed. By shifting resources into more cost-effective vehicles, a manager can increase Awareness while using fewer resources.

Taking a Holistic View of Business Success

A key strength of the 4A framework is its ability to encompass every aspect of the firm in service of its marketing objectives. By focusing a firm's activities towards achieving a clear set of directly measurable, customer-focused objectives, the approach also liberates managers from purely functional preoccupations. Managers throughout the firm should be thinking of what they can individually and collectively do to raise each of the A's for the firm's targeted customers. This approach views the entire business as a holistic system in which marketing is not solely responsible for satisfying customers.

For example, to get consumers to accept a product, every aspect of the purchase and usage experience must add value. Consider the Sprint Spectrum Digital phone service, first launched in Washington DC in 1996. Sprint's system appeared to have several advantages over its cellular rivals, including a smaller handset, clearer reception, more features (i.e. paging, call waiting, etc.), increased security, no service contracts, and a cheaper monthly access fee (as low as $15/month). However, when the product was first introduced, numerous technical, billing, and service problems arose, causing major headaches for customers. While the product was superior, the overall customer experience was decidedly inferior. The product eventually achieved success, but only after these "Acceptability" problems were addressed.

Providing Clear Managerial Prescriptions

The 4A's framework can conserve human and capital resources by helping companies avoid marketing failures and preventing the launch of doomed products (those very weak on several or all of the A's). It can also help turn potential failures (those weak on one or two A's) into successes by pinpointing problem areas before the product is launched. Here are five ways in which the framework delivers clear prescriptions to managers:

- *Supports continuous improvement:* It allows companies to continually refine and improve their value proposition. No company ever truly attains a "100 percent" score on any of the A's, but they can certainly get better than where they currently might be.
- *Enables "creative imitation:"* Fast followers can take advantage of the pioneer's

experience to address bottlenecks and raise their own chances of success. The 4A framework makes it easier to diagnose and avoid mistakes and seize on successes. For example, each of Microsoft's Office productivity applications benefited by learning from and surpassing its competitors: Word overtook WordPerfect; Excel overtook Lotus 1-2-3; PowerPoint overtook Harvard Graphics; and Access overtook dBase.

■ *Facilitates course correction:* Technologies, markets and customers can change quickly. The 4A's can be used to make vital mid-course corrections. For example, each successive generation of Apple's iPod has added features and functionality to continually stay ahead of its competitors.

■ *Helps assess competitive threats:* By analyzing other companies' levels on each of the A's, companies can better identify their direct competitors and determine what they are doing right or wrong.

■ *Enables companies and industries to grow the market:* For most industries, world-wide penetration rates are low, especially among the four billion people at the base of the pyramid, who make less than $2 a day. A big part of the reason is companies do not think about the constraints to adoption from a customer perspective, especially in terms of Accessibility and Affordability. The 4A framework can help identify ways to achieve a higher penetration rate sooner. This is clearly what has happened in the cellular industry, which has exceeded even the wildest expectations for growth and market penetration.

In this chapter, we provided a quick introduction to the 4A framework, without getting into great detail about each of the dimensions: how they are defined and how they can be maximized. In the next chapter, we will take a deep dive into the framework, and explore some creative and cost-effective ways in which you can achieve high scores and maximize your product's odds of success.

Chapter 2

Think Like a Customer

COCA-COLA'S OTHER RECIPE

Part of our inspiration for the 4A's comes from Coca-Cola, which has long been renowned for the zeal with which it guards the formula for its flagship soft drink. Less known is another recipe that Coke has long used in its marketing, which it calls the three A's: Acceptability, Affordability, and Availability. Over the years, it added a fourth A, "Activation." Since 1996, Coke has emphasized Activation's core elements: "pervasive penetration, best price relative to value, and making Coke the preferred beverage everywhere."[1] Here is how Coke's European bottling company, Coca-Cola HBC (CCHBC), describes how it deploys its 4A's:

■ Availability—CCHBC reaches out to consumers by placing its full range of products not just within an arm's reach of desire, but by providing the right package, in the right location, at the right time.

■ Affordability—By offering a wide variety of desirable, quality products, in the package appropriate for each market, for each occasion, and for the right price, CCHBC gives consumers affordable choice.

■ Acceptability—Relentless control, effective customer service, outstanding efficiency, and the best route to market, combined with a detailed knowledge of consumer needs, guarantees that CCHBC products are acceptable to consumers across every market.

■ Activation—Consumer motivation for choosing CCHBC products comes through providing them at the right price for the right brand, in the right location. By placing them in interesting and enticing point-of-purchase displays, by making them available via precisely placed coolers, or vendors, or racks, or fountains, and by making them relevant to the lives of purchasers, CCHBC activates consumer demand.[2]

For any company that competes in underdeveloped markets, one of the principal challenges is to create and deliver products that are readily available and widely affordable. Coke has been highly creative in both arenas.

For more than 60 years, Coke relentlessly invested in creating global availability for its drinks. The legendary Robert Woodruff, former chairman of the company, said in 1923 that Coca-Cola should always be "within an arm's reach of desire." Even today, this clear, compelling objective is the driving force behind the company's efforts to make its products ubiquitous. It is worth citing here two examples among many. In South Africa, taxis feature coolers filled with Coke's soft drinks; in the Netherlands, commuter trains come with vending machines emblazoned with Coca-Cola's familiar logo.

Just how pervasive is the brand called Coke? Consider author and brand consultant Brad Van Auken's account of a trip he took to Peru's hinterlands: "We had spent several days traveling down Rio Madre de Dios on a riverboat, moving deeper and deeper into the Amazon river basin, jungle, and Manu World Biosphere Reserve. When we finally encountered a riverside village of indigenous people and thatched huts, what was waiting for us? A Coke sign and fresh Coke."[3]

As for that other A—Affordability—Coke's goal is to make its products a true impulse purchase anywhere in the world. In India, it hit the sweet spot in 2002, when it introduced a 200 ml bottle priced at about 10 cents. This led to sales growth of 40 percent that year, with 80 per cent of new drinkers coming from rural markets.

Coke's marketing prowess is due in no small part to its mastery of its version of the 4A framework. And yet, while our 4A formula owes a debt to Coke's recipe for customer-centric marketing, we believe we've significantly improved on it. We've redefined (and thereby broadened) "Availability" as "Accessibility," which includes a second dimension of Convenience. We've added a fourth A—Awareness—as we believe that Awareness is as critical to market success as Acceptability and Affordability. For a brand as widely known worldwide as Coke, brand awareness ceased to be an issue a long time ago. For most other products, however, it can be a crucial bottleneck to marketplace success. Moreover, for products that are more complex than a soft drink, understanding the product category is an important part of customers feeling they have enough information to decide whether or not to buy. We have also created the two dimensions of convenience (representing the "within arm's reach of desire" ideal established by Coke) and redefined availability to represent the sufficiency of production capacity to be able to satisfy market demand (something Coke historically has not had to worry about, as it generally does not face supply constraints in producing its products).

As the above suggests, a key aspect of the framework we have created is that it uses two distinct dimensions of each A. It also incorporates a precise measurement methodology, takes a broader view of the resources that can be used to enhance the A's, features a multiplicative formula to determine overall Market Value Coverage, and includes other refinements that we detail throughout the book. But before we can dig deeper into the 4A's of marketing, we first need to better understand the four distinct roles customers play in the marketplace.

THE FOUR ROLES OF CUSTOMERS

In every marketplace transaction, customers play four different roles: they seek information about products; they select and acquire the product; they pay for it expending time, effort, and money; and they use or consume it (Figure 2.1). An individual customer or organizational entity might play out one or more of these roles, or combine with other individuals or entities to perform all four. (For example, one person might acquire information about a product and recommend it to a friend, who then selects, purchases, and consumes it.) Either way, if a sale is to be consummated, each of the four roles must be enacted to the satisfaction of the person or entity carrying it out.

It is important for marketers to understand this distinction between customer roles because each role emphasizes different aspects of the transaction. Customers seek different market values from suppliers depending on the role(s) they are playing. If the company doesn't deeply understand the values and characteristics that shape each role, it will not be able to do what is required for the customer to feel comfortable making the purchase.

What are the wants and needs that define each role? The seeker desires enough of the right kind of information about the offering. For users, the focus is on the characteristics of the product or service itself (such as functionality, efficiency, and reliability), as well as its accompanying experiential elements. For the payer, the offering's total price is paramount. The buyer desires a frictionless way to acquire the product. Note that:

- The seeker role is primarily associated with the *Awareness* of the offering.
- The user role is primarily associated with the *Acceptability* of the offering.
- The payer role is primarily associated with the *Affordability* of the offering.
- The buyer role is primarily associated with the *Accessibility* of the offering.

Most marketers have not traditionally divided the roles that customers play in this manner, except in business-to-business contexts, where the roles are very distinct. For example, the organization's decision-making unit or buying center may consist of representatives of the employees who will use the product, the finance people who pay for it, and the procurement people who acquire it. In the consumer market, the separation of roles is evident for many household purchases. Young children use many products, but they are not usually payers or buyers. Older children may be asked to do the shopping on occasion, but they do not typically select what is purchased, nor do they control the budget.

Understanding the multiple roles customers play in the marketplace is crucial to a marketer's ability to devise a marketing program that has a high likelihood of success.

Market Values Sought By Users

Our study of several hundred products indicates that in their role as users, customers seek two types of value: performance value and social/emotional value.

Performance value: This refers to how well and consistently a product serves its principal function. The performance value resides in and stems from the physical composition of the product or from the design of the service. Thus, the product's performance depends heavily on the quality of its design, engineering, and manufacturing.

Customers buying detergents seek performance values such as dirt and stain removal from clothing and protection against color fading. For business products, much of the value is a function of how accurately and reliably a product performs.

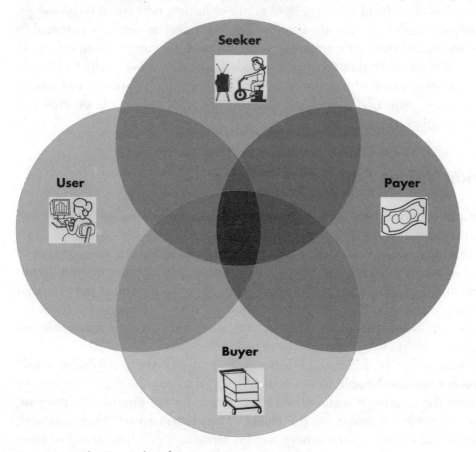

FIGURE 2.1 The Four Roles of Customers

As the performance of business and consumer products improves, consumers' expectations rise as well, to the point where there's now nearly a zero tolerance for error. A hospital's blood-testing equipment must give absolutely correct measurements; machine tools must cut metallic surfaces well within specified tolerance limits; and the seafood delivered to a supermarket or restaurant must be as fresh as the day it was caught.

Social/emotional value: Products are bought and consumed not just for their physical characteristics, but also for the social and emotional benefits they provide. These include sensory enjoyment, attainment of desired mood states, achievement of social goals (e.g. high social status or acceptance by one's reference groups), and what can be called "identity refreshment."

Social value exists when products come to be associated with positively perceived social groups. A recent study underscores the extent to which social approval matters. People who feel excluded will go to great lengths to be part of a group, including behaving in ways they would not otherwise, such as spending exorbitantly, doing illegal drugs, or eating foods that are deeply distasteful to them.[4]

Users driven by social value choose products that convey an image that they believe helps them fit in with a desired group or initiate new social relationships. Additionally, market choices are also based on a product or service's potential to arouse and satisfy the user's emotions. Most experiential consumption offers the promise of emotional value. Examples include watching a movie, eating a favorite dessert, savoring a glass of wine, or enjoying a bubble bath. In business-to-business settings, some might find that attending a convention or industry trade show is a form of experiential consumption.

Market Values Sought by Payers

Customers as payers seek two types of market value: psychological value and economic value.

Psychological value: An offering's psychological value reflects the consumer's willingness to pay what is being asked in exchange for what is being offered. To put a premium on an offering's psychological value, the customer must perceive that the price being asked is fair, taking into account the total costs incurred in acquiring the product. Judgments about whether the price and costs are reasonable are always made within the context of the product's benefits.

Economic value: In addition to being willing to pay the price being asked, customers must also be able to economically afford to pay the price.[5] Customers must have the income or accumulated assets to pay for the purchase. In the past, this was a major constraint on the ability of marketers to sell their products; customers had to save up the money needed to make a purchase ahead of time. Today, the widespread availability of credit and financing, especially in developed economies, makes it easier for customers to pay for goods and services. Of course, it also enables some of them to buy things they can't afford. Responsible marketers should never encourage such consumption.

Market Values Sought by Buyers

In their role as buyers, customers are concerned with availability value and convenience value.

Availability value: For buyers, a key market value is the availability of the product. Availability refers to an adequate supply of the core offering as well as necessary accompanying services such as pre- and post-purchase advice and assistance in maintaining the product's usability. In many situations, marketers successfully stimulate market demand but are then unable to close the deal because they lack sufficient supply. This could be due to poor sales forecasting, inadequate manufacturing capacity, a shortage of key components, transportation bottlenecks, or other unanticipated factors. To cite just one prominent example, in July 2010, LG Electronics announced that it could not keep up with demand for Apple's wildly popular iPad and would not be able to fulfill all orders for the device's displays. Similarly, Boeing was plagued with problems of delivering the Dreamliner aircraft for more than three years!

Convenience value: Acquiring a product requires time and effort. The effort includes the distance the customer must travel to acquire the product. Companies should not place a significant time constraint on when customers can acquire the product; ideally, it should be available any time the customer needs it. Customers must also be easily able to locate and purchase the merchandise. The more the company can reduce the amount of time and effort that consumers expend in acquiring the product, the greater the convenience value.

Market Values Sought by Seekers

Most humans are seekers by nature, constantly searching for ways to improve their lives. This also applies to their roles as customers, especially in advanced consumer economies. The relentless pace of innovation, growing ever more rapid, ensures there's always something new on the horizon that has the potential to contribute to a customer's life experience.

What do people seek? Of course, it depends on the individual and his or her circumstances at any particular moment. However, we can generalize to say that people desire happiness, fulfillment, satisfaction, new and exciting experiences, and solutions to problems. Fundamentally, people continually look for ways to improve the quality of their lives. Mature customers, who are a growing proportion of many

countries' populations, generally look to meet higher level needs such as enlighten-
ment or "self actualization," in Abraham Maslow's parlance. They are searching for
offerings that enable them to maximize their own potential.

To improve the quality of their lives, consumers continually absorb information
about products and services. Seekers are at different times either passive or active
in their search for information. When in the passive mode, they are not highly
motivated to seek out and act on information. They don't have an urgent need, but
remain open to receiving information that could prove beneficial to them in the
future. Active seekers, on the other hand, search for information and are primed to
act (provided the offering meets the criteria laid out by the other A's). In contrast
with passive seekers, they "lean forward" rather than "lean back" in their search for
and processing of information. Anyone who walks through a retail store's doors is
an active seeker, especially when she claims she's "just browsing."

Our research suggests that the seeker role has two key dimensions: *education* and
inspiration. As learning animals, humans look to continually enhance their mastery
over the domains in which they live and work. They seek to educate themselves to
gain expertise and confidence in what they're doing. Beyond education, people also
seek inspiration—the spark that will ignite their imagination, which will enable
them to experience life in a new and compelling way. Inspiration is essential to
creating in consumers the motivation to act on the information they gather. The
human desire to be inspired is great; as evidence, consider that seven of the top ten
selling books on Amazon.com in May 2008 were described by their authors,
publishers, or reviewers as inspirational.

The information revolution that we have experienced for the last two decades
has dramatically transformed the role of customers as seekers. The biggest impact
has been to diminish the role of marketing approaches such as mass media advertising in fulfilling the needs of customers as seekers. Most customers are no longer
content to be passive recipients of poorly targeted information. Few television
commercials are watched with any significant degree of attention. There are excep-
tions, of course. According to the TV advertising analytics firm Ace Metrix, recent
TV ads for the Kindle, iPad, and HP Printers scored far above "the norm" for certain
demographics of viewers. But this is generally the case only for new and newsworthy offerings that have captured the public's imagination in a significant way.
Increasingly, interested customers are becoming active participants in the process.
Even information that used to randomly come to consumers now typically reaches
them by design. For example, Google's sophisticated use of context-based advertising puts relevant information in front of potential customers at the very moment
they're searching for related information or referring to certain products or activities in their e-mail communications

As we suggested earlier, we have designed the 4A framework to correspond
closely with what customers are looking for in their various roles. Figure 2.2 shows
the direct connection between the market values sought by customers and the

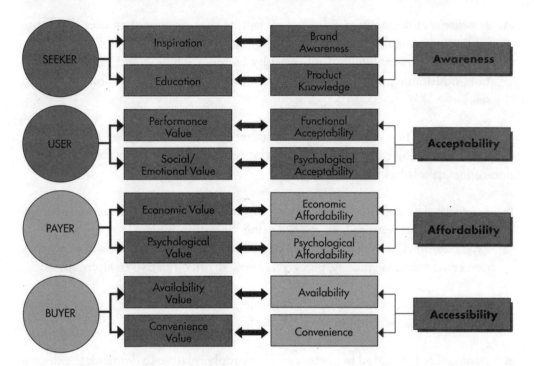

FIGURE 2.2 Customer Roles and Market Values

components of the 4A's. The 4A's represent a straightforward way of ensuring that marketers pay attention to all of the requirements that must be met to satisfy customer needs in each of their four roles.

THE 4A'S OF MARKETING: DEFINITIONS

Now that we've unpacked the roles that consumers assume in their pursuit and purchase of a product or service, let's dig deeper into the definitions of each of the A's:

Awareness: The extent to which customers are informed regarding a product's characteristics, are persuaded to try it, and are reminded to repurchase it. It has two dimensions:

- *Product knowledge* (indicated by factors such as interest, understanding, involvement, relevance).
- *Brand awareness* (indicated by factors such as brand recall, brand associations, perceived brand characteristics, brand attraction).

Acceptability: The extent to which the firm's total product offering meets and exceeds the needs and expectations of customers in the target market. It has two dimensions:

- *Functional Acceptability* (indicated by factors such as core attributes and capabilities, functionality, ease of use, quality, reliability).
- *Psychological Acceptability* (indicated by factors such as brand image [reputation, positioning, personality], styling, social value, emotional value, perceived risk).

Affordability: The extent to which customers in the target market are economically and psychologically willing to pay the product's price (monetary as well as non-monetary). It has two dimensions:

- *Economic Affordability* (the ability to pay, indicated by factors such as income, time and effort required, assets, financing, fit within budget).
- *Psychological Affordability* (the willingness to pay, indicated by factors such as perceived value for money, perceived fairness, price relative to alternatives).

Accessibility: The extent to which customers are able to readily acquire and use the product. It has two dimensions:

- *Availability* (indicated by factors such as supply relative to demand, the degree to which the product is kept in-stock, related products and services).
- *Convenience* (indicated by factors such as the time and effort required to acquire the product, the ease with which the product can be found within and across locations, packaging in convenient sizes).

For a company to reap our framework's full benefits, it must achieve a high score on all four A's. Each of the A's is measured on a "0–100 percent" scale for a given target market. In other words, we measure the fraction of the target market that finds the offering to be acceptable, the fraction that finds it affordable, and so on. A simple formula is then used to calculate the "Market Value Coverage" (MVC), which is a measure of how well the overall marketing program succeeds in ensuring that prospects have the greatest likelihood of turning into actual customers:

$$MVC = \text{Acceptability} \times \text{Affordability} \times \text{Accessibility} \times \text{Awareness}$$

The framework, by design, is not "compensatory." That is, the elements do not substitute for each other; a company cannot make up for a severe shortcoming on one A by greatly increasing its emphasis on another. To succeed, a company must do well on all four dimensions. To fail, however, a company need only fail on *one* of the dimensions, even if it performs brilliantly on the others. If two of the dimensions are at 100 percent, but the other two are only at 50 percent, the program can achieve a maximum of only 25 percent of the target market (100 percent x 100 percent x 50 percent x 50 percent). If all four A's are at 25 percent, the maximum achievement potential is only 0.39 percent. (Of course, if a company registers a zero on any one A, it doesn't matter how it performs on the remaining three—the marketing campaign will most certainly fail.) This property is depicted in Table 2.1.

To achieve high Market Value Coverage, marketers must create high value in all four areas. Customers don't make trade-offs across the A's; they need all four criteria to be met. However, managers often accept trade-offs, such as raising Acceptability at the expense of Affordability. The most successful managers are those who refuse to accept trade-offs and instead strive to deliver simultaneously on all the A's.

DYNAMICS OF 4A'S OF MARKETING

Technologies, markets, and customer expectations can change quickly. Therefore, each A is *dynamic* rather than static. What's "Acceptable" today may not be acceptable a few months from now, and vice versa. A competitor's new product or service can quickly change the Acceptability of an existing product or service. The same is true of each of the other A's. For example, an innovative distribution channel can quickly disrupt "established" distribution networks. Just consider the effect that the launch of Amazon.com had on traditional bookstores. Or recall the effect that Wal-Mart's November 2010 announcement that it would offer free shipping for the holidays had on Amazon, which was forced to match the Bentonville behemoth's offer.

Any offering that remains stagnant over time is likely to see its Market Value Coverage deteriorate. It is therefore important that companies regularly audit their 4A's performance, to monitor slippage and initiate immediate corrective action.

TABLE 2.1 Generating Market Value Coverage

Product	Acceptability Value Coverage %	Affordability Value Coverage %	Accessibility Value Coverage %	Awareness Value Coverage %	Market Value Coverage %
A	100	100	100	100	**100**
B	100	100	100	50	**50**
C	100	100	50	50	**25**
D	100	50	50	50	**12.5**
E	50	50	50	50	**6.25**
F	25	25	25	25	**0.39**

Keep in mind that the 4A's are all *outcome* variables; they don't impact each other directly. We treat each of the A's as independent from the other A's, which allows us to use a multiplicative formula for Market Value Coverage. However, the A's can and often do move in tandem when particular marketing actions are taken. There are many instances of such "co-variability" between two or more A's. For example, well-designed point-of-purchase displays can simultaneously create Accessibility and Awareness. Similarly, marketing efforts aimed at creating a high level of Awareness also make it easier to raise Accessibility, as retailers are more likely to carry a product if they know that the firm is trying to pull customers in. When LEGO launched an aggressive marketing campaign to flag its new line of board games, Toys "R" Us and Target made sure to stock up on the toys.

Affordability and Acceptability can also move in tandem. When a product is defined in a particular way, it results in a certain portion of potential customers viewing it as affordable—that is, priced fairly relative to the value they see in it. If you add value to a product (e.g. adding more memory to an iPod model) while maintaining its price, it makes the offering more acceptable and more affordable.

Improving a product's design can also make an offering more acceptable (functionally and psychologically), more affordable (such as by cutting maintenance and upgrading costs through the use of a modular design), and more accessible (by making the product easier to ship and store), as well as raising Awareness (e.g. through newsworthy innovations). Some other examples of marketing actions that can simultaneously impact more than one A:

- Packaging innovations can improve Acceptability, Awareness, and Affordability.
- Educating the customer to be able to use the product in more compelling ways can improve Acceptability, Awareness, and Affordability.
- A well designed, comprehensive website can improve all four A's.

Possible new marketing initiatives should be evaluated on the basis of their net impact on MVC. For example, if a marketing initiative simultaneously raises two of the A's by 20 percent each, it would raise MVC by 44 percent (1.2×1.2). Another marketing initiative costing the same may raise one A by 40 percent but lower another by 10 percent; its net impact would be to raise MVC by only 26 percent (1.4×0.9).

As we mentioned earlier, good managers strive to resist easy trade-offs. Any manager can increase Affordability by cutting prices drastically and reducing revenues per customer. Any manager can increase Acceptability by greatly adding to the costs of production. Truly creative and breakthrough management consists of breaking these and other trade-offs. Managers must practice what we call *oxymoron management*: simultaneously achieving seemingly contradictory objectives. In terms of the 4A's, this means doing things like the following:

- Increasing Affordability while also increasing revenues per customer.
- Increasing Acceptability while lowering unit costs.
- Raising Awareness while decreasing spending on advertising.
- Increasing Accessibility while lowering channel conflict (which arises when too many dealers sell the same product).

Given the productivity crisis bedeviling marketing (which we discussed in Chapter 1), a critical benefit of the 4A framework is its ability to identify ways in which marketers can do more with less.

Sequencing the A's

Companies must not only score highly on each of the 4A's, they must also get the sequencing right. The challenge is tougher than it sounds, largely because consumers and marketers engage the A's in very different ways.

From the customers' perspective, the purchase process starts when they become aware of a company's offer through incidental exposure, information from the media, or through word-of-mouth. When customers have a latent need or desire for the product, they are *attracted* to it and are motivated to take the next step.

Customers next *assess* the value proposition being offered. This requires a simultaneous weighing of the offer's Acceptability and its Affordability. If a range of product variations is offered, customers may go through a cyclical process of assessing the Acceptability and Affordability of the various options. For example, a customer contemplating buying an HDTV may look at several combinations of screen size, resolution, and price points before arriving at an internal consensus on which choice offers the best blend of Acceptability and Affordability.

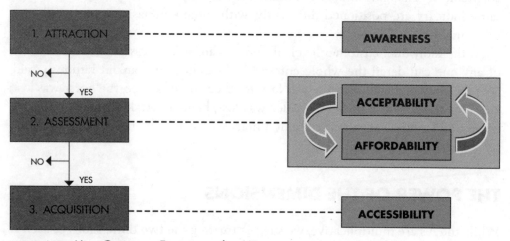

FIGURE 2.3 How Customers Experience the 4A's

Having determined that the product is both acceptable and affordable, customers next move to the acquisition stage. Whether they take this step depends on the offering's Accessibility.

From the marketer's perspective, however, the sequence is different. Marketers must first focus on creating a compelling value proposition, which as we discussed earlier consists of ensuring that the product or service is acceptable and affordable. This too is an iterative process, as marketers must consider various combinations of features, functionality, options, and price points in order to come up with the strongest possible value proposition for the target market. Then, and only then, should marketers determine how best to ensure that customers are made aware of the offering and can easily acquire it.

To get the most out of the 4A's, marketing managers should follow the sequence described above: Acceptability and Affordability, followed by Accessibility and Awareness.

Why the A's are Weighted Equally

Instead of treating all A's as equally important, we could view some as having a greater influence over a product's success than others. Some have observed that in packaged goods, the competitive battle is largely won and lost based on brand image and promotions, while in product categories such as automobiles, the product itself takes on greater import. It is certainly possible to develop a weighting scheme that adjusts according to the importance of individual A's over the total success of the product.

However, the potential value of such a scheme should be assessed against the additional complexity it introduces into what is otherwise a simple and elegant framework. Any weighting system must be industry-specific as well as dynamically adaptable to changing industry conditions. Further, different companies in the same industry are positioned differently, with some emphasizing one marketing mix variable over another.

At the individual customer level, all four A's are still necessary, and the absence of any one can derail the whole enterprise. As Benjamin Franklin famously said, "For the want of a nail, the shoe was lost; for the want of a shoe, the horse was lost; and for the want of a horse, the rider was lost, being overtaken and slain by the enemy, all for the want of care about a horseshoe nail." The best course of action for any company is to nail all 4A's.

THE POWER OF THE DIMENSIONS

While the A's are multiplicative, we suggest treating the two dimensions of each A as additive, which means that it is possible (though not desirable) to make up for a shortcoming in one dimension by overcompensating in the other. For example, extremely high psychological acceptability can overcome a relative lack of functional acceptability. Very high psychological affordability or willingness to pay can induce people to buy who really cannot economically afford a product. However, as we discussed earlier, this is not usually a responsible thing to do. In fact, marketers are rightly criticized for enticing people to buy pricey products they clearly can't afford. For example, Nike's Air Jordans are extraordinarily popular with children in inner cities who really can't afford the $100+ shoes, but buy them anyway.

Marketers have traditionally placed greater emphasis on one of the dimensions of each A and underplayed the second dimension (Table 2.2). Marketing can thus create additional value by giving balanced attention to both dimensions. At most companies, the second dimension is generally not under the marketing group's direct control. For example, decisions made by the engineering and operations groups tend to determine functional acceptability, and the finance department often has the last word on pricing.

For each A, marketing largely controls one dimension, but not the other. Those are the dimensions that marketing must manage obliquely or indirectly, by leveraging the efforts and resources of other entities within and outside the organization. The scope (and need) for cooperation is far greater on the second dimension, especially with competitors. For the second dimension, companies must go beyond using traditional marketing dollars—first internally, by leveraging the capabilities of other departments, but also externally, such as by undertaking cooperative actions using industry resources and trade associations.

Even for the dimensions that marketing has emphasized, it is beneficial to incorporate some fresh thinking into how to better deliver them. For example, marketers have traditionally sought to create psychological acceptability using promotional techniques. They would be better served by focusing more on factors such as true innovation-based differentiation. Toyota's Prius became a highly psychologically acceptable car because of the highly sophisticated hybrid technology that Toyota developed and implemented in the car.

Improving on the second dimension can often be a much larger challenge. For example, improving economic affordability (the ability to pay) requires

TABLE 2.2 Unbalanced Emphasis of A's Dimensions

	Overemphasized Dimension	Underemphasized Dimension
Acceptability	Psychological Acceptability	Functional Acceptability
Affordability	Psychological Affordability	Economic Affordability
Accessibility	Convenience	Availability
Awareness	Brand Awareness	Product Knowledge

breakthroughs in technology as well as in mindsets. Japanese consumer electronics companies licensed many innovations from American laboratories and niche companies and converted them into mainstream products by innovating around the second dimension of the 4A's, especially functional acceptability and the ability to pay. For example, Sony and JVC licensed VCR technology from industry pioneer Ampex, which sold VCRs for $50,000 each to commercial customers. The Japanese companies created a mass market for VCRs by redesigning the products to make them easier to produce in large quantities, and set a price point of $500 that would be attractive to individual consumers.

Acceptability Dimensions

Marketing has generally done well in creating psychological acceptability, usually by associating products with certain users. Much of the utility that marketers have created has been in terms of associating products with a particular setting, socio-economic group, individual personality, or an emotional need. For example, for 100 years, Lux soap has been sold largely through the endorsements of celebrities ranging from Joan Crawford and Judy Garland to Sarah Jessica Parker and Anne Hathaway in the US, as well as leading actresses and models in India, Pakistan, and many other countries.

Although the light from Hollywood and Bollywood stars has shone brightly on brands like Lux, marketing needs to focus more on functional acceptability: bringing the quality, design, and reliability of today's products in line with customers' expectations. This is the "hard" stuff that ultimately matters more to customers. The literature shows that frustrated users who believe they can improve on the products that are available to them create many innovations. Marketing can harness their energy through crowdsourcing innovations as well as use other creative ways to improve functional acceptability.

Affordability Dimensions

It's only a slight exaggeration to suggest that in almost every marketing brain-storming session, one of the animating questions is: How can we motivate customers to pay a higher price? Trouble is, by focusing almost exclusively on customers' willingness to pay, marketers neglect customers' *ability* to pay. Many customers in advanced countries live below the poverty line, and cannot afford essentials like food and healthcare. Many of them pay interest rates of 100 percent or more on borrowed money. However, taken together, people who live in relative poverty nevertheless have enormous purchasing power that companies should not ignore.

Consider what Ratan Tata is doing in India. Tata is emerging as a visionary business leader of India's largest business conglomerate. He is looking to achieve a breakthrough on the "ability to pay" dimension of Affordability, by reaching out to vast numbers of lower-income families in India and many other developing countries. In 2003, Tata Motors announced that it would produce and sell a safe and sturdy compact family car, the Tata Nano, for about $2200 by 2008. (Widely heralded as the "world's cheapest car," the Nano was launched in March 2009.) Here is how Ratan Tata explained his vision:

> It is propelled by the opportunity, but there is also a social or dreamy side to it. Today in India, you often see four people on a scooter: a man driving, his little kid in front, and his wife on the back holding a baby between them. It's a dangerous form of transportation, and it leads to accidents and hospitalizations and deaths. If we can make something available on four wheels—all-weather and safe—then I think we will have done something for that mass of young Indians.[6]

While the jury is still out on whether the Nano will indeed become the runaway hit that many have expected it to be (given that several other companies have picked up the gauntlet that Tata has thrown down and have launched very low priced cars of their own), the intention behind the venture is clear and admirable. Tata is using the same philosophy to bring another "luxury" within reach of the middle class: hotel stays. The company's Ginger chain of budget hotels includes cyber cafés, ATMs, safe-deposit boxes, 24-hour restaurants, meeting rooms, and gymnasiums. They offer air conditioned rooms with a flat screen television and Internet connectivity, a mini-fridge, a tea/coffee maker, hot water, toiletries, same-day laundry services, and 24-hour check-in—all for about $20 a night. Here, then, is a service for which many middle-income people are now willing and able to pay.

Accessibility Dimensions

Marketers have emphasized convenience, such as offering 24/7 service through call centers. However, they have often failed to create the necessary infrastructures to provide true product availability to all their customers. In some cases, availability requires the creation of new and innovative distribution channels. But creating broad availability is a non-trivial matter, since it must be built upon a robust infrastructure.

As we discussed at the opening of the chapter, near-universal availability has been the key secret to Coke's success. The challenge is to duplicate in the retail environment some of the key innovations in the manufacturing sector, such as just-in-time (JIT) supply functions. As customers buy products, products need to be replaced immediately. This requires a very sophisticated logistics and supply chain management system. Unfortunately, service and support infrastructures are often inadequate, even in developed markets.

Creating availability is especially key in developing markets. The Eveready Battery Company gets this. It dominates the Indian market for batteries because it has developed a formidable distribution network that covers the length and breadth of the country. In urban areas, the company relies on a traditional system comprising of distributors, retail stockists, wholesalers, and retailers. For the much larger but underserved rural market, its unique distribution system relies on more than 1000 vans, each of which calls on 50 to 60 retail outlets per day. Taken together, Eveready's batteries and flashlights are available in more than two million shops—a core reason why the product lines command 45 percent and 80 percent market share respectively.[7]

Awareness Dimensions

While most marketers do a good job of creating brand awareness, few are truly adept at creating product knowledge. Most companies focus strictly on informing customers about their brand's attributes and its unique selling proposition. Most advertising highlights little more than the brand and its overall image.

However, the reality is that in many product categories, most customers are severely lacking in product knowledge. For example, few customers understand the basics (let alone the intricacies) of financial service offerings such as "variable life insurance" or "defined benefit" pension plans.

Once customers are made aware of how a product works and what it can do, there is a greater possibility of market expansion. For example, Bayer and other companies have educated customers about the many benefits of aspirin and have been able to expand the market as a result. In some product categories, such as wine, most customers lack brand awareness as well as product knowledge; there is thus a dual opportunity for marketing to create value.

LEVERAGING THE FULL SPECTRUM OF RESOURCES

One of the reasons that marketing has delivered less-than-optimal value to corporations is that it has relied exclusively on resources bequeathed by the budgeting process. To achieve high marks on each of the A's, marketing can and must leverage other resources within and outside the organization, such as R&D, public relations, logistics, and operations. Marketing can also harness external customer resources such as word-of-mouth and customer-to-customer tech support. These resources impose fewer direct costs on the marketing function and many of them do more to create true customer value.

A broader view of marketing's responsibilities and resources is necessary for a number of reasons. First, "marketing" activities are increasingly performed by other business functions. The actions of departments other than marketing can and do have a direct impact on the A's, and thus on the company's performance. For example, the operations department often undertakes customer service, while R&D departments work to obtain customer insights to guide product-development efforts. The finance group typically conducts analyses to estimate customer-level profitability and it plays a major role in setting prices. Efficient business processes contribute to greater Affordability, while superior customer service results in higher Acceptability.

Second, by leveraging resource pools other than the marketing budget, marketing objectives can often be met in a more resource-efficient way. For example, companies can participate in industry-level marketing campaigns, such as the National Milk Processor Board's highly successful "Got Milk?" effort, to raise a product's Awareness and Acceptability. In fact, according to the Got Milk? website, the blockbuster campaign has scored over 90 percent Awareness in the US. Such cooperative actions can be much more cost-effective—and in the case of Got Milk?, far more successful—than unilateral company or brand-level initiatives.

Another cost-effective addition to the corporate marketing budget can be found in customer-service and support innovations. Many companies are discovering that their customers can serve as a highly effective and inexpensive means of providing pre-purchase guidance to potential customers, as well as technical support to new customers. For example, network equipment maker Cisco's support forums are a community building tool that lets more experienced customers help less experienced customers. Many of the customers who show others how to overcome problems like switching and firewall malfunctions have achieved credentials as Cisco Certified Network Engineers (CCNEs). The certification process costs Cisco very little, but is highly valued by customers since they can use the CCNE "badge" as a résumé builder that helps them win better jobs or earn a promotion.[8]

Table 2.3 depicts the four kinds of resources that marketing managers can use to improve their performance on the 4A's.

Internal Marketing Resources

Historically, marketing's emphasis has almost entirely been on using its own internal resources, specifically resources devoted to the 4P's. Even in companies where marketing has direct control over each of the 4P's (a situation that is by no means universal), individual managers are focused narrowly on optimizing within their domain. For example, product managers are focused on enhancing the product as much as possible given their resources. Promotion managers are concerned with

TABLE 2.3 The Impact of the 4P's on the 4A's

	Acceptability	Affordability	Accessibility	Awareness
Product	PRIMARY BENEFITS	Additional Benefits	Additional Benefits	Additional Benefits
Price	Additional Benefits	PRIMARY BENEFITS	Additional Benefits	Additional Benefits
Place	Additional Benefits	Additional Benefits	PRIMARY BENEFITS	Additional Benefits
Promotion	Additional Benefits	Additional Benefits	Additional Benefits	PRIMARY BENEFITS

designing the most effective advertising and sales promotion campaigns they can given their allotted budgets.

When companies think from a customer perspective, they recognize that each of the P's has a primary impact on one of the A's, but also has important benefits for the other A's:

■ The *product* should not only enhance Acceptability, but also Awareness, Accessibility, and Affordability.
■ The *price* should not only enhance Affordability, but also Awareness, Accessibility, and Acceptability.
■ The *place* should not only increase Accessibility, but also Awareness, Affordability, and Acceptability.
■ *Promotional* efforts should not only increase Awareness, but also make products or services more Accessible, Affordable, and Acceptable.

In addition to the 4P's, managers should look to two other P's that impact the customer experience: people and processes. Especially for service-intensive businesses, these two P's can have a great impact. The people who interact directly with customers obviously have a direct bearing on Acceptability, while the efficiency (or lack thereof) of a firm's business processes impacts its Acceptability as well as Affordability. Finally, the sales function obviously impacts the creation of Awareness and Accessibility. It also impacts the psychological aspect of Acceptability, and the efficiency with which it is conducted impacts Affordability.

External Marketing Resources

There are two primary external marketing resources: retailers and a company's own customers. Each can be a powerful catalyst for sparking a successful campaign.

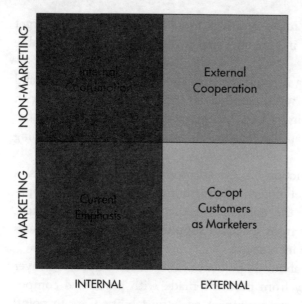

FIGURE 2.4 Leveraging the Full Spectrum of Resources

Retailers: Companies that distribute their products through retailers must work in concert with their retail partners to ensure that all the A's are optimized for customers. Achieving this requires a partnering mindset between producers and retailers, rather than the adversarial one that remains quite common. Having a product available at the "right" retailers can raise Acceptability. Retailers can help create higher levels of Acceptability (by helping to customize the offering), Awareness (through product demonstrations and knowledgeable sales staff), Accessibility (through sound inventory management that ensures that products are in stock), and even Affordability (by taking smaller markups and offering financing options). Highly successful retailers such as Costco do all of these things, and thus enjoy very strong relationships with their suppliers as well as customers.

Customers: The most effective marketing is often free marketing, the kind provided by happy customers who become passionate advocates for the brand. Properly leveraged, a company's satisfied customers can be its best sales force. As we detail in Chapter 6, companies can facilitate strong word-of-mouth and foster customer-to-customer support groups.

Internal Non-Marketing Resources

Internal non-marketing resources include functional areas such as R&D, operations, purchasing, customer service, IT, and human resources. In some cases, the impact of these areas on the A's can dwarf the impact of the 4P's.

R&D: The R&D department can help increase a company's Market Value Coverage by prioritizing efforts that improve each of the A's. For example, features, functionality, and aesthetics can make offerings more acceptable to the target market, and they can be designed in a manner that makes them highly affordable to manufacture and assemble.

Operations: The operations area is responsible for the production of goods and services. It is concerned primarily with the efficiency, reliability, and quality with which products are produced. Its impact on Acceptability and Affordability to the customer is obvious. Operations can also improve Accessibility by better matching supply and demand.

Purchasing: The purchasing function has gained prominence in recent years as companies have reduced their level of vertical integration. In other words, companies increasingly make fewer of the components that go into their products, choosing instead to procure them from specialist suppliers. In essence, companies are becoming "a mile wide and an inch deep."

It is estimated that on average, about 80 percent of the value companies deliver to their customers comes directly from products made with purchased components.[9] Thus, suppliers can have a strong impact on Affordability. Case in point: Japanese automobile manufacturers have demonstrated the efficiency enhancing benefits of just-in-time manufacturing systems that rely heavily on supplier collaboration. And companies such as Toyota increasingly rely on suppliers to invest in R&D and develop breakthroughs that improve their own products and lower their costs.

Customer service: Once people make an initial purchase, the likelihood that they will remain customers depends heavily on the quality of service they receive. In most companies, the marketing department does not control the customer service function. Marketing must work closely with customer service to ensure that customer expectations are continually met and exceeded.

IT: Information technology is fast becoming a core activity and essential competence for all companies. Today, IT capabilities are increasingly embedded in products, and are also an integral part of every other aspect of marketing. IT clearly has a huge impact on each of the A's. For example, the IT function can play a significant role in improving Acceptability by:

- Enabling ready customization: Customers can "program" the product to work in the manner that they prefer.
- "Informationalizing" the offering by creating smarter and better-connected products that generate more revenue and achieve competitive advantage. For example, high-end cars now come with sophisticated self-diagnostic and communication capabilities that provide customers with immediate access to emergency services and a greater sense of security. See Figure 2.5.
- Creating value added services around the product, such as sophisticated billing and accounting services provided by credit card companies. These can be

sources of competitive advantage or can serve as additional revenue streams from corporate clients looking for better expense controls.

■ Enabling self service, such as home-banking, which simultaneously increases customer convenience and lowers costs to the supplier.

IT can enable greater Affordability by, for example, enabling the metered usage of corporate-software applications, making them more affordable to less-frequent users. IT can greatly improve Accessibility and Affordability by improving logistical capabilities, since information and inventory are often direct substitutes. A robust online presence can decrease the need for bricks-and-mortar outlets, even if the product is not sold online, since a website can direct customers to a store in their vicinity.

Human resources: All of a company's employees, not just those in marketing or customer service, can serve as brand ambassadors. It is important that marketing work with HR to ensure that the company hires employees who have a customer orientation, and provide them with training that will help them to continue to put the customer first.

Consider Starbucks, whose success is in large measure due to its employees' ability to sell a coffee experience to more than 30 million customers globally every week. Realizing that satisfied workers (or "partners," as Starbucks calls its employees)

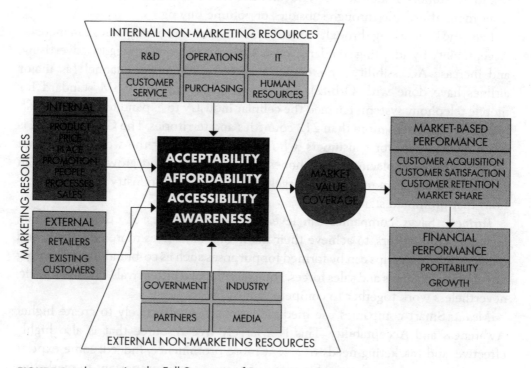

FIGURE 2.5 Leveraging the Full Spectrum of Resources to Enhance the A's

ultimately translate into greater profits, the Seattle-based coffee giant makes employees' happiness a big priority, paying them an above-minimum wage salary and providing comprehensive health benefits to all (part-time as well as full-time). Starbucks trains every employee in the art of making a good cup of coffee, in tailoring every cup to the customer's specifications, and in delivering consistently pleasing customer service. While some inevitably fall short, the company strives to ensure that every barista is not just a server but also a seller of the Starbucks experience.

External Non-Marketing Resources

This includes areas such as government, industry, partners, and the media. These resources are especially valuable as they often do not cost anything but can be highly effective.

Government: The actions of the governments at various levels can have a powerful impact on a product's overall market value coverage. For example, the government can make products more acceptable by creating rules and regulations, such as safety standards for bicycle helmets and child car seats. The government can make certain products such as credit cards more acceptable by reducing the risk to consumers of identity theft. It can make some products such as pharmaceuticals more affordable through subsidies or volume buying.

Industry: By working through industry trade associations, companies can increase Acceptability by adopting standards, raise Awareness through category advertising, and increase Accessibility by creating a shared distribution channel (as major airlines have done with Orbitz). For example, creating the GSM standard for mobile telephony systems enabled the cellular industry to expand to more than 1.5 billion people across more than 212 countries and territories. The GSM standard is a compelling draw for consumers, who can roam much of the world and switch carriers without replacing their phones. Similarly, the rapid growth of ATMs in banking and DVDs in movies was largely due to efforts of industry trade organizations that promoted standards.

Partners: Savvy companies can leverage the capabilities of other companies, including competitors, to achieve their marketing objectives more effectively and efficiently. Partnerships can be formed for purposes such as co-branding and sharing distribution channels and sales forces. For example, two bitter rivals, HP and Oracle, nevertheless work together to compete against IBM.

Media: Smart companies use media relations very effectively to create higher Awareness and Acceptability. This is a largely free resource that is also highly effective, and marketing needs to give it more prominence. Indeed, some experts argue that the public relations function is becoming more important to marketing than advertising.[10]

It should be clear from the preceding discussion that marketing managers can leverage the resources of a variety of organizational entities and institutions to achieve their objectives of increasing the 4A's. The ability to leverage a particular resource to impact a particular component of Market Value Coverage is highly situation-specific. In Chapters 3–6, we will present detailed examples of how all resource pools can be leveraged to enhance each A.

KEY ISSUES

The 4A framework has elicited overwhelmingly positive reactions from our students and consulting clients. Typical responses are that it simplifies the often mysterious and overly complicated marketing process, and that it yields immediate insights into the problem they are trying to analyze and solve.

Upon thoughtful reflection, those who are newly exposed to the framework do come up with questions and concerns. While we certainly do not assert that the 4A framework is even close to perfect (we know of no framework that is), we have found that many objections reflect confusion or misunderstanding about the framework rather than its inherent limitations. In part, this is due to the terminology we have used for each of the A's. No one word (especially when constrained to begin with the letter "A"!) can fully capture all the nuances that shape each of these constructs. Though imperfect, the words we have chosen come the closest to capturing the essential elements for building and sustaining a successful brand.

Here are some of the more commonly raised concerns about the framework and our responses to them:

1. "The difference between the 4A's and the 4P's is only semantic—they are the same thing."

One of the seeming weaknesses of the 4A framework resides in its close proximity to the 4P's. Until explicitly elaborated, the framework may be mistaken for an exercise in semantics. However, the 4A's are far more than that. They offer managers a set of conditions that must be fulfilled, if the company hopes to attract and retain customers. Once managers understand that, the question then becomes, "How can I deliver on each of these?"

As discussed earlier, when you start to think about Acceptability, for example, you immediately see that the product's characteristics looms large, but they are not the only component. To attract and hold a consumer, many other factors must come into play—from the various service elements surrounding the product to the image that the brand possesses. The same holds true for each of the other elements. The corresponding "P" has a great deal to do with each "A," but it is far from being the only determinant.

2. "The framework ignores competition."

Customers—not competitors—ultimately assess the company's performance on each A. If the company achieves high marks on all four, it needn't be overly concerned with the competition. Having said that, remember that each of the A's reflects customers' *perceptions*, which are shaped by the presence of competing alternatives. The Acceptability level of a product immediately goes down when a compelling alternative becomes available.

3. "You need more than four A's to capture the richness of markets and marketing. Candidates include Adaptability, Assurance, Automation, Activation, Affect, Attitude, Action, Appropriateness, Affinity, Anticipation, Accountability… the list goes on."

As the classic commercial for Ragu spaghetti sauce says, "It's in there!" All relevant factors—including all those beginning with "A"— can indeed be classified into one of the 4A's. Some others are discussed in Chapter 7.

4. "Branding doesn't relate to the 4A's."

Branding cuts across all of the 4A's because it has implications for each one. Acceptability includes brand image and customer perception of the brand promise. Affordability includes the willingness to pay, which is a function of the brand perception. Accessibility is affected by the brand's power within the distribution channel and its ability to retain prominent shelf space. Awareness refers to the brand's visibility and customer mind-share.

5. "The Market Value Coverage measure isn't always robust—it can vary a lot based on small changes in the A's."

This is an important concern, since the fact that the 4A's yield a single number for MVC is one of its key strengths. The multiplicative formula allows us to roll up the four variables (and their sub-variables) into a single, easily digestible number, which can be compared across companies and even across industries.

However, it is fair to suggest that the final outcome is very sensitive to the accuracy of the inputs (the scores on each of the A's). An overly conservative or liberal estimation could greatly distort the final result. While we acknowledge that the MVC is sensitive to small variations in the levels of the A's, it is not the absolute MVC score that ultimately matters, but how it changes over time in response to marketing actions. Managers should calibrate it to a baseline level, and then undertake corrective marketing actions and observe their impact.

CONCLUSION

No matter how masterful one may be as a marketer, the marketplace drives the ultimate success of a product. Success begins and ends with satisfying the customer.

This is why 4A analysis is so powerful. By design, the 4A framework is directed more toward customers' needs and wants than the 4P framework.

The framework presents the four key areas that a firm can research in detail and thereby adjust the way it spends its resources to enhance its market coverage. Can it cut advertising costs and still retain the same level of Awareness? Can these dollars be spent to bring up other weak areas, such as product quality and customer service? The 4A's guide managers in answering such questions.

Nevertheless, the 4A framework is just a tool. It must be tempered with sound business judgment. If a firm chooses to act, it must know exactly what it expects to achieve. It must evaluate the associated costs. Pouring too many resources into a problem can be just as disastrous as not doing anything.

McKinsey, the management consulting firm, has said that it is important to distinguish between companies that are healthy and companies that are merely profitable. Healthy companies enjoy fruitful relationships with all their stakeholders, make decisions based on their long-term impact, and are able to ride out short-term crises without panicking.

Companies that are highly profitable in the short term could have serious underlying issues that are temporarily masked but will eventually have to be dealt with. Likewise, it is important for companies to ask whether their marketing group is in good health. They must understand its aches and pains and its hidden diseases. The 4A's framework offers a diagnostic tool that can help identify the onset of an illness, although the "treatments" may not always be self-evident or easy to implement.

The 4A framework provides marketers (and indeed, all managers in every kind of organization) with a new pair of glasses that can be used to analyze the fit between customers, markets, and the firm's total offer. It permits more in-depth marketing analysis and is a useful tool for assessing a marketing program's performance. It helps to clarify the often-cloudy nexus between the elements of the marketing mix and key indicators of marketing performance such as market share, customer satisfaction, profitability, and growth.

In the next four chapters, we will take an in-depth look at each of the A's.

Chapter 3

Managing Acceptability

INTRODUCTION

Success in the marketplace is never guaranteed, even for companies that understand that the marketing team must innovate just as much as the R&D team. There are simply too many imponderables that can get in the way of success, and predicting customer behavior has never been and will never be an exact science. However, market *failure* can certainly be assured when companies ignore the essentials. The paramount element in the 4A's framework is "Acceptability." While all four factors are necessary, the core requirement of any marketing effort is to ensure that the offering delivers true, unquestioned value to target customers. If the product or service doesn't achieve high marks on the Acceptability scale, customers won't even begin to consider Affordability, Accessibility, and Awareness. Companies may achieve some short-term success with sub-standard offerings through saturation advertising campaigns and massive pre-launch hype; they can also buy sales in the short run by making the price attractive enough. But *sustained* success means that the offering must achieve and maintain a high level of Acceptability.

While the product itself is obviously a key part of the picture, achieving Acceptability does not end with creating a superior product; many other elements come into play. For example, when it was launched in 1975, Sony's Betamax was in most respects superior to rival offerings from JVC and other machines based on the VHS standard. However, what made the Betamax unacceptable to most customers had little to do with the product's quality, features, or capabilities. The VHS camp simply enjoyed an overwhelming advantage in terms of the availability of pre-recorded content.

Betamax's decline was hardly an isolated incident. To cite one among many other examples, by the mid-1990s, a similar standards-based disadvantage had relegated Apple's personal computing products, widely acknowledged as superior in terms of quality and ease of use, to a marginal position.

Other factors that can lower Acceptability for otherwise fine products include inordinately high or incorrect customer expectations; poor service elements surrounding the product's purchase and use; a shortage of "high touch" elements for high-tech products; and a lack of compatibility with other, related products that the customer already owns.

How can a low score on Acceptability negate high scores on Affordability, Accessibility, and Awareness and ultimately scupper a product's potential for success? Consider a product offering in the late 1970s that launched as an overnight wonder—the Vegamatic. As anyone who caught the Vegamatic's breathless and ubiquitous television commercials could tell you, this Swiss Army knife for the kitchen "sliced, diced, grated, and shredded" any piece of produce that came in its way.

Homemakers were certainly made aware of the many wonders of the Vegamatic, which promised to make kitchen appliances obsolete. The product was sold in all the major department and appliance stores, and by mail order, making it readily accessible. It was priced within reach of most consumers—less than a single electric kitchen appliance and not much more than the price of a good knife or vegetable peeler. However, the product's initial design did not meet the expectations of its targeted customers: young women who were looking for fast and easy ways to get through their kitchen work. Product safety was also a concern; it only took one slip of the hand to lose considerable skin from one's knuckles.

It wasn't until a later release of the Vegamatic 2.0 that its producers incorporated safety features such as a handle to prevent users from injuring themselves. Even so, it was too little, too late. While the initial offering captured a small portion of the target market, the product never became the ultimate kitchen appliance that it set out to be.

Had the Vegamatic's marketing team truly analyzed the product's Acceptability, they would have thought beyond its quality or functionality, and tried to anticipate how the market would react to their newfangled appliance. Instead, they learned a difficult lesson: a "superior" product (based on objective measures) does not always win. Rather, it's the product that fits best with the needs of the target market— needs that may be unarticulated and thus difficult to decipher. For example, some products are overengineered or have too many features, whereas customers may be looking for something simpler and easier to use. (Later in this chapter, we discuss the failure of the Apple Newton, which suffered from this problem.)

For consumers to truly accept a product or service, the total offering must deliver real value to the target market. And that means companies must understand what their target market desires and then design the product and its accompanying elements (such as service and accessories) to best meet those needs. Of course, recognizing and fulfilling the customer's needs is not so easily accomplished. But once achieved, the hard part is over.

Delivering on the Acceptability requirement is especially vital in these times of rapid technological innovation. At first blush, many techno-driven products appear highly attractive, but further investigation reveals little likelihood of consumer acceptance. In recent years, widely heralded technological innovations, such as web-based grocery shopping and videoconferencing, have floundered despite offering added convenience and savings. Most consumers instinctively resist innovations; it is up to marketers to figure out how to overcome such skepticism.

When marketers take a product-centric view, they tend to focus on the device's color, shape, size, functional features, and other attributes. When taking an "Acceptability-centric" perspective, they must focus on the offering's tangible and intangible aspects and assess the total impact on customers. As Boeing has demonstrated with its aptly named Dreamliner 787, intangibles like time- and space-saving innovations could well be the factors that ultimately determine whether the product is not only acceptable, but desirable.

BOEING'S DREAMLINER: BETTER AIR TRAVEL, AT LAST

If ever there was an object lesson in how *not* to excel at experiential marketing, the airline industry seems to provide it in abundance. This is an industry that for a long time has managed to abuse not only its employees and customers, but also its investors.

Air travel has seen few improvements of note in the past few decades. Other than ill-fated experiments with very expensive in-flight calling (the now defunct Airfone) and cramped and highly expensive supersonic flight (the late unlamented Concorde), the only tangible improvement, from just a handful of airlines, has been the gradual introduction of more entertainment options. But that paltry offering has been more than offset by reduced seating comfort, greatly diminished in-flight service, and ever more harrowing airport security measures. No wonder air travel has gone from being a pleasurable experience to a dreaded ordeal. The vast majority of travelers care for little more than getting the lowest price on every flight.

What is the way out? For decades, airlines have been content to spend their marketing resources on meaningless slogans and irritating jingles, from United Airlines' "Something special in the air" and "Rising" to American Airlines' "We love to fly and it shows." Some of the blame must go to the industry's two main suppliers, Boeing and Airbus, which have offered few substantive improvements in airplane design. Boeing fired nearly 30,000 people between 2001 and 2006 and lost its industry leadership position to Airbus. The latter company gained market share largely due to the backing of the several European governments that are its part owners, as well as preferential purchasing by Europe's national airlines.

But it appears now that Boeing might come storming back to reclaim its industry leadership. It is doing so by designing a new airplane—the 787 "Dreamliner"—that represents the industry's first instance of truly fresh thinking in decades. While Airbus has been pushing its mammoth, 555-seat A380, which promises reduced per-passenger costs to airlines but only more aggravation for travelers attempting to board or deplane the enormous plane, Boeing has chosen to simultaneously focus on better meeting the needs of travelers *and* airlines. For airlines, the new 220- to 300-seat plane will offer 20 percent lower fuel consumption, lower maintenance costs, and increased range. But the new plane's most important innovations are all squarely aimed at increasing the functional and psychological acceptability of air travel.

A fruitful way to increase Acceptability is to identify, from the customers' point of view, the aspects of a product that are most aggravating or disappointing. In the Dreamliner, Boeing has addressed every one of a traveler's pet peeves and then some. For example, today's planes maintain the relative humidity in the cabin at just four percent. This arid atmosphere dehydrates travelers but is necessary to prevent corrosion in the metallic fuselage. The Dreamliner's fuselage, however, is made of light-weight, composite plastics that do not corrode, permitting the humidity level to be set at a far more agreeable 20 percent. It also allows the cabin pressure to be set at a level equivalent to 6000 feet above sea level, instead of the current 8000 feet. The difference is significant, allowing travelers to feel less jet-lagged at the end of their journey.

Other customer-delighting innovations include wider aisles and seats, much more overhead storage space in lockers that descend for easy loading, a smoother ride, much less engine noise, larger windows that can be rendered opaque at the touch of a button, and indirect LED (light-emitting diode) lighting. The LEDs permit color to be adjusted, so that, for example, red lighting can be used at mealtimes to bask food in an appealing glow. To help passengers adjust their body clocks, the entire cabin can mimic nighttime, with LEDs in the ceiling that twinkle like stars.

Boeing's $10 billion investment in the Dreamliner will pay handsome dividends for years, perhaps decades to come. After Boeing started taking orders in April 2004, 44 airlines worldwide placed 567 orders worth more than $75 billion by April 2007, making the Dreamliner the most successful commercial airplane launch in history. By December 2009, when the plane had its much-delayed maiden flight, Boeing had nearly 1000 advance orders.

The Dreamliner's sky-high pre-sales demonstrate that there's no substitute for Acceptability—that a resolute focus on the factors that truly make a difference in how customers experience a product will pay handsome dividends for many years to come. Catchy slogans and pretty tunes do not have nearly the same capacity to drive superior, long-lasting performance in the marketplace.

WHAT IS ACCEPTABILITY?

As we defined it in Chapter 2, Acceptability refers to "The extent to which the firm's total offering meets and exceeds the needs and expectations of customers in the target market. It includes the dimensions of functional and psychological acceptability."

To better understand its role in the marketplace, let's unpack Acceptability's key elements:

Total offering: For an offering to be truly acceptable, it must offer more than the product. Many intangible factors, such as service and installation, determine whether the product is truly acceptable.

Meets and exceeds customer needs and expectations: Crafting a highly acceptable market offering begins, but does not end, with surpassing the customer's expectations. This requires that companies, before they develop their offering, have a deep understanding of their customers and that they thoroughly test before the launch. However, this is a necessary but insufficient condition for success. Customers can often articulate their desires, but rarely their needs. Because technologies ceaselessly, continually evolve, companies are often in a position to solve problems that customers do not know they have. The trick is to achieve a balance between technology's push and the market's pull, to avoid creating products and services that fail to resonate with customers.

Unfortunately, Boeing has experienced numerous delays due to supply chain problems critical with the Dreamliner. As we mentioned in Chapter 2, Accessibility is equally important.

Customers' expectations are most commonly influenced by a company's advertising and promotional claims, as well as by available competing alternatives. Companies need to analyze their advertising messages to ensure that they do not promise more than they can consistently deliver. If its advertising is "succeeding" in creating Awareness but not leading to higher sales, the company must cast a cold eye toward the design of its products and services, and also look for opportunities to improve its production processes.

Acceptability has many components, but they can all be grouped into two main categories: functional and psychological.

Functional acceptability: Functional acceptability includes the attributes that are commonly associated with the product class's target market. For example, today's luxury cars must possess certain attributes: leather upholstery, sun roof, six speakers or more, satellite-based navigation system, anti-lock brakes, dual air bags, keyless entry, roadside assistance, wood grain paneling, V-6 or higher engine, and an integrated communications capability. Functional acceptability also includes factors such as ease of use, quality, and reliability.

Psychological acceptability: While every product or service aspires to achieve a basic functional value, attaining high Acceptability means that marketers must pay attention to the quality of the customer experience in consuming the product or service. Subjective issues can be very important in determining Acceptability. A person's needs, motivations, and general perceptions about value all impact Acceptability. Another essential: an understanding of the customer's subconscious needs and desires. For example, when the Mazda Miata first came out, its "bugs-in-the-teeth, wind-in-the-hair, classically British-sports-car" personality had such a high level of appeal to its owners, some would "pet" it and say good night to it before going to bed![1]

A company's "higher purpose"—the notion that it should embellish the greater good as well as its bottom line—is also an important part of psychological acceptability. Newman's Own has become a spectacularly successful brand and family of products by combining great taste and healthy ingredients, and by donating all after-tax profits to charity.

The two dimensions—functional and psychological acceptability— can also be thought of as "performance" and "personality." To achieve very high levels of overall Acceptability, the product must perform and it must be personable. However, customers may trade off between functional and psychological acceptability, especially for products that are relatively low in price. For example, Chrysler's successful compact, Dodge Neon, made up for its so-so performance with its magnetic personality. Such a strategy can succeed, but only when a competitor offers customers both high levels of functional and psychological acceptability.

A high level of Acceptability is reflected in customer comments such as:

- This product fills a need better than any other product.
- This product is quite distinct from others in its category.
- After I saw this product's advertising, I wanted to buy it right away.
- This product changes the way I feel about the activity for which it's intended (for example, Gillette's Venus razor for women makes shaving a restorative experience; BMW puts the thrill in driving).

Like all the A's, Acceptability is a dynamic concept; it can change due to external factors. For example, GM found that many of its larger cars became unacceptable in the early 1980s, as gasoline prices rose and attractive, fuel-efficient cars became more widely available. This was repeated in 2008 and 2009 after the Great Recession, and led GM to file for bankruptcy protection.

KEY ACCEPTABILITY PRINCIPLES

A product with excellent features may speak for itself, but to succeed, it first must speak to the customer. All too often, marketers fall in love with their products and lose focus of what customers really want—a malady that Harvard Business School professor Theodore Levitt called "marketing myopia." In striving to build "a better mousetrap," marketers fail to attract the mouse. Recall how customers deemed the 1996 Ford Taurus unacceptable, largely because of its overly radical design. And then there was the disaster called Crystal Pepsi, a clear cola that unnerved consumers.

The following detailed examples illustrate three important principles to keep in mind when thinking about Acceptability:

- Offerings should be innovative but not too radical.
- Offerings must surpass customer expectations.
- Offerings should not be overly complex.

The Ford Edsel: Too Radical by Far

Consider the grandaddy of all marketing failures. In 1957, after a decade of planning and investments reaching well over $250 million (almost $2 billion today), Ford launched its Edsel line of cars. *Business Week* reported that the Edsel was the most costly consumer product launch in history.[2] Certainly, no one could accuse Ford of thinking small. From the outset, Ford built seven distinct models of Edsels: two oversized, expensive lines called the Corsair and the Citation; the slightly smaller Ranger and the Pacer; and three station wagons, dubbed the Bermuda, Villager, and Roundup.

Nor could anyone argue that Ford skimped on consumer research. The company hired Columbia University's Bureau of Applied Social Research, at a cost of $50,000, to conduct in-depth, one-hour interviews with 1600 car owners. The resulting data helped Ford position the Edsel in the middle of the market, aiming at "young executives on the rise." However, the surveys didn't gauge consumer attitudes toward the Edsel itself, and therefore failed to offer any insight into the car's chances for success.

Nevertheless, both Ford and the media believed the car would be a blockbuster. Indeed, Ford viewed the Edsel division as the key element in its drive to overtake General Motors in market share. The 1958 edition of *True's Automobile Yearbook* raved about the upcoming launch: "The smart money both in and out of Detroit is solidly behind Ford's new Edsel. It's about as sure to succeed as a straight flush in a two-handed stud game ...."[3]

So why, then, did the Edsel fail so spectacularly? Consumers judged it unacceptable on three fronts:[4]

Overly radical design: For a car aimed at mainstream customers, the Edsel had too many quirky design features. The overchromed vehicle with the vertical "horse-collar" grille was considered garish, even in the era of tail-finned excess. *Time* described the grille as resembling "an Oldsmobile sucking a lemon;" others likened it to a toilet seat.

Unwanted product innovations: The 1958 Edsel featured two imaginative innovations that nevertheless left the buying public cold—a gyroscope-style speedometer that spun under a glass dome, and a push-button gear selector mounted in the steering wheel hub.

An unappealing name: Ford's ad agency, Foote, Cone & Belding, considered more than 6000 names before Ford's chairman, Ernest Breech, decided to name the car after Henry Ford I's only son, Edsel. Subsequent name-association polling revealed that "Edsel" brought to mind such unflattering words as "Pretzel" and "Weasel."

The magnitude of the Edsel's failure was colossal by any standard. The company sold 109,466 units in 26 months, only a quarter of its two-year goal. Ford lost an estimated $350 million on the car (approximately $2.4 billion in 2005 dollars). To put it another way, it would have cost Ford less money to have simply given away 100,000 comparable cars from its Mercury line.

There's a reason why popular cars like the Honda Accord and Toyota Camry sell so well—their ho-hum, plain-vanilla designs largely conform to the mainstream consumer's expectations. The same could not be said of the Edsel, whose "out-there" design proved a turn-off for middle-of-the-road car-buyers. While obvious, it's also true: for a mainstream product to succeed, mainstream consumers must broadly accept it.

Ford appeared to have learned some valuable lessons from the Edsel's failure, most importantly that it could not dictate what customers should buy. With its launch of the Mustang several years later, Ford focused on developing a car that was rakish and sporty, but still fell within the bounds of what people expected in a roadster. After losing its way for a number of years in the 1970s, Ford again redis-covered its formula for success with the launch of the 1986 Taurus—a car designed to give mainstream car buyers everything they could ask for in a family sedan. However, the radical 1996 restyling of the Taurus once again proved too much for buyers, and Ford lost considerable market share as a result.

Given that consumers' tastes are constantly changing, achieving and maintaining a high level of Acceptability is far from easy, but absolutely necessary.

Apple's Newton: Unfulfilled Expectations

Unlike the Edsel, the Apple Newton MessagePad was aimed squarely at a well-defined segment of technology-savvy early adopters. However, it, too, ranks as a major failure, due again largely to problems with Acceptability (and to a lesser extent, Affordability).[5] Like many products that score poorly on Acceptability, Apple's "personal digital assistant" was almost too successful with the other two elements (Awareness and Accessibility), which ironically contributed to its failure.

Apple launched the Newton with incredible fanfare, fueled by a $12 million introductory advertising campaign and a host of celebrity user endorsements. As a result, the product was eagerly anticipated, not only by the Mac faithful but also by legions of Windows users. Apple's aggressive distribution strategy ensured that customers could quickly and easily obtain the product. After introducing the Newton at the MacWorld trade show, Apple quickly expanded distribution nationally to authorized Apple dealers, computer superstores, and campus resellers. Such was the enthusiasm surrounding the product that a chain of specialty stores was founded specifically to sell Newtons—Newton Source, with outlets in New York, San Francisco, and Los Angeles.

The market was primed but unfortunately, the product was far from ready for prime time. Launched August 2, 1993, the Newton aimed to help people organize their work and communicate ideas with great speed and clarity, anywhere in the world. However, Apple overpromised and underdelivered in numerous ways. Aside from its portly look and poor usability, the original Newton's biggest disappointment was its extremely poor handwriting recognition. One Newton retailer reported that when you wrote "Apple Newton" in "fairly neat block letters," it came back as "It Pie Warm!" Because the writing technology was considered one of Newton's biggest selling points, the flaws quickly alienated high-tech buyers. The handwriting recognition failure was widely reported and ridiculed in the media, including in a series of memorable Doonesbury cartoon strips. Where once it was an object of fascination, the Newton quickly became the butt of countless jokes.

Though Apple recognized the problems, it took two years to release the improved Newton 2.0 operating system, which was based on extensive customer feedback and testing. Then in 1996, approximately three years after the first-generation launch, Apple introduced the Newton MessagePad 2000, with access to the Internet and the ability to share data with Macs and Windows PCs. While improved, the product could never get past its earlier shellacking from the critics and ultimately delivered too little, too late. And yet, Apple kept at it, launching the MessagePad 2100 in 1998. *PC Magazine* was just one among many publications that gave the 2100 a thumbs-down review. Finally recognizing the handwriting on the wall (something the Newton could never do), Apple pulled the plug on the line.

What do we learn from this failure? A few lessons stand out:

Get it (almost) right the first time: It is extraordinarily difficult to recover from a fiasco like the one the Newton endured. The "pioneer advantage" that Apple sought by being the first to launch a robust, PDA platform was no guarantee of enduring success; research has shown that there are plenty of opportunities for fast followers to succeed where first movers stumble, as Palm later proved in this same category (see below).[6] Lacking extensive testing and bulletproofing, the Newton simply couldn't survive the onslaught of criticism that quickly followed its launch.

Iterate rapidly: No first version of a product can be perfect, though it must strive to come a lot closer to that standard than the Newton did. The key to continued success is to come out with Version 2 rapidly—literally within months of the first version. Sony has historically done this well; the company gears its engineering and product development efforts to fast learning and rapid iteration in the marketplace.[7]

Share the crown jewels: Apple, as it has done through much of its history, refused to share its proprietary technology and license its operating software to third party developers. Had it done so, a number of other companies would have stepped up to continue Newton's development, and the Newton OS could have emerged as a de facto industry standard, operating on a number of different hardware platforms. Instead, Apple quickly ceded market leadership to Palm.

The Palm Pilot: The Power of Simplicity

Achieving high acceptability means delivering the *right* amount of the right attributes, not the maximum amount. Simplicity is a key design objective, as simpler products are almost always preferred over complicated ones. Apple's iPod succeeded not just because of its aesthetics and "cool factor," but also because of its extraordinarily intuitive interface. With the cost of computing power falling so dramatically, companies can now build interfaces that adapt to the way that customers like to do things, rather than forcing customers to learn new ways.

Founded in 1992, Palm Computing built much of its strategy around its less-is-more approach to design. When it launched the Palm 1000 and Palm 5000 organizers in March 1996, the devices were an instant success, becoming the fastest selling computer products in history. Not content to rest on its laurels, Palm introduced two next-generation devices in March 1997: the PalmPilot™ Professional and PalmPilot™ Personal Edition models.[8]

Palm accomplished with its organizers what Apple couldn't with the Newton—it put a useful handheld computer in millions of pockets and purses. The key to the device's success resided in its extraordinarily high level of Acceptability in the marketplace. The *Wall Street Journal* echoed many other rave reviews, asserting that the Palm "inspired a new design principle: size and simplicity are more important than whizzy technology."

The Palm was a perfect example of a user-centered design that delivered valuable solutions to huge segments of the population. Customers responded to the Palm precisely because it gave them easy access to a few essential features that they could use in real life. In contrast to the Newton, which confused people by trying to do too much (and not very well at that), the Palm Pilot focused on doing just enough. An important element in its success was the fact that the Palm was designed as a companion to PCs, not as a replacement. The device's ability to easily synchronize its contents with a desktop application on a PC or a Mac was a breakthrough in the seamless, synergistic blending of two technologies.

Another key to Palm's simplicity and convenience was the fact that it was so portable. All Palm models were light and small, fitting conveniently into pockets and purses. All featured instant-on power and ran on a single battery charge. Most Palms also offered a nifty "gee whiz" feature—the ability to wirelessly zap, through an infra-red link, electronic business cards and data files to other Palm users.

Last but not least, Palm was savvy about the need to create a broad community of users and developers around its standard. The company encouraged third party application development, with the result that literally thousands of software applications soon became available for the Palm platform. This helped Palm stay in front of its competitors, since the software could only be used on Palm devices. And starting in December 1997, Palm licensed its operating system to companies such as IBM, Symbol, Handspring, and Sony, thereby increasing its chances of surviving against Microsoft's competing Pocket PC operating system.

Palm did virtually everything right to make and keep its offering highly Acceptable. As customer needs and expectations grew, Palm responded by adding color screens, expanded memory, and Internet connectivity, but it never succumbed to "feature creep" by trying to do too much. By 2004, over 40 million Palm OS devices had been sold worldwide, largely because Palm made its handhelds highly Acceptable by keeping things simple.

WHEN SMART COMPANIES DO DUMB THINGS

Even smart companies are not immune to blind spots when it comes to achieving a consistently high level of Acceptability for their offerings. Consider the performances of 3Com and Sony. 3Com was the Ethernet networking pioneer and the company that acquired the Palm business from US Robotics in 1997 and then spun it out as a stand-alone company in March 2000. Sony, of course, has been synonymous with stylish, well-designed technological marvels in consumer electronics for almost 50 years.

Around 2000, both 3Com and Sony decided to target a niche in the computing marketplace that had been much discussed in the trade press but had not yet seen any successful product launches: the Internet appliance.

As envisioned by many, the Internet appliance would be a low cost device that consumers could use to surf the Internet and communicate via e-mail. It was thought that such a device would appeal to experienced PC users and novices alike. The former could use it to make Internet access and e-mail capability available in "critical areas" around the house. Non-PC users would get Internet access for web surfing and e-mail without having to buy a larger and more expensive device. Technology pundits predicted that many of the purchases for the latter group would in fact be made by PC owners—the "let's buy one for Grandma" notion.[9] Everyone, it seemed, was convinced that such a gizmo would be the next big thing.

3Com took the first plunge into the market with its October 17, 2000 launch of Audrey, named for the actress Audrey Hepburn. Envisioned as the first in its line of Ergo Internet appliances, Audrey was a small, toaster-shaped box crafted by the famed IDEO design house. The device sported a color touch screen, a wireless keyboard, a microphone for voice e-mail, and other enticing features.

3Com envisioned Audrey as a convenient device for keeping a family wirelessly connected and virtually informed from anywhere in the house. This would be accomplished in three ways: 1. Convenient and immediate access to favorite pre-selected Internet content; 2. Quick and easy e-mailing or voice mailing by recording a message and sending it with the tap of a stylus; 3. Seamlessly tracking and coordinating plans, appointments, and special events on a family calendar.

The device's launch was accompanied by high expectations within the company and much hoopla in trade publications. But a short six months later, 3Com dropped the curtain on Audrey and offered full refunds to anyone who had purchased the appliance. What went wrong?

While Audrey sported some sexy features, it also had many shortcomings. Among them:

- A poor display—the type of screen "found only on the very cheapest of laptops, only smaller."[10]
- Web pages that weren't reformatted on Audrey's browser, so users needed to scroll horizontally to view the entire page.
- Only nine, pre-set Internet channels were available for viewing—guaranteed to frustrate the avid Internet surfer.
- The system processor was so slow that it took a long time to load pages.
- The cramped keyboard made typing difficult.
- The device lacked infra-red hot synching capability, requiring Palm owners to buy extra cradles or make Audrey their primary computer.
- Audrey couldn't connect with three of the day's largest Internet Service Providers.

So while Audrey was sleek, stylish, and smartly targeted to its core market—the reasonably affluent, technologically adroit family—its many failings rendered it ultimately unacceptable. No surprise, then, that Audrey bombed.

What about Sony's eVilla Network Entertainment Center, an Internet appliance launched in June 2001 (a few months *after* Audrey's demise)? Surely, Sony would not repeat 3Com's mistakes?

As it turned out, not only did Sony do a rerun of some of 3Com's blunders, it added a few of its own.

Weighing in at 32 pounds—and sporting a boxy design that resembled a vintage Mac desktop—the eVilla was not exactly svelte. However, its bulk was offset by its excellent flat panel display, which was configured vertically, in the portrait orientation, rather than the landscape orientation common in most PCs.

But then there were the problems. The eVilla had a weak 266 MHz processor and a mere 64 megabytes of memory. Users looking for secondary storage had to settle for the Memory Stick, Sony's proprietary and expensive storage technology. Worst of all, the eVilla used the obscure, BeIA operating system instead of Windows and could only accommodate a narrowband 56 Kbps Internet connection—a huge drawback at a time when broadband access was rapidly becoming more available and affordable. That wasn't all:

- Users were stunned to discover that they could not customize the seven pre-selected websites, which were chosen by Sony and favored its business partners.
- Parents could not filter the websites for children.
- The eVilla did not support any version of instant messaging.
- Customers had to sign up with Earthlink (for $21.95 a month)—they could not use any other ISP. This represented an additional cost to those who were already using another ISP.

As 3Com did with Audrey, so Sony did with eVilla: it pulled the plug just months after the device's launch. Thus, Audrey and eVilla joined other Internet appliance failures such as Gateway's Touch Pac and Netpliance's I-opener. Perhaps the debacle was just a classic case of a product category that existed everywhere except in customers' minds. More likely, the failures were due to the unassailable fact that no company figured out a way to deliver an Internet appliance that truly offered high levels of functional and psychological acceptability to consumers.

SUCCEEDING IN MATURE PRODUCT CATEGORIES

The Acceptability threshold rises with category maturity and competitive intensity. 3Com and Sony tried and failed in targeting "blue ocean" categories that had not yet been exploited and lacked a template for success. On the other hand, companies that can create high levels of Acceptability can succeed dramatically even in mature product categories where opportunities for new product innovation appear limited. To succeed in a competitive market, an offering must go beyond basic Acceptability: companies must provide surplus value over alternatives and sell solutions rather than products.

Consider the women's shaving market, long treated as an afterthought by the shaving industry's mostly male leaders. For many years, the industry viewed a woman's razor as simply a pink version of a man's razor, perhaps with an unimaginative tag like "Lady" added to the product's name. Trouble is, women's shaving needs are very different from men's shaving needs, and men's products hardly appeal to women. Women usually shave in far from optimal conditions (such as in the shower), whereas men generally shave in front of brightly lit mirrors that are often magnified. And women must shave, sight unseen, the parts of their bodies that are hard to reach and difficult to navigate.

It took a while, but Gillette, the shaving industry's kingpin, eventually recognized the wide-open opportunity to craft a razor specifically for women. In 1992, Gillette launched the Sensor for Women. Despite a hefty price tag (with replacement blades costing over $2 each), the Sensor was an unqualified success, accounting for 50 percent of the sales of all refillable razors within three months of its launch. By the end of the decade, the company had sold 100 million Sensor razors and 1.1 billion refill cartridges. The Industrial Designers Society of America and *Business Week* even hailed the Sensor as one of its "Designs of the Decade," citing it as "the first razor to really address women's shaving needs."[11]

Gillette continued to raise the product's Acceptability level, coming out with the Sensor Excel for Women a few years later and the Venus in early 2001. Protected by more than 50 US patents, and sold with the tagline "Reveal the goddess in you," the Venus features advanced triple blade technology, a rounded, pivoting cartridge head that molds to a woman's curves, rubbery oval cushions designed to stretch and smooth skin, an indicator strip that wears off when the cartridge needs to be replaced, and a no-slip handle. Who knew that so much engineering could go into the humble razor?

Gillette's meticulous attention to the details of what constitutes Acceptability for its target market is noteworthy, and accounts for the company's extraordinary success in this market. Gillette also focused on the psychological aspects of Acceptability. The company recognized that women do not think of shaving as a gratifying experience, but an afterthought. So the company sought to put some glamour into shaving and make it less of a chore, by creating a product that tries to make women feel feminine, confident, and empowered.

Consider another example of an exciting new product in a dull mature product category—in this case, a great product that literally rescued a company that was teetering on the brink of bankruptcy. In 1997, Apple was widely given up for dead. Its line of computers had steadily lost market share for many years, no prospects of a turnaround appeared imminent, and by January 1998 its stock price was in the basement, languishing at $6.

In May 1998, however, Apple's fortunes began a dramatic turnaround, as CEO Steve Jobs announced the launch of the iMac, a bold new redesign of the company's flagship Macintosh computer. The unique shape, translucent colors, 40 percent performance edge over the fastest PCs and a host of other product enhancements led to a frenzy of consumer demand. The iMac quickly became the biggest computer launch in CompUSA's history, outselling all desktop PCs combined in its first month. Amazingly, 50 percent of iMac buyers were first-time users, sparking a sharp upswing in the company's stock to $20 by January 1999 and nearly $70 by early 2000.

MANAGING TO FAIL IN GROWING MARKETS

While Gillette and Apple offer compelling lessons on how to succeed in mature, seemingly unattractive markets, we can often learn more by digging into failures.

That's why we present, in this section, examples of major companies that launched promising new products into fast-growing markets—and still found a way to slip up.

In 1995, the PC industry was growing at 30 percent a year, and Microsoft's grip on the market for operating systems was tightening into a stranglehold. And yet, the company hadn't locked in the significant number of potential customer uses who were indifferent towards technology. Microsoft set out to attract them by creating what it called a "social interface." The result was the oddly named Microsoft "Bob," an interface designed to make PCs easier to use for people who were new to computers and even intimidated by them.

Bob was installed on top of the Windows operating system and came with eight tightly integrated applications, including a Letter Writer, Checkbook, Calendar, Household Manager, and so on.[12] When users fired up their PC, they confronted a virtual home for launching applications. Unlike the Windows interface with its icons and pull-down menus, users saw a room filled with common objects. Clicking on an object would start a particular application. For instance, clicking on the calendar on a wall would launch the calendar program; clicking on the writing desk would launch the letter-writing program.

Bob also featured a cartoon character that asked the user questions (via speech balloons) to determine what he or she wanted to do. Users could select from three home styles and seven different rooms; they could also select from a cast of 12 animated cartoon characters, including a purple elephant named Hank and a green worm named Digger. Each guide had a unique personality; Rover the dog was particularly helpful, while Scuzz the rat seldom provided any advice. A family could share Bob, with each member having his or her own room.

The full force of Microsoft's formidable marketing machine launched Bob as a blockbuster program, which retailed for $99 (the same price as a Windows upgrade or a mainstream application such as Word). However, while the price seemed right, the market decided that Bob wasn't the best man for the job. Microsoft lowered the price to $55, but to no avail. The target market remained disinterested, and the product was soon withdrawn.

Bob failed because it did not meet the test of Acceptability with consumers in several ways:

■ Inane interface: Bob's interface seemed geared to young children, who were perfectly comfortable with the graphical user interface already available on Windows. Adults hated the cartoon characters, whose constant questions and encouragement came off as condescending.

■ No need for it: At the end of the day, even newbies had no need for a "social interface." They could get by just fine by purchasing highly readable user guides (such as the Dummies series), viewing videotapes, or relying on tips from friends and family.

■ No way out: While all Windows programs had a consistent interface and menu structure, Bob presented a unique (and unfamiliar) way to interact. There was no other program like it, and that was a problem. For neophyte users who were ready to graduate to Windows, Bob amounted to a dead end—there was no pathway to migrate from Bob to other programs.

■ Demanding hardware and software requirements: Worst of all, Bob was a resource hog that required many customers to buy new computers or upgrade their existing machines with new processors and extra memory.

In the end, Microsoft's vast resources couldn't sway Bob's target customers, who pronounced the product psychologically unacceptable (read: irritating cartoon characters) as well as functionally unacceptable (read: dead-end program). And no amount of price cuts could bring customers back.

Bob seemed to be a case of trying to solve a problem that didn't really exist, and doing a poor job to boot!

SUMMARY OF ACCEPTABILITY LESSONS

We have looked at a large number of examples of products that delivered high or low levels of Acceptability. Here are some of the key lessons we can take away from these examples:

TABLE 3.1 Acceptability Lessons

Product	Lessons
Sony Betamax	■ Try to establish an industry standard—with new technologies/formats, don't try to go it alone
Boeing Dreamliner	■ Focus on Acceptability for immediate (airlines) as well as final customers (passengers) ■ Break trade-off mentality
Ford Edsel	■ Get quality right the first time ■ Don't be too radical with design for mainstream products
Apple Newton	■ Don't overpromise and underdeliver ■ Don't try to do too much with a single product ■ Make sure the technology is ready for prime time
Palm Pilot	■ Appreciate the power of simplicity
3 Com/Sony	■ Beware of blind spots and sacred cows ■ Provide flexibility—don't lock customer into unattractive options
Gillette Sensor for Women	■ Create products specifically designed for each segment/market
Apple iMac	■ Come up with an irresistible design that creates "product lust"
Microsoft Bob	■ If it ain't broke … Don't try to solve a problem that doesn't exist ■ Simple-minded is not the same as simplicity: don't insult your customers' intelligence with dumbed-down products

IMPROVING PSYCHOLOGICAL ACCEPTABILITY

As we discussed in Chapter 2, marketers have tended to focus heavily on psychological acceptability, especially since it goes a long way in improving customers' willingness to pay. Ways to improve psychological acceptability include:

- Brand image
  A brand's image is a critical component of psychological acceptability. Customers use brands not only as a way to identify products and form expectations about product quality, but also as a way of branding themselves. Brand identity and self-identity are inextricably linked, especially for products with which customers have a high level of psychological involvement. For example, Tiffany & Co. and Goldman Sachs have historically benefited greatly from their sterling brand reputations, which attract customers in large numbers and allow them to charge a premium price for their offerings. Of course, Goldman Sachs' reputation has taken a substantial hit in the wake of the bank bailouts, and the company needs to rebuild itself to regain client trust.

- Packaging and design
  Marketers can move beyond brand image and use the product's packaging as a means to communicate to customers and create psychological acceptability. For example, perfume is marketed in very attractive containers, which have come to mean as much to customers as the perfume itself. Marketers can also use design to greatly enhance a product's psychological acceptability; consider the iPod's and iPad's look and feel, which has much to do with the device's overall appeal. We will discuss design in greater depth later in this chapter.

- Positioning
  Positioning refers to how the customer perceives the product—what it stands for and how it relates to other products in its category. Based on the needs and characteristics of the target market, a product should be positioned to ensure that customers find it psychologically acceptable. To succeed, an offering must occupy a leadership position in an area that its targeted customers care about. Possibilities include being the leader on value, prestige, social responsibility, responsiveness, ease-of-use, environmental issues, relationships, service, and flexibility.

- Service guarantees
  Companies should offer service guarantees that create greater psychological acceptability. For example, Caterpillar guarantees customers a 48-hour response time for repairs, which reassures farmers, heavy-equipment operators, and other construction business owners that they won't sustain long-term losses when a machine breaks down.

- Risk reduction
  Customers generally are risk averse and resist change. The more radical the

offering, the more skeptical the customer is. Companies must reduce the social or professional risk that customers perceive. When it dominated the mainframe computing market, IBM was renowned for encouraging the notion that customers could not go wrong with Big Blue. The company used this perception to club its competitors, by allegedly sowing fear, uncertainty, and doubt (FUD) in the minds of corporate customers if they thought of switching to another company's products.

IMPROVING FUNCTIONAL ACCEPTABILITY

Marketers have not paid adequate attention to the functional dimension of Acceptability, as we discussed in Chapter 2. Some ways in which companies can increase functional acceptability include:

- Enhance the core benefit
  Sofa beds have long been derided, as most of them fail to fulfill their primary purpose well: provide a good night's sleep. Most people sleep fitfully on sofa beds, largely because of the metal bars that spear them in the back. No wonder that sales of sofa beds peaked years ago (in 1993, when 2.7 million were sold in the US) and have since fallen steadily; only 1.7 million were sold in 2003. People are increasingly turning to futons, air mattresses, and other options, all of which are growing in sales.

  However, many older customers are uncomfortable with futons and the like, as they are often associated with dorm rooms. One shopper who reluctantly opted for a futon said she would have willingly paid more for a sofa bed, if only she could have "found one that looked good, was smaller and had a pullout mattress that was comfortable." To reverse the trend, furniture designers are returning to the basics of what defines a good sofa bed, starting with the notion that people must be able to actually sleep on it. For example, American Leather has come out with a sofa bed called the Comfort Sleeper that uses a sheet of wood instead of metal bars. The opportunity remains for furniture makers to create a sofa bed that offers true bed-like comfort but is still suitable for a family room.[13]
- Enhance performance and safety
  Most products carry some inherent degree of usage risk. One important way to improve functional acceptability is to enhance the product's ability to protect the user. For example, skiers face a very high risk of torn knee ligaments. Working with MIT's Center for Sports Innovation, ski boot maker Lange has designed a fast-release boot that reduces force on the knee by 30 percent to 60 percent, thus avoiding many devastating injuries.

  The same lab has worked with many other companies to improve their products' safety performance. Case in point: Working with New Balance, the Center helped design a new shoe for triathletes to wear after hours of biking and swimming.[14]

■ Enhance usability

Many products are simply too difficult to use. How many times have you struggled with the alarm clock in a hotel room or the faucet in the shower? Improving the human–machine interface is a surefire way to improve functional acceptability. Technology-intensive products are an especially fruitful area for usability enhancements.

■ Simplify

As digital products go mainstream and older customers start adopting them (sometimes reluctantly), they are often intimidated by all the features and capabilities at their disposal. Many are unable to make use of more than a small fraction of the features they own. One company that has taken this to heart is Philips Electronics NV, which has formed a "Simplicity Advisory Board" of outside experts to help it reexamine all of its products.

According to Philips' top marketing executives, consumers are saying, "Many products complicate my life instead of making it easier." Vodafone, one of the world's largest cellular telephone operators, is also discovering a huge, latent demand for simplicity. It surveyed 5000 Europeans and found that many consumers in the 35-to-55 age group were deeply confused by their phones. Many did not know their own cell number, or how to use basic functions. They didn't know how to respond to text messages and felt intimidated in the company's retail stores—they simply could not understand all the acronyms and jargon used by the young staffers.[15] The simplified Jitterbug by Samsung has been a great success for the silver-hair generation.

■ Increased reliability

Customer expectations for product and service reliability have never been higher. Spurred by continuous improvements in manufacturing processes, quality levels have been rising and defect levels have been declining for decades. The "Six Sigma" quality improvement movement has greatly contributed to this trend. Companies such as Rolls-Royce have leveraged their extraordinary reliability to steal market share in their industries.

■ Greater capabilities

In addition to becoming simpler to use and more reliable, products also become more capable over time. Enhanced capabilities must not come at the expense of ease of use or overall robustness. Good examples of products that have increased their capabilities without making trade-offs include the Blackberry and Apple's iPhone.

People buy products to solve problems. Marketers should strive to solve those problems in the most compelling way without creating other difficulties for customers. This is the essence of creating a high degree of functional acceptability.

THE CRITICAL IMPORTANCE OF DESIGN

Acceptability is above all a design issue. No single factor contributes more to a product's Acceptability (or lack thereof) than its design. Design impacts both functional and psychological acceptability, as well as each of the other A's. It represents an area of highly leveraged spending for marketing. In this section, we discuss the multifaceted strategic role that the design function has come to play.

Design addresses far more than a product's functionality and aesthetics; today, it is a highly complex function. When fully understood and applied, the principles of design can lead to exciting results:

- Empirical studies have shown that an additional dollar spent at the design stage leads to an average of $47 dollars in incremental profits during the life of the product.[16]
- According to the Industrial Designers Society of America (IDSA), the average company realizes sales of $2500 for every dollar spent on design. For companies with revenues over $1 billion, the average rises to $4000.
- Over 80 percent of a product's production costs are locked in at the design stage, even though only a tiny fraction of that is actually spent on design.
- According to estimates by Dataquest Inc., a product change that costs just $1000 at the design stage can cost up to $10 million during the final production stage.

Despite these impressive numbers, most companies do a poor job harnessing the true power of design. For instance, some companies have proven adept at designing products that are easy to manufacture and assemble, but the products themselves are uninspiring. Dell is renowned for its manufacturing prowess, but has often suffered on the design front. Mobile-service providers rejected the PC maker's first attempt at launching a competitor to Apple's wildly successful iPhone, pronouncing the design of Dell's prototypes as relentlessly "dull."[17]

On the other hand, Hewlett-Packard's tremendous success in the laser and inkjet printer markets was made possible by product designs that were simple to use, easy to manufacture, and often immune from breakdown. The company sets a blistering pace for its competitors, consistently improving its products, which are already market leaders. Its laser-printer market share is nearly 60 percent, more than five times higher than that of its nearest competitor—even though it uses the same Canon "engine" that many of its competitors use.

The basic requirements of good product design are timeless and well known: function, aesthetics, and reliability. Function does not imply designing products to serve the largest combination of needs, as many multifunction products reflect design overkill and can confuse the customer. (The Swiss Army Knife is an exception.) Less can often be more in designing products. Many electronics companies are retreating from an everything-but-the-kitchen-sink design philosophy to one that emphasizes robust performance and easy function. Vodafone has launched a cell phone called "Simply," which lacks a camera, browser, and other common bells and whistles. Not surprisingly, it's extremely easy to use.

Another increasingly important consideration is "universal design"—the notion that as the population ages, products must be easy and safe to use, especially by the elderly and the disabled. Examples include walk-in bathtubs, easy-to-open detergent boxes, and OXO kitchen utensils with large rubber grips.

Products must conform to customers' sense of the aesthetic. Great design evokes in consumers something akin to "product lust." Even mundane products such as small appliances are often bought because of their style and appearance.

Companies develop distinct design identities that become as much a part of their overall identity as their brand names. Manufacturers must strive for a high degree of integrity and thematic consistency in their design elements within and even across product lines. Honda Motor Co. achieves such consistency across lines as diverse as cars, power equipment, lawnmowers, garden tools, and motorcycles.

Reliability is probably the single most important factor for consumers, since it is directly related to a product's uptime. This translates to the need to design products to not only minimize breakdowns but also to permit speedy repair. One way to achieve this is through modular design, whereby the overall product consists of a number of modules that easily fit together. A modular design coupled with self-diagnosing modules can dramatically reduce the costs of setting up and running a product service network; uptime can be maximized with minimal investments in inventory or in highly skilled repair technicians. For example, most of Xerox's high-end copiers and GE's sophisticated medical diagnostic equipment are designed with these characteristics.

The lack of early and close coordination between design and engineering can lead to products that are difficult to manufacture. In fact, such neglect can doom potentially outstanding products. For example, the Danish company Bang & Olufsen has long been admired for outstanding product design. The company's high quality electronic entertainment equipment is good enough to be placed in museums. However, the company's products are assembled in a tedious process: workers use pliers to insert individual transistors into circuit boards. As a result, the company's products are extremely expensive, and it has been steadily losing money and market share.

The use of approaches such as "Design for Manufacture and Assembly" (DFMA) is fast becoming a strategic necessity; no company can hope to compete globally (or even locally) for long without making full use of such methodologies. Essentially, DFMA is a series of software "expert systems" that can take an existing design and streamline it, making it easier to manufacture. This generally involves greatly reducing the total number of parts, and redesigning those parts so that they are exceedingly easy to assemble (through the use of snap-together assembly, for example).[18]

Products that allow customers an accessible entry point can give a company a competitive edge. The most important reason for IBM-compatible personal computing's explosive growth was its open architecture and modular design. Customers are also increasingly looking for products that are recyclable and environment-friendly. To respond to this, companies must choose materials, components, and supplies that are less hazardous, as they are doing now with air-conditioning coolants.

The notion of design for *dis*assembly has been used by a number of companies, including BMW and U.K. Kettle. In the latter case, key issues involved in the kettle design included two-way snap-fit and break points, coding of all parts, using labels of similar material to facilitate separation when recycling, and the total absence of fasteners. The product was very successful; it was so well designed that the Museum of Modern Art was its first customer.

To sum up, leveraging design is a key competency for companies. Of course, no company can do *all* of the above. They must prioritize and figure out what approaches work best for them. When the design is right, Acceptability usually follows.

DELIVERING ACCEPTABILITY BY LEVERAGING ALL RESOURCES

At most companies, the marketing function does not do a good job of getting the people who design, engineer, and manufacture products to do so in a way that maximizes customer satisfaction. Marketing groups often lack the clout and credibility to align the efforts of R&D with the needs of customers (IBM is a notable exception; its researchers work directly with customers[19]). Marketing must bring the voice of the customer to bear on all the other internal functions of business, each of which directly or indirectly contributes to customer satisfaction.

Of course, other functional areas are not inherently hostile to the idea of incorporating customer needs into their operations. Each area attempts to do so in its own idiosyncratic way, and some are better at it than others. But the key problem is that they may hear the voice of the customer in a different way. Just as marketing is (or should be) responsible for coordinating a company's communications to its customers through IMC (integrated marketing communications), it must also take responsibility for providing a holistic view of what customers want and need from the company and communicating those wants and needs to all the relevant entities within the company.

Here are some examples of how marketing can leverage a broad set of resources to enhance Acceptability:

Product: Greater ease of use leads to functional and psychological acceptability. This is one of the key elements that make the iPod highly acceptable. Its single, unobtrusive button is a gateway to what is now a seemingly limitless number of apps. Likewise, Google, unlike other search engines, has stuck with a plain, stripped-down design for its search page. This makes the page load faster for those who just want to do a search. Though the company has added many new services, it has kept its homepage the very essence of simplicity.

Increased robustness and functionality makes a product more psychologically acceptable. For example, Hyundai used to be known for low prices, no-frills, and poor reliability. Over time, the company has improved its cars, to the point where they can now compete with Honda and Toyota. One telling piece of evidence of Hyundai's improvements in the reliability arena: the company no longer needs to offer a ten-year, 100,000 mile warranty to gain customers' trust.

User centered design increases functional acceptability. For example, Carhartt has become synonymous with durable, no-nonsense outerwear for workers. Having originally designed work wear for railroad workers in the 1890s, Carhartt gained prominence after World War II, when it came to be seen as the authentic creator of the "original equipment for American workers."

Price: Hitting the pricing "sweet spot" leads to high functional and psychological acceptability. For example, Motel 6 launched the first, no-frills budget hotel for families and business travelers, priced at $6 per night. By providing a clean, comfortable room for that price, Motel 6 exceeded customer expectations for functional as well as psychological acceptability.

Offering higher quality at an affordable price increases the product's psychological acceptability. For example, when they were introduced, disposable diapers were high-priced items that were only meant for occasional use. P&G's research indicated that if they could bring the price down, many people would make disposables their everyday diapers. The company aggressively reduced its costs and lowered its prices, which helped create the $25 billion disposable diaper industry.

"Price fairness," real or perceived, makes the offering more psychologically acceptable. The same holds true for companies that use everyday low pricing rather than constant price promotions. For example, many retailers use localized pricing, which means their prices vary from one store to another. This makes customers suspicious of the prices, and lowers the psychological acceptability of shopping there. But the German supermarket chain ALDI charges the same prices in all of its stores. This has helped make it Germany's third most trusted brand, after Siemens and BMW. Another example is Jordan's Furniture, which sells its furniture at every day "Under Prices." Customers can purchase good quality furniture when they want to, without having to wait until an item goes on sale. This policy has helped make Jordan's one of the most successful furniture retailers in the United States.

Place: Especially for services, place is an important element in functional acceptability. For example, Bay Bank used place as well as IT to become a dominant player in the Massachusetts consumer-banking market. It invested heavily in ATMs when they were a relatively new phenomenon. The bank quickly grabbed a majority of choice locations around the state and created a much larger presence than any other competitor.

Proximity to customers increases a service's psychological acceptability, since it is "there when you need it." Bay Bank's placement of ATMs in locations where people spend their money, such as malls, ensured that customers always had cash near at hand.

Edward Jones, by opening branch offices in local communities, helped its investment representatives build personal, face-to-face relationships with customers. By forging a sense of trust with customers, a firm increases the psychological acceptability of its products or services.

Then there's Samsung, which leveraged retailers to redefine its brand and steal market share from companies such as Sony. To help overcome its image as producer of cheap, knock-off electronics, Samsung moved from discount retailers like Wal-Mart to retailers with stronger reputations such as Best Buy.

Well-trained dealers help enhance the overall customer experience and therefore the functional and psychological acceptability of products. Toyota spends a lot of money improving the capabilities of its dealer network. The dealers now know within 15 minutes, instead of several days, which cars are on the assembly line. They also have a system that enables them to do a "virtual swap" with other dealers in order to meet customer needs. Dealers are now able to offer more customization to customers, leading to a richer customer experience and higher overall Acceptability.

Communication: Open and honest communication—including a willingness to admit mistakes—enhances consumers' trust in a company's service or product. The 1982 Chicago Tylenol deaths, which occurred when seven people died after taking pain-relief capsules that had been laced with cyanide, created so much fear among consumers that many predicted the brand would never recover from the crisis. But Tylenol's parent company, Johnson & Johnson, responded immediately by pulling all Tylenol capsules off the market and exchanging all that had already been purchased with Tylenol tablets, which cost the company more than $100 million. Company executives communicated continuously and openly with customers and other stakeholders. The result: Johnson & Johnson won so much positive media coverage for its handling of the disaster and it emerged from the ordeal stronger than ever.

People: Employees play an important role in improving and increasing the functional as well as psychological acceptability of services. For example, the Four Seasons hotel chain counts on its staff to improve the brand's Acceptability. It has introduced what it calls a "familiarization stay" as part of its employee orientation, in which all workers, from housekeepers to front desk clerks, are given a free night's stay for themselves and a guest, along with free dining. The employees are asked to grade the hotel on measures such as the number of times the phone rings when calling room service to how long it takes to get items to a room. After six months of service, Four Seasons employees may stay up to three nights a year for free. Once they have been with the company for ten years, they get 20 free stays.

While Four Seasons' "familiarization stay" is a powerful perk, it also helps employees understand what it feels like to be a customer. And employee feedback helps the company improve the Acceptability of its service for customers.

Similarly, snowboard maker Burton actively encourages its employees to experience its boards and accessories. All employees are provided with free season passes to a ski resort; they also receive a 50 percent to 60 percent discount on most company products. Burton even closes for what it calls "powder days"—if two feet of snow falls within 24 hours, employees can grab their boards and head for the slopes. When a blizzard blanketed Vermont with several feet of fresh snow and Burton declared a powder day, founder and chairman Jake Burton told the *First Tracks* online ski magazine that "Nothing makes me happier than giving the people who work here the opportunity to experience the essence of a sport that they are making accessible and fun for so many others." Now that's how you create ambassadors for your business.[20]

Aligning employee passions with the needs of customers results in greater functional and psychological acceptability. Timberland is known for its strong commitment to the environment and social responsibility. Employees get a $3000 credit for buying a hybrid car and can take up to 40 hours per year to do volunteer work in the community. In a similar vein, outdoor apparel and equipment company Patagonia offers its employees an environmental internship, whereby any employee can take up to two months off in a year with full pay and benefits to volunteer with an environmental organization of their choice. The adoption of such policies aligns a company's core values with employees' passion, increasing employee loyalty and brand acceptability.

Processes: Since the manufacturing and marketing process plays an integral role in creating and selling the product, it can contribute significantly to its Acceptability. For example, GE is a leading innovator in implementing "Six Sigma," a highly disciplined quality control process designed to eliminate defects. Six Sigma "black belts" have helped GE put world-class quality into its products, thereby attracting customers all over the world.

Then there's the 3M Corporation, which has had a sustainability program called "Pollution Prevention Pays" (3P) in place for more than 30 years. The processes implemented as a result of this program have created more functionally acceptable products. For example, a new process for making abrasive backing improved product performance while reducing air emissions and costs. An additional benefit is that environmentally friendly products are easier and less costly to dispose of. The 3P program and resulting process improvements have won the company significant recognition, including numerous awards from the US Environmental Protection Agency and a spot on the Dow Jones Sustainability Index. The upshot: 3M has come to be known as a model global citizen, enhancing its psychological acceptability to customers and to employees.

Sales: A low-key, service-oriented approach to selling can enhance Acceptability. For example, Barnes & Noble has a very different approach to selling books compared to traditional bookstores. Its stores provide comfortable surroundings, including ample public space, reading chairs and a café that features Starbucks coffee. Customers can go to a Barnes & Noble and thumb through or read several books without any pressure to buy.

Another example: ING Direct's three storefronts in Philadelphia, which are more like cafés than banks. The informal setting has increased Acceptability by making customers more comfortable with the potentially nerve-wracking process of managing their money.

R&D: When R&D focuses on solving customers' problems, it drives Acceptability. 3M places such great importance on R&D that it requires 30 percent of its sales to come from products that did not exist four years earlier. This intense focus on innovation forces a continuous round of improvements to products, which raises functional acceptability. A superior R&D team innovates better quality products, which are more acceptable to customers.

If a company has a reputation for investing heavily in R&D, it increases its psychological acceptability in the minds of customers and employees. For example, Google is known to be a company that spends heavily on R&D (13 percent of revenue as of September 2009, far more than it spends on marketing), which contributes to its image as an innovator whose work benefits society as a whole.[21]

Operations: Efficient operations result in speedy and reliable service and increased functional acceptability. FedEx is known for its operational efficiency. It has a fast and reliable package delivery system, covering over 220 countries with 672 aircraft serving 375 airports worldwide, 894 stations, ten air express hubs, 29 ground hubs and more than 70,000 motorized vehicles for express, ground, freight, and expedited delivery services. Fast and reliable operations also increase psychological acceptability. Customers using FedEx can feel confident that their packages will arrive on time. The FedEx package has also attained some status value, signifying the importance of its content.

Dunkin' Donuts promises its customers a consistent and speedy experience in its stores. It carefully studies employee efficiency behind the counter. It seeks to create the most efficient store layout and reduce the number of employee steps and functions. When it launched a new espresso drink, Dunkin' Donuts did not want to risk slowing down its morning coffee business with the new product. So it worked closely with a supplier to create an entirely automated machine, allowing stores to continue offering fast and efficient service to customers.

IT: The strategic use of information technology can greatly enhance the functional as well as psychological acceptability of a company's offerings. FedEx was the first transportation company to offer web-based package tracking. Customers could see the status of their packages in almost real-time. UPS drivers used maps, 3 × 5 note cards, and their memory to figure out the best way to run their routes. All that changed in 2005, when UPS began to implement a $600 million route optimization system that each evening maps out the next day's schedule for drivers. The sophisticated software designs each route to minimize the number of left turns, thus reducing the time and gas that drivers waste waiting at stoplights. The system has reduced drivers' daily mileage, eased the burden on substitute drivers, and shortened training time for new ones, while improving customer service.

Customers: Customers can help improve the Acceptability of products by providing unadulterated feedback to companies. Ernie's Seafood utilizes a variety of methods to seek customer feedback, such as personal interaction, point of purchase receipts, a customer feedback phone number and e-mail. Dell has listened to customers' complaints about tech support, and instituted a new type of support whereby a Dell associate logs on to the customer's PC remotely and fixes the problem. The Harley Owners Group (HOG) has more than 1 million members and over 1100 chapters. All members share the passion of riding a Harley Davidson bike. HOG members play a major role in promoting the Harley image—some even participate in a think tank that seeks to brainstorm new features for Harleys.

Government: Government certification and endorsements enhances a product's Acceptability. The Food and Drug Administration plays a big role in enhancing the Acceptability of pharmaceutical products. The EPA's Energy Star program has created enormous psychological acceptability for branded products due to the recent spike in energy costs and concerns about global warming.

Industry: Educating customers about the benefits of a product category increases its psychological acceptability. Back in the 1980s, milk was perceived as an uncool drink for children, and the consumption of milk declined. Then in the early 1990s, the nation's milk processors came together and funded a program called the "Milk Processor Education Program," which improved the image and Acceptability of milk with the "Got Milk?" campaign. Pork producers and other industries have pursued similar initiatives.

Industry certifications can also increase functional and psychological acceptability. The International Standards Organization (ISO) ensures that products meet high quality standards, and guarantees the functionality and interoperability of certified products.

Partners: Partners aid in educating customers about a product or service's benefits and thereby enhance its Acceptability. Unilever partners with parents, health educators, teachers, community leaders, and government agencies in India to promote health education through a program called Lifebuoy "Swasthya Chetna" or "health awakening." The program is aimed at educating people in rural India about good hygiene practices. As a result, sales of Unilever hygiene products rose 10 percent. The program has also improved the overall image of Unilever in the Indian market.

Partnerships can help enhance the psychological acceptability for both parties. The partnership between L.L. Bean and Subaru enhances the psychological acceptability of Subaru's cars, positioning them as the ideal vehicles for people who thrill to the outdoors, as well as providing additional exposure for L.L. Bean.

Treating suppliers as customers increases Acceptability for a company's own customers. Toyota treats its suppliers as customers, establishing close relationships with them. Toyota's managers learn about their suppliers, visit them, respect them, and care about their future, working with them to improve their processes and make them more efficient and innovative. By doing so, Toyota is able to attract high quality and reliable suppliers, giving them the ability to decrease time-to-market and achieve significantly lower costs than their competitors.

Public opinion/media: Public opinion impacts the *zeitgeist* of the moment and thus helps determine what is acceptable and what is not. The public's opinion of fatty foods and the ever-increasing waistline of the American consumer have caused the fast-food industry to revamp its food offerings, adding healthier fruit and vegetable choices. Popular restaurant chains such as Applebee's are embracing the more health-conscious consumer by offering a whole menu section endorsed by Weight Watchers.

With environmental activism and awareness increasing globally, locally and organically grown produce has become more mainstream, greatly increasing the Acceptability for a company like Whole Foods. Rising environmental consciousness has led GE to launch its "Ecomagination" initiative, designed to meet customer needs in a more sustainable way. Projects include a 200 ton, "Prius-on-rails" hybrid locomotive; a new jet engine that delivers a 15 percent improvement in fuel efficiency with half the emissions; better wastewater recycling technologies; and a hydrogen infrastructure that could lead to a carbon free transportation network. This initiative has increased the Acceptability of the GE brand.

While no company can do all of the above, the examples illustrate the richness of the possibilities that exist for companies to enhance the Acceptability of their offering in creative ways. Companies should look at the range of possibilities and prioritize the most likely high impact areas where they can positively impact Acceptability without spending too much.

THE INTERNET AND ACCEPTABILITY

Companies can use the Internet as a cost-effective tool to work more closely with their customers and improve Acceptability. Working online with customers can greatly improve communications and the efficiency with which new product designs or modifications to existing products are implemented. Having a more interactive relationship is now possible due to the power of the information age and the integration of technology. Customers can now be a part of the product design process, allowing companies to use real-time feedback to make changes that make the offering more acceptable.

Information technology has also allowed designers to infuse products with intelligence and responsiveness. As society moves toward more distributed intelligence, more and more inanimate objects will become "thinking machines." Designers of even the most mundane products can contemplate adding intelligence and connectivity to their products. For example, appliance makers such as LG are exploring the customer appeal of smart, connected refrigerators.

Companies can leverage the Internet to make their products more responsive. Responsiveness includes the dimensions of product intelligence, connectivity, and integration. Product intelligence has several aspects. High-value products should be made self-diagnosing through the extensive use of sensors. When feasible, these sensors should be linked to an automatic data interpretation and reporting system. For instance, Fuji-Xerox in Japan has developed a copying machine that runs a detailed set of diagnostic tests every 50 copies; it analyzes the results using a built-in rule-based software system. If it anticipates a problem, the machine automatically contacts a service center and schedules a preventive maintenance visit; it also alerts the service department as to what parts need to be replaced.

Such a design and service philosophy is becoming widespread: General Electric has a similar system for some of its medical diagnostic systems. Many cars now use satellite or cellular communication systems to send performance data to service facilities and trigger reminders to make service visits.

Design for intelligence also means intelligent product performance. Consider the extensive use of "fuzzy logic" systems by some Japanese manufacturers. Fuzzy logic is based on fuzzy set theory, and incorporates reasoning that is approximate rather than precise. By using this technique, they have designed a variety of "smart" products, including smooth-shifting automatic transmissions, fast and always-available elevators, energy-efficient air conditioners, and one-button washing machines that choose the optimal wash cycle from 600 possibilities.

CONCLUSION

The Holy Grail for marketing success starts with a great offering that meets customer needs as well as possible. When customers are new to a product category, the psychological barrier is the more important one. Once consumers become experienced in a product category, functional factors become more important. Marketers must pay balanced attention to both dimensions of Acceptability, and continually innovate to stay ahead of rising customer expectations. They must accomplish all this in a cost-effective manner, which can best be done by leveraging all possible resource pools to maximize all facets of Acceptability.

In the next chapter, we examine the second half of the value proposition equation: the Affordability of the offering.

Chapter 4

Managing Affordability

INTRODUCTION

Would you buy a $100,000 Volkswagen? While the very idea seems ridiculous, consider the fact that Volkswagen launched just such a car in 2003. The Phaeton was the brainchild of Volkswagen chairman Ferdinand Piëch, who bet that such an over-the-top creation would add some golden luster to the Volkswagen brand. Not surprisingly, the Phaeton was a bust. When it was introduced to the US market in 2004, the car barely registered any sales. After Volkswagen offered a $10,000 buyer incentive, a total of 1433 Phaetons were sold that year. In 2005, sales declined to 820. Volkswagen finally pulled the Phaeton from the US market after the 2006 model year, with a grand total of 3354 cars sold. Toyota sells that many Camrys in the US every three days.

The costly failure had nothing to do with the car's features and quality. By any objective measure, the Phaeton was one of the world's great sedans. After all, Volkswagen knows how to do luxury: it produces Bentleys and Audis, two of the world's premier marques. The problem is that while Bentleys and Audis aren't branded as Volkswagens, the Phaeton was. And as the British motoring journalist Jeremy Clarkson put it, "To what question is the answer a £68,000 Volkswagen?"[1]

Clearly, most customers are not willing to pay that much money for a Volkswagen when they can buy a high-end Mercedes-Benz, Lexus, Audi, or BMW for the same amount. To make matters worse, Volkswagen sold the Phaeton at its regular dealerships. Luxury car buyers expect luxury service and a high-end purchasing experience, neither of which was available through Volkswagen dealers. Moreover, Volkswagen is primarily targeted towards younger buyers in the US, while the Phaeton was clearly a product aimed at older and more affluent buyers. Finally, the very name Volkswagen stands for and has always meant "the people's car," which the Phaeton is most certainly not.

While other aspects of its marketing could have been refined, the fact remains that the vast majority of potential customers are not willing to pay $100,000 for a car that has a VW on its grille. Volkswagen would have been far wiser to have launched the car as an Audi or a Bentley. Big spenders would have been more willing to pay the price for what was, after all, one of the world's most opulent cars. Unfortunately, the company does not appear to have learned this lesson, and continues to insist that Phaeton will be its luxury brand going forward.[2]

Obtaining good value has been and will remain an eternal quest. Markets run on voluntary exchange, in which both parties to a transaction need to feel like they have made a profit. For sellers, the definition of profit is straightforward: it is the excess of revenues over costs. For buyers, the profit comes from a perceived, greater net benefit than costs incurred. The benefits to customers go beyond the core product offering, and the costs that customers incur include monetary as well as non-monetary elements. Monetary costs include the total cost of ownership over the lifetime of the product, including switching costs and service costs, and any residual value that the product may have at the end of its usable life. Non-monetary costs are often ignored or underemphasized in thinking about what is truly afford-able to customers. They include the time and effort that customers must invest in order to acquire and use the product.

For every Phaeton that failed because the perceived net benefit *wasn't* greater than the cost incurred, there are many brands that deliver great value while making a profit. Southwest Airlines "democratized the skies" by introducing dramatically lower fares. This enabled it to compete not just with other airlines, but also with trains, buses, and even driving. Southwest typically chose to focus on short haul routes, for which alternative modes of transportation were an option. In its early years, Southwest often quadrupled in one year the volume of passengers that flew between the cities it served.

Charles Schwab dramatically changed the economics of retail investing by offering discount stock trading to consumers. Dell cut huge chunks of cost out of its operating model and delivered customized computers directly to customers for far lower prices than its competitors. Mercedes-Benz went the other direction from Volkswagen, launching its C class at a relatively affordable price point, while very much maintaining its identity as a true Mercedes-Benz.

A classic case of achieving great success by focusing on Affordability was Henry Ford's Model T. Through his innovations in manufacturing and assembly, Ford succeeded in dramatically lowering the cost of production so that the car's price fell from $850 in 1909 (equivalent to $20,000 today) to $290 in the 1920s (equiv-alent to $3191 today). When the Model T was launched, competing cars sold for $2–3000. Along with designing a sturdy, reliable, and versatile car, Ford also doubled the prevailing wage for his employees to $5 a day. For the first time, the workers who built cars could actually afford to drive one home.

Ford succeeded in making people more willing to pay as well as enhancing his own employees' ability to pay. No wonder, then, that more than 15 million Model

T's were sold, a number that wasn't surpassed until 1972, by Volkswagen's Beetle (a car that most certainly delivered a net benefit that went beyond its sticker price). Here is how Henry Ford himself described his philosophy for the Model T:

> I will build a car for the great multitude. It will be large enough for the family, but small enough for the individual to run and care for. It will be constructed of the best materials, by the best men to be hired, after the simplest designs that modern engineering can devise. But it will be so low in price that no man making a good salary will be unable to own one—and enjoy with his family the blessing of hours of pleasure in God's great open spaces.[3]

WHAT IS AFFORDABILITY?

As we have defined it here, Affordability refers to two characteristics that customers must possess in order to move ahead with a transaction. These are the willingness and the ability to pay. The willingness to pay reflects the *economic desirability* of the proposed transaction: does it make sense from the customer's viewpoint to engage in the exchange that is being proposed? The answer to this question is "yes" when the amount of value the customer stands to gain significantly exceeds the total cost that the customer will incur. As we mentioned earlier, this total cost includes non-monetary elements such as time and effort, which are valued differently by different customers, at different points in time.

The ability to pay reflects the *economic viability* of the proposed transaction from the customer's perspective. A purchase should not endanger customers' economic well-being; it is the responsible marketer's job to ensure that customers are not pressured into making decisions that will put them in a financial bind in the future. This calls for long-term thinking and a deep sense of responsibility on the part of the marketer.

Of course, too many marketers engage only in short-term thinking, by pushing products and services to people who clearly can't afford them. Such a tactic often reaps a quick gain. But the long-term consequences—for customers and for the company's brand—can be devastating, as foreclosed homeowners and scorned banks have learned painfully over the past few years. As part of their reward for selling subprime mortgages to people with low credit scores, banks and financial-services firms occupied the bottom tier (and earned a "poor" rating) of the Reputation Institute's 2010 survey of the world's most reputable companies. Once sullied, a company's reputation is not so easily cleansed.[4]

For a transaction to be desirable from both the seller's and the buyer's perspectives, both the ability and the willingness to pay must be high. If either dimension is lacking, the transaction should not and usually will not take place. As we will discuss later in this chapter, marketers can explore a number of ways to enhance both the willingness to pay as well as the ability to pay of customers.

As we will also see, there are many creative ways for companies to arrive at a price point that beckons consumers without bleeding their credit cards. For example, customers' ability to pay can be increased by offering them the use of the product as a service, rather than requiring them to take direct ownership. Such an innovation is built around the notion that the amount of value people extract from a product is directly proportional to the amount of use they make of it. In reality, the "capacity utilization" of many products can be extremely low, which means there's an opportunity for creative marketers to offer a piece of the product, rather than the whole thing. The rising popularity of "fractional ownership" of a variety of different types of products, such as luxury cars, yachts, vacation homes, and corporate jets suggests that it's a viable way for people to afford products that would otherwise be unaffordable. A valuable by-product of this way of thinking is reduced environmental impact on the planet.

There is a substantial difference between a marketer who has a pricing mindset and one who operates from an Affordability mindset. Marketers with a pricing mindset tend to focus heavily on the interests of the seller. They seek to find an "optimal" price or pricing approach that will result in maximizing the seller's profit. Almost by definition, this tends to be a short-term approach that is largely devoid of truly creative thinking. In recent years, companies have become increasingly sophisticated in their ability to micromanage prices on almost a real-time basis, in order to maximize profitability. However, it often seems that the customers' interests are lost in the process.

On the other hand, the idea of "Affordability" stresses what the customer is willing and able to pay, rather than what the company is able to set as the highest price. It is based on value rather than cost. And building value is more of a creative endeavor than leveraging cost-accounting skills. Of course, understanding costs is important, but it should come after an analysis of Affordability. Such an approach could be called "Affordability-based costing;" the objective is to determine what kind of cost structure is needed to operate profitably under the proposed Affordability-based approach to pricing. For example, after Peachtree Software lowered the price of its accounting package from $5000 to $199, it started charging for customer support, converting that activity from a cost center to a profit center.

True, people buy things they cannot economically afford, as the subprime mortgage crisis so powerfully demonstrated. And some argue that an Affordability mindset could possibly discount the reality of impulse purchases and spontaneous spending. A common attitude is, "What good would car salesmen be if they only sold what consumers could afford?" In our view, they'd do a lot of good. When they match vehicles with customers who can afford them, car salesmen (and saleswomen) begin to build long-term, trust-based relationships that stand a better chance of yielding repeat sales.[5]

An Affordability mindset differs from a pricing mindset in that it *starts* with the customer's perspective. Marketers must deeply understand the drivers of value from the customer's perspective; based on these insights, they must then seek to incorporate as much value as possible into their offerings. They must also, especially in the case of significant purchases, understand the customer's financial realities, and determine whether the customer can truly absorb the added cost that purchasing the product would entail. In the long term, this approach makes sound economic sense; customers who are unable to keep up with their payments are not likely to be profitable for the company.

The ultimate objective of a well-thought-out approach to maximizing both dimensions of Affordability for customers (while preserving profit) is to ensure that the overall value proposition is so strong, the customer can't afford *not* to buy the product. Such a proposition might sound utopian, but in fact, it's the hallmark of any good market exchange. After all, if the purchase doesn't enhance the customer's welfare, why should the customer do the deal?

While a price mindset tends to focus on what consumers are willing to pay today, an Affordability mindset captures the initial purchase as well as the longer-term cost of ownership. An Affordability mindset removes the often hidden barriers that inhibit people from moving ahead with a purchasing decision. It also removes the necessity for the marketer to engage in a hard sell.

Marketers are accustomed to working with corporate customers to make the "business case" for a proposed transaction. This is a very constructive approach that should be honestly and transparently implemented in consumer buying situations as well. If a company is not legitimately able to make such a case to a customer, it should revisit its fundamental value proposition for the markets it's targeting.

Peachtree Software: A Radical Approach to Affordability

Peachtree Software is an example of a company that benefited itself and its customers greatly by adopting an Affordability orientation. It was the first company to provide off-the-shelf accounting software that ran on personal computers. IBM chose Peachtree to produce a full-featured accounting system for its then top-secret PC project. When the IBM PC was launched in 1981, Peachtree was the only accounting software available for it.

Peachtree sold its software as eight separate modules, with a total price of approximately $4800. While the price tag was steep, it compared favorably to the $25,000 and more that businesses would have to spend to develop their own, customized accounting systems. Peachtree's software could be customized for a modest additional charge, a good deal for customers who could afford it. Peachtree used its own sales force—and almost no advertising—to sell its software.

In the mid-1980s, however, the company was struggling to compete with lower-priced rivals such as DacEasy's $50 accounting product. Taking a calculated, market-based decision in 1986, Peachtree dramatically lowered the price of Peachtree Complete® Accounting for DOS, from almost $4800 to only $199, and placed an ad in the *Wall Street Journal* announcing the price reduction. The new price point made Peachtree affordable to a much larger market. With the company selling the software directly to customers, demand exploded. Sales rose from $50,000 a month to approximately $1.5 million a month.

Peachtree president Bill Goodhew described the company's pricing strategy this way: "The approach we took was that DacEasy was $50 software that you could buy for $50. Peachtree has $5000 software that you could buy for just $200. It's a great value."

An important aspect of Peachtree's new pricing strategy was that sales were not the only revenue stream—there was also service. The company established 35 local support centers around the country, each staffed with trained accountants, and charged customers for the accountants' advice. Within a matter of months, the support services as well as the software were profit centers.

Peachtree's success demonstrates the power of thinking in terms of what customers can afford, rather than what the company can get them to pay. It also shows that cutting price can be a shrewd strategic move, especially when it's coupled with a newly created source of revenue and also leads to a significant expansion of the potential market.

CREATING AFFORDABILITY

Before we look at how companies can improve economic affordability (the ability to pay) and psychological affordability (the willingness to pay), here are some basic approaches that companies should consider to improve affordability overall:

1. Make the product worth more in the customer's mind through functional improvements such as adding desirable features or improving quality.
2. Make the product worth more in the customer's mind through psychological factors such as improving its image or lowering risk.
3. Lower the effective price (i.e. everything the customer has to give to get the product) to the customer by reducing the time or effort required to purchase and use the product.
4. Break through psychological price barriers by changing the product's size or form factor, as Unilever and others did in developing markets by creating single-use sachets of their products.
5. Devise a creative pricing mechanism that better links price to value and removes upfront barriers to purchasing.

6. Make the product more affordable to the payer by enticing others to pay part of the price. This could include advertisers, employers, or the government; for example, many governments provide tax rebates for socially desirable products such as hybrid and electric cars.

7. Create product variations to meet the expectations of those customers with less ability and willingness to pay. For example, Apple has created the Mac Mini and the iPod Shuffle to appeal to customers who cannot afford its standard offerings.

8. Use performance-based pricing. This is a clever approach that aligns Acceptability and Affordability. In performance-based pricing, the seller is paid based on the actual performance of its products or service. For example, advertising agencies have traditionally been paid 15 percent of media billings. This practice actually provides agencies with a counter-incentive to create more compelling advertisements, as research has clearly shown that if mediocre advertisements run more often than better quality ads, they can achieve the same impact. Marketers have gradually been shifting towards performance-based pricing, which rewards agencies for advertisements that are more effective in achieving the company's stated goals. When their campaigns deliver superior results, advertising agencies' profit margins rise—a classic win-win outcome for the agency and the client.[6]

9. Make products more affordable by removing the many hidden cross-subsidies across products, customers, markets, and channels. For example, the use of Activity Based Costing can reveal where the company is actually making money and where it is losing money. It can then adjust its prices accordingly.

Since every customer is different, it is important to take a customized approach to Affordability. Just as marketers are increasingly able to precisely match customers with the right product, they must also learn to match customers with the right price. Many products today can be readily customized to the requirements of individual consumers. The challenge is how to customize Affordability to each customer, and thereby maximize overall profitability without alienating customers (by appearing to be unfair in your pricing approach).

An effective way to achieve price customization is through multidimensional pricing, whereby the company uses two or more price parameters instead of just one.[7] For example, consider a company selling industrial gases packaged in steel containers. Under a traditional one-dimensional pricing scheme, the company charges by weight, say $2 a pound. A standard pricing strategy makes it easy for customers to compare prices across suppliers. But there's an alternative approach, which is to offer a pricing scheme that combines a daily rental fee for the cylinder with a lower per-pound price. This allows customers who use gas at a faster rate to get a lower price. The supplier can now use two variables along which to effect price changes. If the two price components are managed well, profit can be increased.

Consider how the Deutsches Bahn (German Railroad) took a multidimensional approach to its pricing. For many potential customers, the company's simple, distance-based pricing couldn't compete with driving. The company then started offering a "BahnCard" that sold for $300 per year for first class and $150 for second class. Customers who bought these cards were then entitled to a 50 percent discount off the standard per-kilometer rate. The pricing innovation made train travel much more competitive with driving (and other forms of transport), once customers recovered the "sunk cost" of buying the BahnCard, and ultimately increased the company's profit by more than $200 million a year. When companies customize the product or service's price around the market's willingness and ability to pay, customers follow.

Defying All Odds: The Tata Nano

On January 10, 2008, Ratan Tata, the chairman of Tata Group, proudly drove the company's new car, the long-awaited Nano, on to the stage at the ninth Auto Expo in New Delhi, India. Five years earlier, he had been struck by an all too familiar sight on Indian roads: a family of four balanced precariously on a two-wheeler as it weaved its way through traffic in the rain, trying to avoid puddles, potholes, and cows along the way. A deeply compassionate leader who helmed a company known for its commitment to improving the lives of ordinary people in India, Tata soon confirmed what he had already suspected: India had one of the highest traffic fatality rates in the world. The average person in India simply could not afford to provide safe and comfortable transportation for his or her family. For Tata, putting cars within reach of millions of Indian families was more a matter of restoring human dignity than simply improving traffic safety.[8]

Tata challenged his engineers to produce a safe, comfortable, reliable, fuel-efficient, and environmentally friendly car for the then unheard-of price of Rs. 100,000 (approximately $2200). This would be about half the price of the lowest priced car then on the market, and was not much more than the average price of a two-wheeler. His competitors scoffed at the very idea, and said, in essence, "We believe it when we see it." Tata stuck to his guns. "If you could position an all-weather car that is not a glorified scooter or a stripped-down car, then I believe there would be a market potential for one million cars a year," he told *The McKinsey Quarterly*.

Today, the Tata Nano (which means "small" in Gujarati, the language of the Tata's founders) is very much a reality. The stylish, attractive car has garnered major worldwide publicity and more than half a million pre-orders. It has won rave reviews in the automotive press, and has the potential to dramatically alter the economics of the global auto industry. The car has many design and engineering innovations (the company has filed 34 patents for it), and is fully expected to uphold Tata's famed reputation for rugged overengineering, while delivering

73 mpg on highways. The car is expected to boost the Indian economy, create entrepreneurial opportunities for millions and has the potential to expand the Indian car market by 65 percent.

The Tata Nano sets a new standard for Affordability in the automobile market. In fact, its Rs. 100,000 price tag has become an integral part of its identity. With the enormous worldwide publicity that it has received, the Nano is set for years and years of high demand with virtually no advertising needed. Its launch event in January 2008 was carried live on all of India's major news networks, and made the front page of the *New York Times* and numerous other newspapers worldwide. In many ways, the Nano launch even surpassed the anticipation surrounding the launch of the Apple iPhone in June 2007.

After its launch, the Nano did run into some production delays (due to a last minute shift in the location of its factory) and quality problems, which the company has worked on to fix. An interesting marketing challenge it is facing is that in a market in which incomes and aspirations are rising rapidly, the ability to pay is becoming less of an issue for existing car buyers, who are looking to trade up in terms of size, comfort, and luxury. Tata will have to concentrate its efforts on first-time car buyers and those accustomed to buying two-wheelers.[9]

IMPROVING ABILITY TO PAY

Marketers have historically paid inadequate attention to the issue of customers' ability to pay, and have instead focused almost exclusively on creating a high willingness to pay based on intangibles such as brand image. As a result, they have ignored vast numbers of potential customers worldwide, especially in emerging markets. With the recent emphasis on "bottom of the pyramid" markets—as well as the recognition that with high unemployment, consumers are spending less—companies are beginning to focus on improving their customers' ability to pay.

A customer's ability to pay is a function of their income statement and balance sheet, for both business and consumer markets. In other words, customers need to have enough income and free cash flow to pay for the purchase, or have enough assets to finance the purchase.

When assessing ability to pay, it is useful to distinguish between necessary and discretionary purchases. "Engel's Law" states that as people's incomes rise, the proportion of income they spend on food goes down, even though the absolute amount of money spent on food goes up. The same could be said of other necessities as well. This suggests that in prosperous economies, the ability to pay for most necessities is not a constraint on most customers. By the same token, the ability to pay for necessities is a serious constraint in less prosperous economies. In such situations, companies must work even harder to help people afford goods and services that can improve the quality of their lives.

When improving the customer's ability to pay, it's important to ask whether, from the customer's perspective, the planned purchase is an expense or an investment. An investment (like real estate) potentially appreciates over time or is instrumental in generating income (e.g. factory equipment). An expense, of course, doesn't offer such benefits. It therefore makes sense to expend greater effort to create the ability to pay for products that can be viewed as investments. Conversely, it is irresponsible on the part of marketers to create the illusion of an ability to pay for products that have little or no long-term value.

Another way to think about Affordability from the customer's perspective is to separate the short term from the long term. If a customer's ability to pay is lacking in the short term, but is quite assured in the long term (because of rising income), it makes eminent sense to come up with creative financing approaches that could allow the customer to afford the product immediately.

Here are some ways in which companies can try to increase customers' ability to pay:

■ Leasing
The leasing phenomenon began in Europe (mostly in the United Kingdom), when it was called "hire purchase." It was a means of paying for large household items such as furniture and white goods. Customers would pay for the product in installments over a period of time and were charged interest on the loan. Modern leasing began in the business market. The objective is to lower or eliminate the upfront capital cost to the buyer, making the purchase an operating expense instead. Many companies prefer not to expend capital if possible. Leasing has become very common in all kinds of industrial equipment purchases; most airlines, for example, do not buy planes any more but lease them from companies such as GE Leasing. Even the military now leases some of its aircraft. In the consumer world, leasing has caught on in the automobile industry.

■ Creative financing
As mentioned earlier, when customers have the ability to pay in the long term but not in the short term, it makes sense for marketers to come up with creative financing approaches. That's how the savings and loans banks created the 30-year mortgage in the United States. When the US government stepped in to provide guarantees for mortgages, it made such financing options even more attractive for lenders and borrowers alike. Creative financing can and should also be used for important infrastructure projects, which can have a significant impact on economic growth.

■ Third party pays
For people who lack the ability to pay, a good strategy is to leverage a third entity that stands apart from users and payers. Consider the rise of Blue Cross Blue Shield, which was created by doctors. After the Great Depression, many

people stopped going to doctors, as they could not afford to. Some doctors decided to create organizations that would offer insurance, to make the cost of healthcare more predictable and affordable. By 1944, with US unemployment at a record low level of 1.2 percent, companies started using the promise of healthcare benefits as a way to lure workers away from other companies, since they were prevented by the prevailing wage freeze from paying employees more. Over time, this tactic greatly increased the demand for healthcare services.

■ Tiered offerings

Rather than lower prices across the board to attract customers with lesser resources to pay, it makes more sense to segment the market into price tiers. Sears, with its Good-Better-Best strategy, was very good at this. Taken together, the company's offerings in a broad range of price categories were affordable for almost everyone. In the hotel business, Marriott has created a range of properties, such as Hampton Inn, Courtyard, and Marriott Marquis, that are priced according to the depths of the target customers' pockets. Many other chains have followed suit.

■ ASP model

The Application Service Provider (ASP) model converts a product into a service. Instead of making an upfront purchase, companies have the option to use the service as needed and pay accordingly. A good example of this is salesforce.com, which offered its suite of sales automation and customer relationship management applications on the web to customers on an as needed basis. The alternative is to go through an expensive, time-consuming, and unpredictable installation of a software system such as Siebel. In a sense, the offering is like a utility that customers can tap into when they need to. Other examples of the ASP approach include on-demand computing, metered pricing for software and the use of "Centrex" instead of PBX telecommunications services, where companies can use up-to-date phone facilities at the local phone company's central office. This subscription-based approach gives customers a "right to use" rather than a "license to own," and generally makes these offerings more affordable. The most recent example is the emergence of cloud computing, especially for small businesses and individual consumers.

■ Fractional ownership

Fractional ownership, where customers buy a share of an expensive product instead of owning it outright, has become increasingly popular in recent years. While it began with vacation properties and private jets, fractional ownership now extends to recreational vehicles, yachts, motorcycles, and exotic cars. Buyers typically pay the seller to handle scheduling and maintenance. The assets are usually sold after a few years, and the proceeds are divided among the owners. For example, fractional ownership pioneer NetJets charges $406,250 for a one-sixteenth interest (the equivalent to 50 hours of annual flying time) in a Hawker 400XP. In addition, owners are charged a "monthly management fee," which covers indirect operating costs such as pilot salaries, training, hangaring, insurance, and owner support. They also pay an "occupied hourly fee" that covers flight-specific direct operating costs such as fuel, maintenance, catering, and landing fees.[10] The economic logic behind fractional ownership is strong. It allows people access to better and more expensive products than they could afford on their own, and also removes the burdens of maintaining and selling the product once there is no longer any need for it.[11]

■ Micro packaging

In developing markets, companies need to think small, in contrast to the "super size" culture of developed markets. In India alone, Unilever sells over $1 billion a year of shampoos and other products in small single-serve sachets, which typically cost a few pennies and are readily affordable to the masses, who generally cannot afford to buy a larger size package at one time.

■ Market-based product design and pricing

Music and movie companies have long bemoaned the fact that their products are routinely pirated and sold for deeply discounted prices in many countries around the world. The companies have tried many different tactics to curb piracy, including more elaborate copy protection schemes and the enactment and stricter enforcement of tough anti-piracy laws. None of these approaches have proven effective. In China, 90 percent of all CDs sold are pirated. The fact remains that most consumers in these markets simply cannot afford to pay the prevailing retail price for DVDs and CDs. Few Mexicans can afford to pay 130 pesos ($12) for a legitimate CD, so most buy pirated ones for about a dollar. Now, some companies have decided to try a new tactic: sharply lowering prices on legitimate DVDs and CDs that are sold in developing countries. For example, Warner Bros. has started to sell DVDs in China for $2.65 for basic discs (with English and Mandarin tracks) and $3.38 for enhanced versions with extra features.[12] Software companies such as Microsoft are trying the same tactic, coming up with much cheaper versions of their products for emerging markets. Such approaches are still profitable, since the variable cost of producing a copy of a software program (just like a DVD or CD) is close to zero.

The Origins of Consumer Credit

Any discussion of improving consumers' ability to pay must consider that double-edged sword called credit, which has always played a prominent role in the American economy. As the author and historian Lendol Calder observes, "A river of red ink runs through American history. Americans have always lived in debt. The Pilgrims came over on the installment plan." After all, London merchants financed the New World expedition; in exchange, the Pilgrims agreed to forego all profit for seven years.[13]

Even in the seventeenth century, American attitudes towards credit were ambivalent. Certain kinds of debt were deemed acceptable, others not. Moralists referred to "productive" debt and "consumptive" debt. Borrowing money to buy a farm or start a business was considered a productive debt; borrowing for personal consumption was considered consumptive—that is, decidedly unhealthy. By and large, this seemed a fairly sensible prescription for avoiding financial difficulties.

Until the Industrial Revolution took root, consumers did not have a plethora of tempting products to choose from. But in the 1910s and 1920s, American factories began producing an immense range of new consumer products, such as washing machines, phonographs, radios, refrigerators, and more. Though manufacturing was rapidly becoming more efficient, most products remained beyond the reach of the vast majority of consumers. The result was that people saved for years before buying a big-ticket item. For example, the average family had to save for about five years to buy a car.

The company that recognized the disparity between price and ability to pay as a huge opportunity was none other than General Motors, which built the modern consumer economy's foundations by inventing the credit system.

In 1919, the world's leading carmaker was still the Ford Motor Co., whose iconic Model T—with its low price, high reliability, and simple "any-color-as-long-as-it's-black" marketing philosophy—continued to sell at an extraordinary rate. GM made a range of cars, such as Oldsmobile, Buick, and Chevrolet. The cars were available in many colors and were more stylish than the Model T, but they were also a lot more expensive.

To compete with Ford, GM began offering auto loans. In 1919, the company established the General Motors Acceptance Corporation (GMAC) to sell cars "on time," as the practice was known. The early loans were quite conservative, requiring as much as 35 percent down and the rest due in installments over the course of a year. Henry Ford, who held strong beliefs against using debt to finance products like cars, refused to follow suit. Instead, Ford offered customers the old-fashioned lay-away plan, under which they could deposit $5 to $10 with their local Ford dealer every week until they had enough money accumulated to take delivery. Needless to say, this "weekly payment plan" was a failure.

GM soon overtook Ford in the market. In 1928, Ford was finally forced to set up its own auto loan subsidiary to compete. Spurred by GM's innovation, consumer attitudes toward credit and debt began to change rapidly. The country had long made thrift a virtue. But now, with so many manufacturers dangling so many enticing products in front of them, consumer resistance crumbled. By 1930, the majority of durable products were bought on installment plans, including two-thirds of all cars.

Except for a brief respite during the Great Depression, the consumer credit market continued to grow explosively, especially after World War II. By the year

2000, GMAC alone had lent over $1 *trillion* to car buyers! And it had expanded into home mortgages, other kinds of loans, and credit cards.[14]

Given this history and prominence of credit in the American economy, it is important for companies to rethink how they should use credit to improve consumers' ability to pay, without driving them deep into debt.

AFFORDABILITY AND ACCEPTABILITY

Keep in mind that an offering's Acceptability and Affordability together determine the overall value proposition. If both are high, the value proposition is strong. If one factor is weak, the value proposition is weak. If both are weak, the value proposition is virtually non-existent.

For example, in 1999, Harman Kardon and Microsoft launched the Take Control TC1000 remote control, which could be programmed to operate up to 15 devices. Despite the obvious appeal of replacing the glut of remote controls crowding most American family rooms with one unit, the product was a total failure. Viewed through the 4A's value-proposition lens, the reasons for Take Control's demise become clear:

- *Acceptability:* The portly unit weighed in at nearly a pound, used four AA batteries, and measured 7.5 × 3.4 × 1.8 inches. Its backlit, LCD touch screen was relatively hard to read. Configuring the device took well over an hour, even for technologically sophisticated users, all of which led consumers to say "no" to the Take Control.
- *Affordability:* Take Control was priced at an unbelievable $349—at a time when consumers could buy a VCR for well below $100 and a DVD player for less than $200. Harman Kardon and Microsoft's oversized, hard-to-use unit offered a value proposition that any consumer would be more than happy to turn down—and just about everyone did.

"Willingness to pay" captures the customer's personal value equation: Is the value I will derive from this product greater than the total cost that I will incur in acquiring it? "Acceptability" has to do with whether the offering meets the consumer's requirements, regardless of price.

Increasing an offering's Acceptability increases the customer's willingness to pay, but does nothing to impact their ability to pay, which is purely a function of their resources. Lowering the price increases a customer's ability to pay but does not impact Acceptability; however, it can increase the willingness to pay because the value equation appears better to the customer. In other words, the customer feels she is getting better value when the price is lower. For example, she may be unable and unwilling to pay $100 for a Broadway play, but at a price of $50, she is able and willing to pay.

An expensive product that is beyond a customer's ability to pay (such as a Rolex watch or a Rolls-Royce) may be functionally and psychologically acceptable to a customer. However, if customers can't afford the product, they obviously won't buy it. Companies can entice customers with a significant sale, which often increases their willingness as well as ability to pay. Another way to augment consumers' willingness to pay is to introduce an economy line of products under the same brand name. Indeed, when BMW melded prestige and value with its 3 Series, the company doubled its worldwide auto sales within three years of the car's launch. More than three decades later, the 3 Series remains the best-selling car in its class.

IMPROVING WILLINGNESS TO PAY

A customer's willingness to pay occurs at two levels. At the first level, customers are willing to pay if they view the price as reasonable. They consider a number of factors before making a decision, including the price of competing products, the cost of substitute products, their perception of what goes into making the product, and the value they expect to derive from the product. In the absence of direct substitutes or competing products, willingness to pay is very much a function of the value created in the mind of the customer.

At the second level, customers are willing to pay if they are convinced that the value they are receiving from the product far exceeds the price they are being asked to pay. In these cases, customers believe that it would be highly unwise of them *not* to buy the product at the offered price. In other words, customers are not only willing, they are *happy* to pay the price.

The 1995 Chevrolet Lumina's success story demonstrates the value of understanding what customers are willing to pay. In 1993, sales of the Lumina sedan and Lumina coupé had slipped from a peak of 225,000. A Lumina marketing team quizzed more than 2000 customers and learned that the sedan's target buyers put price and value at the top of their lists; next in line were dependability and safety. Based on their survey results, the team decided to price the Lumina below the Ford Taurus, settling on a base sticker price of $15,995. By addressing consumers' foremost concern, the Lumina team dramatically increased sales.

An advertising campaign that highlighted the Lumina's low base price and strong value helped make customers aware of the Lumina's unique Affordability compared with its competitors. The results were that the Lumina's sales increased by 75 percent in 1995 calendar year and its market share in the mid-size sedan segment nearly doubled to 12 percent.

Another model for improving customers' willingness to pay comes from the fast-food industry, which has long appealed primarily to people looking for an inexpensive meal in a hurry. But as consumers began to put a higher value on health consciousness, some companies have seen an opportunity to create a new niche of fast food that's healthy and priced at a premium.

A prime example is Panera Bread, whose sales grew at a 33 percent annual rate between 2001 and 2006, while net income rose even faster at 50 percent per year. Panera's average customer check comes to $8.51, much higher than the industry average of $4.55, which allows it to generate more revenue per store than its competitors. Panera's primary appeal is freshly baked breads and pastries that contain no unhealthy transfats and a menu that is revitalized every two months with a new sandwich or salad. The willingness of customers to pay higher prices for its products enables Panera to offer better food, ambience, and service than its rivals. Employees are well paid and receive good benefits, resulting in a turnover rate that's less than one-third of the industry norm. The future of the chain seems secure for now, with many parents refusing to take their children to traditional fast-food restaurants. As one parent says, "[Panera's] prices are a little more expensive than fast food, but it's well worth it."[15]

Willingness to pay is a function of the customer's life priorities, as well as budgeting (how much of their discretionary income they have allocated to different spending categories), alternative uses for resources, and contextual factors such as location and convenience. Some factors that *inhibit* a customer's willingness to pay include a perceived lack of fairness or transparency in pricing and a significant mismatch between the expected and actual price. If the price is significantly below what the customer associates with the product, it can damage the product's image and lower the customer's willingness to pay. If the price is too high, the customer does not see a viable value proposition, and is therefore unwilling to pay the price.

The business world is rife with stories of customers with the ability but not the willingness to pay. Recall our earlier example of the failure of airphones. More recently, airlines appear to be making a similar mistake, this time with their pricing of Wi-Fi service in planes. For example, AirTran charges $14.95 per flight for Wi-Fi use. Most of AirTran's flights are 2 to 3 hours in duration, and the vast majority of its passengers do not believe that comparatively brief access to the Internet and e-mail is worth the price. Innovative products that strike customers as overpriced are also prone to willingness-to-pay problems. As we have shown, Apple's Newton and Motorola's Iridium failed because targeted customers who could afford them were simply unwilling to pay for them.

Marketers have traditionally tried to create a greater willingness to pay by focusing on certain psychological aspects of pricing, such as ensuring that prices end with a "9," in hopes of convincing customers that the price is lower than it actually is. Conversely, marketers of luxury products have long understood that if the price is too low for a prestige brand, the brand will have less of an appeal. In such cases, a premium brand's allure increases as its price increases.

Willingness to pay is also a function of the customer's ability to "make" rather than buy a product that they perceive to be of poor value. For example, some airlines have started to produce many of the replacement parts they need for maintenance, since Boeing often charges what the airlines consider exorbitant prices. American Airlines started making a small replacement part in its own machine shop for $5.24 each, rather than paying Boeing's price of $146. This do-it-yourself approach saved American $170,000 a year, just for the one part. Since over half of a plane's parts get replaced over a typical 30-year lifespan (many repeatedly), the savings can be substantial.[16]

Another product category in which very high prices and high margins have created similar pressures is inkjet cartridges. The ink that sits inside inkjet cartridges sold by major manufacturers is perhaps the world's most highly priced liquid, running as high as $8000 per gallon! Numerous companies and franchises have emerged to offer customers far more affordable alternatives to new cartridges purchased from the manufacturer. Until 2002, Hewlett-Packard made all of its profits as a company from the sale of replacement cartridges. Refilling cartridges only costs 60 to 70 cents, while new ones retail for $20–30. By 2004, refillers had captured about 20 percent of the market.[17] In recent years, printer manufacturers have gradually started to lower their cartridge prices, and Kodak has made a virtue of its relatively inexpensive cartridges ($10 for black, $15 for color).

Here are some ways that companies can improve customers' willingness to pay:

■ Build more value into the offering
  The most powerful way to improve willingness to pay is to dramatically improve the value proposition to the customer. Consider the following examples:
  The toothbrush market has long been divided into two distinct categories: inexpensive manual toothbrushes that retail for approximately $2–3 and expensive, rechargeable power toothbrushes that can cost as much as $130. Not surprisingly, the latter only occupied a tiny share of the overall market in which revenues have been stagnant for some time. The vast majority of customers were neither able nor willing to spend that much on a toothbrush.
  In recent years, several companies have introduced products that bridge the gap between price and performance. Battery-powered toothbrushes offer many of the advantages of rechargeable power toothbrushes but at a much lower price. For example, in 2003, Gillette launched the Oral-B CrossAction Power at a retail price of $6.99. The slender instrument is a marvel of engineering: a high-efficiency motor encased in a waterproof body, 2596 bristles angled in five different directions and mounted at three different heights, and a sophisticated suspension system that oscillates 7200 times a minute. The product followed on the heels of a rival toothbrush launched by Procter & Gamble: the $7.99 Crest SpinBrush, which has a head that pulses as well as oscillates.[18]
  These innovations have injected new growth and higher profitability into a

sector that had long been stagnant. They demonstrate the power of offering value-added products at prices that customers are not only willing, but are happy to pay.[19]

Especially in a business-to-business marketing context, companies must be able to make the case for why their product or service surpasses their competitors', in terms of delivering better benefits to customers. For example, the food service marketing and distribution company Sysco commands higher prices than its competitors, mostly because it demonstrates true value to the customer for its thousands of products. For instance, it sells organic, fresh cut onions at $14.44 for 21 pounds, compared to its competitor's price of $12.56 for 50 pounds of uncut onions. However, when factoring in the labor cost of slicing onions and the yield of usable product from the competing supplier, the cost for an 8-ounce portion of Sysco's offering comes to just 36 cents, compared to 67 cents for the competitor. The lesson: a product's total value isn't always reflected in its price.

Like Sysco, 3M delivers superior value to its customers and distributors not by lowering its prices, but by finding applications and support services that reduce the overall cost of total solutions. It does so by investigating how its products are used and then suggesting cost-saving modifications in those applications. It uses tools such as Quality Function Deployment (QFD) to evaluate the value of individual product attributes to customers. 3M consistently focuses on the value of its offerings (based on savings) over substitute processes or competing products.

Other examples of adding value-added services include full-service brokers who offer financial advice in addition to trading services, and retailers that add value through a more engaging experience and greater expertise, service, and selection.

■ Adding intangible benefits
Airline lounges and gated communities enhance their appeal by offering greater exclusivity. Airline lounges used to offer their services for free, but are now able to charge significant amounts. Their value has grown due to the greater use of hubs and international travel, which increases layover time for travelers. Gated communities are based less on security and more on creating a sense of community and exclusivity. Intangible benefits can also be created through the use of exclusive brands.

■ Lowering risks through performance and satisfaction guarantees
Every transaction carries a certain amount of risk. If the perceived risk is high, customers' willingness to pay decreases. Companies that can offer customers greater assurance that they will indeed receive what they are paying for can increase their customers' willingness to pay. Offering extended warranties and additional forms of optional protection to customers can result in increased revenues.

■ Packaging

Companies have been able to create in consumers the willingness to pay by making products appear more attractive through creative packaging. Many companies excel at this. Consider perfume: it is not the scent, but the lush packaging that often makes the difference. The same is largely true for chocolates. The wine industry is belatedly seizing on the power of packaging, as is the beverage industry in general.

■ Better positioning

Marketers position products for price, prestige, and value. From a willingness to pay perspective, the strongest position that any brand can attain is "best value." For example, Caterpillar does not strive to be the price leader in its industry. Instead, it focuses resolutely on being a quality leader that delivers value in innovative ways.

Despite charging a premium price, Caterpillar can still make the case that it offers superior economic value, because the cost of owning its machines over their lifetime is actually less than that of even its most aggressively priced competitors. The machines have a higher resale value, and often can be rebuilt because of their extremely strong frames. To close a deal, Caterpillar provides customers with software that helps them understand the machine's true value equation by factoring in the acquisition price, operating and maintenance costs, insurance costs, and resale value.

Caterpillar offers its customers multiple ways in which they can meet their needs while maximizing Affordability. Customers can go to dealers with a specific job in mind (e.g. "I have to remove this much dirt") and be quoted a fixed price for using the equipment to do the job. They can then rent machines and tools by the day. Caterpillar also offers customers an innovative "forward repurchase program," under which the company agrees, at the time of the sale, to repurchase a machine after a given number of years at an agreed upon price. The machines can be returned to any dealer, who then makes additional profits by reselling them.

Caterpillar also has a very innovative "barter" program, whereby it accepts merchandise—from steel to TVs to generators—in lieu of cash. The company has set up a highly profitable subsidiary, called Caterpillar World Trade Organization, to manage its barter operations. This is a classic win-win; customers who could not otherwise afford its machines benefit from their use while also benefiting Caterpillar and its shareholders.

■ Better targeting

By targeting the right segments with the right offering, marketers can create high willingness to pay. For example, in the past few years, many sports teams have moved away from pricing their tickets based strictly on the location of the seat. They now vary pricing based on the day of the week, the time of day, and the quality of the opponent. By doing so, they have expanded the range of prices they offer; their lowest prices are now much lower than before, and the highest prices are much higher. In making this move, teams are recognizing what ticket scalpers have always known: that the value of a ticket depends much more on factors other than seat location. This approach tailors price to reflect value, which always increases a customer's willingness to pay.

■ Bundling/unbundling

Phone companies often bundle different products and services into one price package. This makes people more willing to pay the price, since they perceive that they're receiving incremental value at a lower, incremental cost. But for certain market segments, unbundling can also be attractive. For example, until 2005, Verizon required its DSL customers to also keep their local phone service with the company. As a result, it lost many potential customers who wanted their DSL service unbundled from their local service.

As companies as disparate as Apple and Dow Chemical have demonstrated, unbundling can yield long-term benefits. The iPod's success is in part due to the fact that people are very willing to pay 99 cents for a song, but not $15 for a CD. Dow Chemical now splits out and charges separately for many add-on services in its commodity-plastics business. For varying fees, it offers faster delivery, pay-per-use technical support, and consulting services.[20]

■ Leveraging the razor-and-blade principle

The razor-and-blade business model was pioneered by King Camp Gillette, inventor of the safety razor, who discovered that he could ensure the sales of his blades at a reasonable profit margin if he could convince enough people to use his razor. He started by giving his razors away to increase the market for blades, and the rest, as they say, is history. By 1915, 14 years after its founding, the Gillette Safety Razor Company's blade sales exceeded 70 million units.[21]

The razor-and-blade model also transformed the cellular telephony industry. Handsets used to cost as much as $3000 upfront, and few customers could afford them. Some companies started offering the handsets at a deep discount, while requiring customers to sign multiyear contracts for cellular service. As a result, the industry has experienced explosive growth, as we discussed in Chapter 1.

As these examples illustrate, there is great potential to enhance customers' willingness to pay. Marketers need to be highly creative in how they think about this issue.

THE ULTIMATE IN AFFORDABILITY: FREE

There's affordable, and then there's free. While it may seem ludicrous at first to suggest that "free" can be a viable price, there are plenty of examples in the information sector and beyond to suggest that this can indeed be the case.

The free approach has long been used as a cross subsidy: you get the razor or cell phone for free, and pay for the blades and the minutes. Increasingly, however, the economics of many key industries are changing in a way that enables companies to price their products at or near zero, even without a cross subsidy. For knowledge intensive products such as microprocessors, memory chips, software, and even pharmaceuticals, the bulk of the costs are fixed. It can cost hundreds of millions of dollars, even billions of dollars, to develop a state-of-the-art microprocessor, operating system, software application, or blockbuster drug. Once the development is done, however, the cost of producing the next incremental unit goes down steeply, in many cases to virtually zero. This is where creativity in pricing becomes not only possible, but also necessary.

In 1984, the author Stewart Brand famously said, "Information wants to be free. Information also wants to be expensive ... That tension will not go away." Nowhere is this more evident than on the web. The vast majority of newspapers and magazines offer their content for free; even the *Wall Street Journal* is planning to switch back to a predominantly free service in the near future. The *New York Times* experimented with a paid model and then switched back to free in 2007. Almost all of Google's services are free to users.

It is a fundamental principle of economics that in a competitive market, the marginal revenue eventually equals marginal cost. In hotly contested markets, the competition eventually drives a product's price down toward the incremental cost of producing the next unit. In the world of the web, that incremental cost so closely approaches zero that it is not worth measuring. As Chris Anderson says, describing the economics of YouTube: "Nobody is deciding whether a video is good enough to justify the scarce channel space it takes, because there is no scarce channel space."[22]

More and more businesses are feeling the impact of "the economics of electronics". Just consider how Google has transformed advertising. Where once it had been an intensively people-oriented business, in the wake of Google, it's now largely automated and software-based. In the world of "human economics," things get more expensive every year. In the world of automation and software, things get cheaper and cheaper. Similar transitions have taken place in banking and travel services.

When thinking about the decline of marginal costs, consider that a cost approaches but never actually reaches zero. Why not charge a small amount instead of nothing? An emerging body of research shows that when the price becomes zero, human behavior changes significantly.

MIT behavioral economist Dan Ariely conducted an experiment in which he offered subjects Hershey's Kisses for 1 cent and Lindt truffles for 15 cents. Three out of four subjects chose the truffles. Then Ariely reduced the price of each by one cent, so that the Kisses were now free and the truffles were 14 cents. The order of preference switch led around dramatically; 69 percent now preferred the Kisses!

This experiment demonstrates the powerful impact on consumers of "free." One explanation for the result: the ratio of prices between the two products went from 15 to infinity.

The power of free certainly isn't limited to candy and software. Amazon's offer of free shipping for orders over $25 induces a great many customers to order a second book to qualify. In France, when customers were mistakenly told that the shipping cost would be 20 cents, the number of people buying the second book declined steeply. As author and *Wired* editor Chris Anderson observes,

> From the consumer's perspective, there is a huge difference between cheap and free. Give a product away, and it can go viral. Charge a single cent for it and you're in an entirely different business, one of clawing and scratching for every customer … People think demand is elastic and that volume falls in a straight line as price rises, but the truth is that zero is one market and any other price is another. In many cases, that's the difference between a great market and none at all.[23]

Anderson suggests that when costs drop to near zero, it is far better to let the price fall all the way, rather than charge a few pennies. Or to put a twist on a familiar quotation, while a service, no matter how cheap, can still be metered, at a certain point, it's too cheap to matter. This maxim explains why micropayments—tiny amounts that customers would be charged for various web-based services—never took root.

The economics of "free" usually work by inviting a third party, usually advertisers, into the transaction between buyers and sellers. The third party pays to gain access to the market created by the seller. This is the model that has been long used in the media business, wherein media companies provide content for free to their customers and then sell advertisers the opportunity to pitch to those customers. The web is enabling an extension of this business model to other industries beyond media, and to other payers beyond advertisers.

In his book, *Free: The Future of a Radical Price*, Chris Anderson cites six ways to achieve "Free:"[24]

- *"Freemium:"* Web software, services, and content are free to users of the basic version, while fewer users pay for the premium version, which is priced to cover the costs of the freebies and still make a profit.
- *Advertising:* Free content, services, software, and more. Free to everyone.
- *Cross-subsidies:* Free products that "entice you to pay for something else." Free to everyone.
- *Zero marginal cost:* Free material that can be distributed at virtually zero cost. Free to everyone. Online music is a good example. Many artists give their music away and make money on concerts, merchandise, and licensing. Others

view music-making as a creative endeavor and are not necessarily in it for the money.

■ *Labor exchange:* Free websites and services. Free to all users. In using the site, users generate content that's valued.

■ *Gift economy:* Free everything, such as open source software or user-generated content. Free to everyone. Examples include Freecycle, which offers second-hand items to anyone willing to take ownership, and Wikipedia.

Traditional economics is based on a presumption of scarcity. It is therefore predicated on making trade-offs. But when some of the things that create the most value for people don't require trade-offs, we must adopt a new economics of abundance, based on non-depleting assets that can be enhanced by further use (such as social capital). In other words, "freenomics" is based on ubiquity. What remains in limited supply are intangibles such as reputation and attention, and these have become the "new scarcities." Business models based on "free" exist largely to build reputation and attract attention, which can then be converted through creative business models into monetary and other forms of value.

Marketers should examine the viability of the economics of free in their business, as a powerful way to create a very high level of Affordability. Clearly, Affordability for the customer can be maximized when the price is set at zero. For that price to be viable, what is needed, from the company's perspective, is an approach that maximizes *profit* when the price is set at zero.

AFFORDABILITY AND PROFITABILITY

As we've previously argued, it's important to remember that in any transaction, both sides must benefit. Increasing Affordability should not translate to lower total profit or even lower margins. For example, car leasing lowers price sensitivity, qualifies more buyers, and generates more profits for sellers.

The test of whether a company is doing a good job of managing the Affordability component of Market Value Coverage is its ability to meet its revenue and profitability objectives while simultaneously delivering high levels of Affordability to customers. As Sheth and Mittal describe in their book *Value Space*, the two primary drivers of creating profitable Affordability are target costing and lean operations.[25]

Target costing requires that companies manage all of their costs so that they yield a profit while meeting their Affordability objectives. Managed costs include developing, producing, distributing, and marketing the product, as well as the costs associated with customer service, warranty repairs, managerial overhead, and other costs that impact the company's profitability. In order to achieve their cost targets, companies must consider every aspect of their activities, from redesigning products so that they consist of fewer parts and are easier to assemble, to using cost-effective materials, to finding more efficient outside suppliers.

While target costing traditionally has focused on developing and launching new products, an emphasis on lean operations must pervade the company's culture. All of a company's processes, production as well as management, must be made more efficient. There are four primary ways to realize this goal. First, they should stream-line their business processes and remove unnecessary steps. Second, companies should automate wherever possible, so long as they don't sacrifice effectiveness or customer satisfaction. Third, companies should look at supply chain management as a way to lower procurement, storage, and handling costs. Fourth, companies should use flexible manufacturing approaches, to ensure that their production system can respond to market requirements without incurring high levels of additional costs.

Companies can improve their efficiency by benchmarking their performance against the best of their competitors as well as their own previous levels. For example, Sysco uses approximately 20 different metrics to keep track of its overall efficiency in operations. These include logistics measures such as shorts, mistakes, cases loaded per truck, and the quantity of product delivered per stop. Then there's NetApps, which competes with the dominant storage-industry leader, EMC, by using a networked storage architecture instead of attaching storage boxes directly to servers. By using small boxes that cost $15,000 instead of high-end boxes that cost $1 million, NetApps enables customers to start small and add capacity as needed. The "total cost of ownership" is far lower, as NetApps' maintenance fees are approximately one-eighth of EMC's.[26]

Companies can offer customers good price value and reap a profit by investing in making their operations efficient. For example, UPS gives its customers software that lets them service their own package shipping and tracking needs. Such customer automation lowers UPS' costs as well as customers' shipping costs and helps them better manage their accounts receivable.

Companies should not undertake cost-saving actions if they detract from customer value. For example, hotels should ask customers whether they would like their linen changed only if they've first determined that the practice adds value (guests feel good about conserving the water and energy that would be used for laundering) as well as saves money.

Companies must never lose sight of the reality that they must deliver high levels of Affordability without sacrificing Acceptability and without adversely impacting profitability. They must aim for a *double win* (improved Affordability and Acceptability) by investing in and perfecting practices and technologies that simultaneously lower costs while improving customer value. This is not as far-fetched as it sounds; many IT-based solutions have precisely this effect. For example, when FedEx switched to web-based package tracking, it lowered its costs and improved value to customers. Banks that get customers to switch to electronic bill paying and home banking experience similar benefits.

Another way for a company to improve its operating efficiency is to better its asset utilization. UPS, long known for "running the tightest ship in the shipping business," is highly effective at extracting maximum value from its enormous volume of fixed assets. For example, since it flies fewer routes over weekends, UPS converts many of its planes every Thursday to passenger planes and leases them to charter services. The cargo bins come out, and seats and other amenities go in. In fact, customers find that UPS planes are more roomy and comfortable than the planes of most commercial airlines! UPS similarly "repurposes" many of its other assets, such as airport equipment, which it requires only after most commercial flight operations have ceased for the night.

DELIVERING AFFORDABILITY BY LEVERAGING ALL RESOURCES

As we have pointed out, "Price" is not the only variable that impacts Affordability. Here are some examples of how companies can leverage many other resources to enhance economic and psychological affordability:

Product: Enhancing a product's quality and reliability increases the customer's willingness to pay. Notwithstanding its recent problems (which we expect will be corrected in short order), Toyota has steadily increased customers' willingness to pay over the years by offering high levels of quality and reliability. When Toyota first entered the US market, it competed by having a lower price. Over the years, it has proved to potential buyers that it builds quality vehicles, and customers have responded by being willing to pay ever higher prices for Toyotas, such as over $100,000 for some Lexus models. This strategy is now being replicated by Hyundai from Korea.

When targeting a lower-income market, companies can increase consumers' ability to pay by creating low-priced products that leverage investments that have been made in more prosperous markets. For example, publishing houses such as McGraw-Hill collaborate with local publishers in India to make their textbooks more affordable to local students. The books, which are published as paperbacks using lower-quality paper, sell for as little as one-sixteenth of their retail price in the US.

Price: Companies can devise innovative pricing strategies that increase customers' ability to pay. In India, the cellular company SMART, in an effort to appeal to low- and lower-middle income customers, developed an over-the-air-recharge technology and offered increments of airtime in small quantities that had not been previously available. Some were as low as 50 cents. Customers could also transfer values of as little as a few cents from one account to another. This new approach generated revenues of approximately $2 million per day within ten months.

Place: Customers are usually willing to pay a higher price for making a more informed purchase. For example, many would prefer to buy a branded television from Best Buy rather than low-end models at other stores, largely because of the assistance they get from Best Buy staffers.

Customers are often willing to pay a higher price to acquire a product or service from a brand they respect. Whole Foods Market sells natural and organic foods at a premium price—some critics have been known to call it "whole pay check"—but it's nevertheless a magnet for consumers who support its mission.

Promotions: Companies sometimes use price-discrimination strategies to promote their products. For example, movie theaters give discounts to students and seniors, creating greater Affordability for these groups. Pfizer has a program through which lower-income customers can buy critical drugs directly from the company at affordable prices.

Companies can create greater perceived Affordability by running promotions that tie into outcomes in which customers are emotionally invested. For example, Jordan's Furniture, a retail chain in the Northeast, ran a promotion in 2007 whereby customers who had purchased a mattress, dining table, sofa, or bed at a Jordan's store between March 7 and April 16 would receive a rebate if the Boston Red Sox won the 2007 World Series, which, in fact, they did. An insurance company underwrote the promotion—Jordan gave away an estimated 30,000 orders for free—which had a significant impact on Jordan's revenues for the year.

People: Customers' willingness to pay is increased if they receive exceptional service. For example, customers choose to fly on JetBlue in part because of the excellent service it offers. At times, the CEO of the company works as a flight attendant to interact with customers and learn how to better serve them. Likewise, Southwest Airlines (NYSE ticker symbol LUV) has long been known as a company that loves its employees and customers "to death."

In 1979, Home Depot changed the home improvement industry forever by creating a warehouse store filled with a wide assortment of products at "everyday low prices." It offered the best customer service in the industry, including many free classes. With its promise to customers that "you can do it, we can help," Home Depot gave customers the tools and knowledge to undertake many home maintenance tasks themselves and save money in the process.

When employees create memorable experiences, customers are more willing to pay. Employees working at Disney resorts, theme parks, and cruise lines are trained to interact with customers in such a way that it creates a "magical" experience. These experiences are what keep customers coming back and paying Disney its relatively high prices.

Processes: Self-service by customers reduces costs to the company and the savings can be passed on to customers, fueling their ability to pay. Many supermarkets now offer customers the option of self-service checkout. IKEA expects customers who come to its stores to select the items they want, retrieve them from the storage center, and bring them to the checkout line. Such innovations let IKEA cut costs and offer lower prices.

Increasing convenience directly impacts customers' willingness to pay. Customers are delighted with the value they receive from Netflix. Every time they think of a movie they would like to see, they simply add it to their queue. Often, these suggestions come from Netflix's outstanding recommendation engine. The company automatically ships them the next movie on its list when the previous one is returned.

Sales: Direct selling can deliver lower costs, leading to greater Affordability. Dell's direct model, through which it offered greater customer value at a lower price, by cutting out intermediaries and letting buyers customize their PCs, was largely responsible for the company's dramatic growth.

R&D: R&D and innovation leads to greater value for customers through the creation of affordable and useful products. Philips, the world's largest lighting manufacturer, has been at the forefront of developing new forms of energy-efficient light bulbs. Its advanced LED bulbs use 80 percent less energy and last up to 20 years, resulting in immense savings for customers and a positive impact on the environment.

Operations: Efficient and effective operations help make products and services economically and psychologically affordable. Toyota's hybrid cars save customers money through lower fuel consumption, but cost approximately $5000 more to build than gas-powered cars. Toyota is working on operational efficiencies that will allow it to produce hybrids at a lower cost. It plans to reduce the size of components and improve battery performance, further improving fuel efficiency and extending the life of the car, which will enhance Affordability to customers.

Customer service: Companies should not sacrifice customer service for efficiency. While Dell did well with its direct model, over time it became synonymous with poor customer service. By cutting costs, it could deliver a cheaper product. However, it decreased the value customers got for their money, especially if they found themselves in need of customer service.

Demonstrating a high level of responsiveness in customer service increases customers' willingness to pay in the future. After JetBlue experienced major customer service problems related to snowstorm delays (the famous 2007 Valentine's Day crisis), the company moved quickly to repair the problem. The CEO apologized, accepted full responsibility, and introduced a Passengers' Bill of Rights. JetBlue service representatives called passengers and personally apologized. These actions cemented greater loyalty among JetBlue's customers towards the airline.

IT: IT can lower the cost of providing services, resulting in higher ability to pay. For example, the news industry has used IT to lower the total cost of providing its services. Users can subscribe online to the *Wall Street Journal* for $70 a year, which is much lower than the subscription rate for the physical paper. Despite the lower rate, online customers are actually more profitable for the paper, because of the savings on paper printing and delivery costs.

IT can also enable value-added and customized features that enhance the offering and thus raise customers' willingness to pay. Netflix's success has much to do with its terrific website, state-of-the-art recommendation engine, and real-time checking of recommendations against inventory. Netflix also now uses IT to deliver programming directly to its customers' computers and television sets, enhancing its value proposition.

For companies with a good value proposition, IT can be a powerful way to increase customer confidence in their prices and thus raise their willingness to pay. For example, Progressive Auto Insurance allows customers to have all the power when it comes to pricing out insurance. Customers can go to Progressive's website and compare prices, even for the company's direct competitors.

Customers: By using existing customers to bring in new customers, companies can save dramatically on marketing costs and thereby offer better value to their customers. Many companies have successful referral programs. For example, the e-mail service Hotmail grew primarily by free customer referrals. Customers can also help solve other customers' technical problems, saving the company significant resources, which helps to keep its offerings affordable. It is estimated that Cisco saves over $500 million a year in customer support costs in part because its user forums let customers consider one another's technical questions and help each other out.

Retailers: Retailers can help make products more affordable, by offering financing at real interest rates. For example, Best Buy often offers 0 percent financing for big-ticket items such as flat screen TVs. Retailers can also encourage customers to experience products in the store, increasing their willingness to pay for those products. For example, Brookstone lets customers experience the comfort offered by the massage chairs it sells. REI, the outdoor sport and equipment retailer, lets customers try out its products and learn about a sport or outdoor activity from REI experts. All of this up-close-and-personal service increases customers' willingness to pay.

Government: Governments can enhance customers' ability to pay for certain products by helping with financing and providing subsidies. For example, the US government, through Fannie Mae, has assisted first-time homebuyers by reducing the amount of money necessary for a down payment to as low as 1 percent. The US government has also long provided subsidies to farmers. The purpose has been to both ensure the nation's food security, as well as maintain low prices. The government has also encouraged the purchase of fuel-efficient hybrid cars by offering a $2000 tax rebate for a number of years.

Governments can also help raise Affordability by creating or mandating the adoption of industry standards. While the US government has historically been reluctant to play this role, governments in Europe have typically pushed for standardization, which has led to greater efficiencies through economies of scale. This is how all of Europe ended up adopting the GSM standard for mobile telephony, while the US still has several different non-compatible standards in its market.

Industry: Companies can work with their competitors through industry trade associations to jointly develop standards, push for favorable government regulations, develop shared infrastructure, and engage in cooperative advertising campaigns. All of these have the effect of making the industry as a whole operate more efficiently and thus be able to offer better Affordability to customers. For example, the big three automobile manufacturers in the US have jointly lobbied the government to help them with high healthcare and retirement costs.

Partners: Partnerships among companies can reduce R&D and design costs, enabling companies to pass on the savings to customers. For example, Renault and Nissan partnered to improve the products of both companies by combining their strengths. This increased customers' willingness to pay for their products. Likewise, Volkswagen and Porsche jointly develop the latest sport utility vehicles to save costs.

Public relations and media: Public relations can be used to enhance Affordability by promoting products to the company's various markets. This saves greatly on marketing costs, which represent a very high proportion of overall spending. For example, before Procter & Gamble launched its Crest White Strips product, it identified key influence groups to market to. It organized conferences for these groups, to introduce the product to them. The PR campaign generated extensive media coverage. Similarly, when iRobot launched its Roomba vacuum cleaner, it received so much free publicity that it didn't have to spend on advertising.

The media can influence the price and quality of products and services and help improve their ability to pay. For example, various consumer magazines such as *Consumer Reports* have a powerful influence on product design and pricing, as they educate customers about the best products in the market. Companies vie with each other to be recognized for delivering good value for customers.

AFFORDABILITY IN EMERGING MARKETS

Affordability is not just about delivering value for money, but figuring out how to deliver appealing products and services to markets where money is tight. On a global level, the greatest bottleneck for customers is Affordability, primarily the ability to pay.

The enormous emerging markets of China and India illustrate the importance as well as the limits of creating high levels of Affordability. Both markets have shown that low prices can be critically important, but they must be coupled with reasonable levels of quality and functionality. In these markets, the lowest priced products do not always win; customers are looking for a combination of attractive prices along with compelling design, high quality, recognized brand names, and convenient distribution. In other words, high Affordability must be coupled with high levels on each of the other A's.

Consider Nokia's and Motorola's experiences in these two markets. In China, Nokia trailed Motorola and aggressive domestic players TCL and Ningbo Bird, newcomers who had captured half the market with inexpensive but stylish phones. Both companies flooded the market with vast numbers of sales assistants. Nokia has stormed back to reclaim market leadership with 31 percent of the China market. It did so by launching a broad range of phones specifically designed for the China market, ranging from inexpensive units to the "L'Amour" line that sells for nearly $500.

In India, Nokia has captured nearly 60 percent of the extremely fast growing market. Its most successful product is the simple but rugged Nokia 1100, which sells for $54. The highly practical phone is designed for Indian conditions, with a dust cover, slip-free grip, and a built-in flashlight. Nokia has held on to its market share even though Motorola has introduced cheaper models, as Motorola's brand name is virtually unknown in India and the company has lacked a distribution system.

Motorola's market share is just 6 percent in India and 10 percent in China. The company has launched a $35 phone in India, and is gradually building up its brand recognition and distribution.[27] As a result of such initiatives, cellular companies have added a billion subscribers over the last five years—after it took them 25 years to reach the first billion. The user base in India alone grew by 100 million in 2008, and is expected to reach 650 million by the 2012. The lesson? Companies that ignore emerging economies like India and China—and in the not-so-distant future, some African countries—leave millions (even billions) of dollars on the table.

Radical Innovation in Emerging Economies

As the author C.K. Prahalad has noted, entrepreneurs in developing countries such as India are creating business models that generate profits while delivering highly affordable yet high quality products and services that serve the needs of the poor. For example, they have pioneered pay-per-use services and the use of single-serve containers, innovations that are now being adapted for more prosperous markets in industries such as telecommunications, financial services, healthcare, hospitality, and even car manufacturing.[28]

These business models are based on being highly efficient users of scarce resources, which in turn allows companies to offer quality goods at rock bottom prices and still make a profit. For example, Indian cellular operators such as Bharti,

Reliance, and Tata are able to offer cellular service for 2 cents a minute and still make a good profit, even though they have to buy the same equipment that their Western counterparts do. Indian companies are offering a package of bundled TV, data, and voice services for $30 a month—a third of what such packages would cost in the US.

The contrast is especially stark in healthcare. The Narayana Hrudayalaya (NH) hospital in Bangalore performs heart bypass surgery for $1500, which is one-fiftieth the average cost in the US. It operates on hundreds of infants for free every year, has a better success rate than most US hospitals, and still manages to operate at a profit! The lower price is not all due to lower wages; the hospital's 25 foreign-trained surgeons earn about half of what they would make in the US, which still enables them to afford a better lifestyle than they could attain in the West.

Companies are also making creative use of technology, heavily using outsourcing (as a way to "import innovation" rather than just lowering costs by exporting jobs), and utilizing their capital investments more efficiently. NH uses remote clinics and mobile testing labs with satellite links to serve poor rural patients. It uses its expensive X-ray, CAT, and MRI machines 14 hours a day, seven days a week, far more intensively than US hospitals use their equipment.

A new hotel chain called Ginger is trying to revolutionize the hotel business in India. In much the same way that Marriott Courtyard started in the US as a way for companies to affordably travel, Ginger offers spartan but spotless, air conditioned rooms with flat panel TVs and free wireless Internet access—all for approximately $22 a night. Amazingly, the hotel has 65 percent operating margins, compared with 35–50 percent for four- and five-star hotels owned by the same company. The company achieves these numbers by operating a 100-room hotel with just seven full-time employees. Virtually everything is outsourced, from room cleaning to laundry to computer support and cafeteria service. The chain spends no money on advertising, relying on word-of-mouth, and most bookings are made online. An innovative element of its growth strategy is to lower real estate costs by offering landowners a share of the hotel's profits in exchange for their land.

Prahalad believed strongly that the approaches being pioneered in developing countries could benefit wealthy countries as well, particularly when it comes to better serving the needs of their own lower-income citizens. For example, approximately 45 million US consumers lack bank accounts because they cannot afford them. Instead, they rely on check cashing services, bond brokers, and other alternatives. Financial institutions can learn from banks such as SBI and ICICI in India, which have developed innovative ways to profitably serve poor customers.

In India, open-source operating system Linux has been making gains in the marketplace, particularly with state governments and public schools. Its main attraction, of course, is that the software is free. However, performance can sometimes be erratic, and technical support hard to get.

To counter the Linux threat, Microsoft has launched a new version of its

Windows XP operating system, called the Starter Edition, which sells for just over $20 and comes in ten Indian languages, compared to just English and Hindi for the standard edition of Windows. While the Starter Edition only allows users to open three programs at the same time, and doesn't support advanced networking, it still offers enough to meet the needs of many customers. Understates a Microsoft executive, "We need to demonstrate superior value to our customers."[29] Indeed, delivering superior value is the *sine qua non* for competing in emerging economies.

CONCLUSION

In many ways, we are entering a "golden age" for Affordability, as companies discover the size and impact of "bottom of the pyramid" markets and innovate to come up with radically more efficient business models. The rising impact of the Internet, and the growing proportion of economic activity that is based on electronic technology, augur well for continued gains in Affordability for customers.

   In the next two chapters, we turn our attention to the facilitating factors that marketers must create, once they have fashioned a compelling value proposition.

Chapter 5

Managing Accessibility

INTRODUCTION

For any company, delivering products and services to customers is a significant challenge. In an era of global competition, product proliferation, limited shelf space, and ever rising customer expectations for convenience and instant gratification, building an adequate distribution system is time-consuming and expensive. Most companies attempt to meet this challenge by bringing ever greater amounts of control, precision, stability, discipline, reliability, and most of all, efficiency to their distribution systems. The problem is, the term itself, "distribution system," reflects an inside-out mindset.

At a time when people are using the Internet to assert their individuality and redefine the typical company–consumer exchange, marketers need to flip the way they think about how consumers acquire the company's wares. Instead of attempting to create a frictionless way to *distribute* products to consumers, marketers must clear the way for consumers to *access* products from the company.

As Harvard Business School marketing professor V. Kasturi Rangan has said, "Most channels are constructed from the supplier out, rather than from the customer in."[1] To build channels "from the customer in," companies must develop a deep understanding of how customers best access products and then devise channel strategies that not only meet customers' needs, but the needs of channel partners. The process starts with putting the customer first, before everything else. Of course, that's not a new concept.

In 1935, the late president of Toyota, Shotaro Kamiya, described the company's philosophy as "Customer first, dealer second, manufacturer third." In other words, "The order of persons benefiting from the sales of Toyota vehicles is first the customer, second the dealer, and last the manufacturer. This stance is the best means of securing the confidence of both customers and Toyota dealers, and the results will ultimately benefit Toyota."[2] This philosophy has clearly served the world's largest and most profitable auto manufacturer well.

The impact of putting customers first and streamlining their access to products and services can be gleaned from a few well-known examples:

- Enterprise Rent-a-Car, through its strategy of opening neighborhood locations for car rentals (in addition to the common industry approach of renting at airport locations), has grown rapidly to become the largest US company in its industry. Enterprise created a high degree of convenience for customers by offering to pick them up and drop them off at their homes or other locations. The company has also added a significant revenue stream by partnering with various auto-insurance companies and car dealers to offer courtesy cars to customers whose cars are being repaired.

- Domino's Pizza's strategy of quickly delivering pizzas directly to customers' homes helped it become a multibillion-dollar juggernaut. While the company has backed off from its promise that if it doesn't deliver within 30 minutes, the pizza is free (out of concerns that some of its delivery people were driving recklessly to beat the deadline), Domino's can still attribute a great deal of success to its up-close availability and convenience.

- CNN was the first network to deliver 24-hour news availability, at a time when other television networks offered 30 minutes a day of national news and another 30 to 60 minutes of local news programming. CNN subsequently created a separate channel, dubbed Headline News, which continuously delivered up-to-date news in 30-minute installments.

- Wal-Mart's growth in its early decades came largely from the bottom up. The company specifically targeted small-market, rural areas that had largely been ignored by competitors like Kmart. Those companies grew from the top down, starting with large-market cities and then moving to smaller cities and towns. Wal-Mart was able to offer its customers in those underserved markets low prices and a wide selection of products from which to choose.

- McDonald's used franchising to become the dominant fast-food chain. It frequently maintained control over the geographic locations of its franchised stores, often owning the land on which the stores were built. The strategy ensured that Mickey D's restaurants would be evenly distributed across a given market.

- When Southwest Airlines started operations in the 1970s, only 15 percent of the American public had ever flown. Today, that number stands at well over 85 percent, thanks largely to Southwest's efforts to give people the "freedom to fly." Southwest democratized the skies by serving smaller cities, using more convenient airports, and offering more point-to-point service, a strategy that fueled the airline's sustained success over the years.

- Google's mission to "organize the world's information and make it universally *accessible* and useful" (our emphasis) has helped make its brightly hued logo the web's universal welcome mat for billions of people.

- Apple's App Store has sustained and even accelerated the iPhone's appeal. More than 100,000 applications for enhancing the iPhone's performance are just a click away, which sets a new standard for nearly instant Accessibility.
- Until just a few years ago, most of the world's video content was decidedly difficult—if not impossible—to access. YouTube changed all of that, by allowing users to easily upload video and immediately achieve worldwide Accessibility.

Each of these examples illustrates the power that comes from delivering high levels of access to customers. Each also establishes a blueprint that other companies have used to succeed in their industries and markets.

Sometimes, merely creating availability above the industry norm can have a dramatic effect on sales, suggesting that the channel has room to grow. For example, pantyhose sales went up substantially after the product became available at drug stores, supermarkets, and convenience stores. The same holds true for the consumption of soft drinks in a given building, which goes up substantially when a second vending machine is installed on a higher floor.

For impulse products that are uncomplicated (i.e. have a low information content), Accessibility may be all that is needed to create adequate Awareness as well. This is true for many impulse purchase items that are placed close to the checkout counter.

Creating greater Accessibility leads to a larger total market when "purchase drives consumption" rather than situations where "consumption drives purchase." For discretionary products such as snack foods and beer, the rate at which people consume the product is a function of the amount of supply they have at home; thus, purchase drives consumption. For necessity products such as laundry detergent or motor oil, having more supply does not increase consumption; for such products, people have a certain fixed amount that they need in a given period of time, and thus, consumption drives purchase. Even in the latter case, a brand with broader Accessibility will tend to gain market share at the expense of brands that are not as readily accessible, though the size of the market as a whole does not change.

Accessibility can be a most compelling motivator. For the person running on fumes while driving on a turnpike, a $0.25 per gallon premium may be a bargain— as long as it's accessible. Similarly, the sports fan attending a game may pay several times the free market value for a hot-dog because it's readily accessible.

WHAT IS ACCESSIBILITY?

The notion behind Accessibility is really very simple: ensure your product or service "meets up" with the customer, at the time and place of the customer's choosing. The customer should be able to obtain the product or service with the most minimal amount of effort. While consumers are willing to tolerate more steps to acquire a more desirable (or necessary) product or service, such as booking a flight online, their patience is not only finite, it's also falling.

When a product is difficult to acquire, competitors essentially get a free trial opportunity. This is especially true in the non-durable consumer goods industry. Proctor and Gamble's success has a lot to do with its efficient delivery network. Similarly, McDonald's ubiquitous golden arch ensures that it doesn't miss many customers, even in remote locations. The real secret to Coca-Cola's success all over the world is its distribution system: in the remotest part of the Amazon you will get a bottle of Coca-Cola!

The delivery process must be tuned to minimizing the customer's effort, rather than prioritizing the producer's needs. A cautionary example is Levi's, which rolled out its Tailored Classics line of suits in department stores (because it desired high-volume sales and already had sales relationships with them), rather than in the specialty stores where its target customers habitually shopped.

Accessibility has two primary dimensions:

Availability: In too many cases, companies either have too much or too little availability. They overproduce in anticipation of demand that does not materialize, or they generate a level of demand that they fail to meet because of supply constraints, lack of production capacity, or other bottlenecks. The ideal situation is to match supply as closely as possible with demand and avoid the worst scenario: flooding the market with excess supply, which creates downward pressure on prices and the brand's image.

Convenience: It is not enough that a company produces just enough to meet overall demand. It must also ensure that the right products are available in the right way, at the right time, in the right locations. Time is a non-renewable resource, and with life becoming ever more complex and demanding, customers are putting an even bigger premium on convenience. The result: companies must find truly innovative ways to deliver convenience to customers.

How can companies get creative around convenience and availability, and thereby make their products and services ridiculously accessible? Let's consider three examples.

Zappos: Wowing Customers with Service, Convenience, and Availability

Would you buy a pair of shoes over the web? Millions of people do, thanks largely to the efforts of Zappos.com. Since its founding as shoesite.com in 1999, the company has grown dramatically, reaching $1 billion in annual sales by 2009. Zappos' success is based largely on its exceptional ability to create a very high degree of Accessibility for its customers, along with world class, "Wow" service.

In terms of availability, Zappos stocks an extraordinary number of brands and it maintains significant inventories of each item. This was not the case in the company's early years. Initially, products were drop shipped directly from manufacturers to customers, after Zappos took the order. However, delivery schedules were uncertain and variable, and inventory information was not always accurate. Zappos then experimented with third party fulfillment, leasing space in a UPS warehouse in Louisville, Kentucky. However, this proved inadequate, as UPS could not consistently handle the number of SKUs that Zappos wanted to offer.

Zappos then decided to build its own, state-of-the-art warehouse, with a website that displays up-to-the-second inventory information. For example, on November 29, 2009, the warehouse stocked 1210 brands in 130,948 styles, with 756,688 UPCs and 3,618,277 total products available for immediate shipment. No matter how exotic their tastes, customers can be sure they'll find their preferred style, size, and color—and that their choice will still be in stock.

As for customer convenience, few online retailers can match Zappos. Its website features eight pictures of each item and offers up detailed information that would normally be available only in a bricks-and-mortar store, such as suggestions on which shoes best match the customer's gait. The customer service phone number is prominently displayed on the site, since Zappos actually wants people to call, as it views each call as a relationship-building opportunity. The company offers free, next day delivery on most orders and a 365-day return policy (shipping included). So rather than discourage returns, the company encourages its customers to order as many pairs of shoes as possible, keep what they like, and return the rest. Few companies do a better job of leveraging convenience and availability than Zappos.[3]

L'eggs: Nothing Beats a Great Marketing Strategy

The L'eggs pantyhose success story is a classic illustration of a customer-focused marketing program. In 1971, the Hanes Corporation introduced L'eggs with a marketing strategy that included several novel elements: a one-size product designed to fit most users; a new and eye-catching egg-shaped package, a special free-standing rotating display fixture, and a new system of direct-to-the-store distribution.

L'eggs was the first nationally branded hosiery line to be sold in supermarkets, convenience stores, and drug outlets. Before L'eggs demonstrated that hosiery was as much a convenience item as it was an apparel item, most hosiery was sold through department stores. For customers, this meant that hosiery had to be a planned purchase requiring a trip to a downtown or suburban department store. In the mid-1960s, unadvertised brands started selling in supermarkets and drug stores. By 1969, they accounted for 18 percent of all sales of hosiery. But no brand had a market share greater than four percent, and stockouts were commonplace.

Since hosiery brands were commoditized, customers would simply buy any brand rather than search for a preferred brand. Research showed that customers liked the convenience of being able to purchase hosiery in supermarkets and drug stores, but were frustrated by the fact that their desired brand was frequently out of stock. This caused many customers to start shopping for hosiery once again at department stores and specialty apparel retailers. In essence, customers were being forced to choose between convenience and availability.

As a result of its customer research, Hanes developed a new hosiery product that was coupled with a distinctive marketing program. Hanes' hosiery had a memorable name (L'eggs), distinctive packaging (an egg-shaped plastic container), and a free-standing display that didn't require retailers to give up shelf space. The product itself was a one-size, super-stretch pantyhose that could conform to any woman's shape. The single size let Hanes increase availability while drastically reducing inventory.

Hanes' marketing program was beautifully coordinated. The company devised a classic tagline, "Nothing beats a great pair of L'eggs." The packaging concept was obvious, which accounted for its brilliance: a distinctive plastic egg inside a colored cylinder that represented various colors and styles. The individual packages were housed in a plastic in-store display, called the L'eggs Boutique, which also reflected the brand's identity.

The final piece of the puzzle was another innovation in distribution. L'eggs sales personnel, who arrived at each store driving can't-miss L'eggs trucks, stocked the displays. Inventory was customized to each location, based on historical sales. And Hanes sold L'eggs on consignment; retailers did not have to buy any inventory and were instead credited with their margin on each unit sold.

By 1974, L'eggs was the pantyhose market's leading brand. While each of its marketing strategy's components undoubtedly contributed to the product's success, it is also clear that the components reinforced each other. For example, extensive advertising accelerated consumer trials, which facilitated the retailers' acceptance. And because L'eggs were seldom out of stock, satisfied buyers developed steady, repeat purchasing routines. The company fired on all cylinders, and its ability to deliver outstanding Accessibility (by twinning convenience *and* availability) was key to its success.[4]

Netflix: Revolutionizing the DVD Rental Business

Netflix has revolutionized the video rental business in the United States by providing its over 12 million customers with unprecedented levels of convenience and availability. The company operates 58 distribution centers throughout the country, putting more than 97 percent of its members within one-day delivery postal zones. Since launching the concept of DVD rentals by mail in 1997, Netflix has grown its total subscribers at a compound annual rate of 64 percent.

Starting as low as $8.99 a month, Netflix allows its members to watch unlimited movies and TV episodes (with over 17,000 choices) streamed directly to their computers and televisions, and also receive unlimited DVDs (over 100,000 choices) directly at their homes through the US Postal Service. Netflix involves its customers in its service. The average member has delivered feedback on 200 movies, giving Netflix over 2 billion movie ratings from its members. This has allowed the company to deliver spot-on recommendations to its customers, based on movies they have previously viewed and liked. As a result, Netflix members rent approximately twice as many movies after they join the service.

Before Netflix came on the scene in 1997, the dominant player in the video rental business was Blockbuster. The company was fond of saying that approximately 70 percent of the US population lived within a ten-minute drive of a Blockbuster Store. However, this still potentially requires 40 minutes of driving for each movie rented (two roundtrips of 20 minutes each). The "convenience" of being able to rent movies on impulse was compromised by the effort, time, and fuel required to pick up and return movies.

After some early experimentation with a pricing model that emulated that of physical stores, Netflix finally hit upon its "all you can eat" subscription model, with no late fees, in 1999. From there, the company's growth exploded. Netflix. com has been named the highest-rated website for customer satisfaction for more than eight consecutive surveys since 2005; more than 90 percent of Netflix members recommend the service to family and friends.

Netflix initially relied on traditional promotions to complement its search engine. Much as in physical stores, the website provided standard recommendations to all users. These generally resulted in the recommended movies being quickly rented out. Eventually, Netflix developed its world-class, proprietary recommendation system. After they sign up for an account, customers take a short survey to identify their favorite types of movie. Netflix then recommends additional movies to each subscriber. As a result, Netflix drives well over 70 percent of its rentals from older releases—one more way that the company has harnessed the power of the Internet to provide a personalized experience that goes way beyond what is possible in bricks-and-mortar retail.

Netflix has moved aggressively to make its own DVD-by-mail business obsolete, by becoming the leader in the video-on-demand business. It even launched its own device, called the Roku, which enables instant streaming of online video content directly to televisions and computers. Roku was later spun off as a standalone company that also offers video streaming from companies such as Hulu and Amazon. Netflix has now created its own software that resides on other Internet-connected devices such as game consoles, DVD players, and smart phones such as the iPhone.[5]

Netflix demonstrates the incredible power that comes from providing customers with unmatched convenience, coupled with an extraordinary level of inventory selection, real-time information on inventory availability, and a pricing approach that encourages the growth of the overall market.[6]

IMPROVING AVAILABILITY

Buyers value products that are readily available. But companies can't confine availability to just the transaction; the concept also applies to accompanying services such as pre- and post-purchase advice and assistance. If, say, customer service is lackluster, the brand takes a beating. In 2005, long wait times for customers calling into Dell tech support resulted in hordes of unhappy buyers hanging up on the PC maker's products. Dell itself saw its customer-satisfaction rating fall from the top of the University of Michigan's annual survey to the middle of the pack, as well as the emergence of unflattering websites like ihatedell.net.[7] In many situations, marketers successfully stimulate demand but fail to reap the benefits because of inadequate supply. This is a frequent occurrence in the consumer durables industry. It's not unheard of for customers to wait for months to get a desired car, such as the VW Beetle, the Mini Cooper, and the Toyota Prius. Supplies of hot electronic products such as the Nintendo Wii took a long time to catch up to consumer demand; many consumers camped out overnight in store parking lots to get their hands on the limited stock that was first made available.

The causes of inadequate availability are certainly well known: poor sales forecasting; inadequate manufacturing capacity; a shortage of key components; transportation bottlenecks, or more. And yet, while every marketer's nightmare is to create a hit without enough products, generating too much supply can also backfire. Excessive levels of inventory lead to deeply discounted price promotions, which lowers the product's perceived value. The ideal, of course, is to match overall supply with overall demand as closely as possible. The problem is that this is not a simple challenge.

Companies need to run lean distribution systems that deliver products when and where they're needed, without requiring large amounts of inventory. And that requires up-to-the-minute sales data. The more a company knows about what is selling where, the better it can meet demand without loading up on inventory. The use of automatic replenishment approaches, where point-of-sale data is collected at the retail level and transmitted to the supplier, has helped companies in many industries respond to demand on a just-in-time basis. The idea is to let real-time sales trigger the replenishment of inventory, rather than relying on sales forecasts that aren't always accurate.

In addition to doing a better job of managing inventory, companies must also learn to better manage their suppliers. As much as 80 percent of value creation today is outsourced to suppliers, who provide design, engineering, manufacturing, and logistics expertise. Increasingly, producers act as orchestrators of inventory inflows from numerous suppliers, any one of which can become a bottleneck to shipping finished goods. Fortunately, companies are far better prepared than in the past to effectively manage their supply chains and thereby optimize product availability for customers.

Creating sufficient availability requires companies to tap into existing infrastructures or build their own. The expense that comes with rolling out a new infrastructure can rarely be justified, especially when just a single company or product uses it. It is generally far more cost-effective to leverage an existing infrastructure, such as retail outlets, sales forces, or online storefronts. This often means that competitors must cooperate. For example, many companies in India are leveraging the Project Shakti and eChoupal infrastructures created by Hindustan Unilever and ITC respectively. As we'll show in the next section, models such as these can potentially deliver "win-win-win" outcomes for customers, the owners of the infrastructure, and the other companies that use it.

Penetrating India's Rural Market

Innovations in India's rural market demonstrate the power of leveraging availability. In developing countries such as India, marketing groups have focused primarily on middle-class, urban consumers. Their resources, lifestyles, and geographic concentration has made them attractive targets for packaged-goods companies, especially the multinationals. All that is rapidly changing, as companies are beginning to set their sights on rural and lower-income consumers. This demographic is becoming increasingly important, given their sheer numbers, the fact that their household income is increasing, and the lower level of competitive intensity faced by companies who are able to reach them. The key challenge has been providing Accessibility to these customers.

In India, rural households represent well over 70 percent of the population. According to the rural marketing research company MART, India's rural market already accounts for 46 percent of soft drinks, 49 percent of motorcycles, and 59 percent of cigarettes sold in the country. An estimated 11 percent of rural women use lipstick. In rural areas, the growth rates for many products are much higher than in cities. Coke is growing at 37 percent in rural areas, compared with 24 percent in urban areas. Between 2000 and 2005, sales of color TVs rose 200 percent in rural markets and motorcycles rose by 77 percent.[8]

While growth rates have been high for the likes of cigarettes and soft drinks, rural areas remain underleveraged in many other product categories. This is due to lagging incomes, slowly changing lifestyles, and perhaps most significantly, a lack of adequate infrastructure for delivering products, especially to small villages of less than 1000 people. But in the past decade, two initiatives have been making inroads into India's vast, sprawling archipelago of rural villages.

The aforementioned Hindustan Unilever's Project Shakti (meaning strength) was launched in 2001, with a stated goal of providing entrepreneurial opportunities for rural women (as well as health and hygiene education) and creating a distribution channel for the company's products. The company worked with rural self-help groups to educate women and make them part of its distribution network. The women became direct-to-home distributors of products such as soap, toothpaste, shampoo, and detergent. The result: Shakti distributors now account for over 15 percent of the company's sales in rural India. The project also includes a social awareness initiative called Shakti Vani (voice) and iShakti, a community portal. Leading firms such as Tata Consultancy Services and the financial services giant ICICI are partnering with Hindustan Unilever to enhance the portal and add services such as insurance.

Another successful foray into rural India has been ITC's "eChoupal" initiative, launched in 2000. Originally set up to help ITC purchase soybeans directly from farmers instead of middlemen, eChoupal featured kiosks where farmers could directly access pricing information. Over time, eChoupal has evolved into a distribution system for selling agribusiness goods and services to farmers. The company has even expanded into broader rural retailing, such as its Choupal Sagar, a 7000 sq. ft. store that sells consumer goods as well as agricultural products.

The Shakti and eChoupal examples demonstrate the tremendous transformative power of thinking outside traditional confines and making a concerted, well-thought-out effort to cover previously neglected portions of the market.

IMPROVING CONVENIENCE

You can't improve convenience for customers without first understanding what it implies, for both the company and the customer. And of course, the term means different things to different customers, depending on their experiences and expectations. But broadly speaking, convenience refers to a customer's ability to access a company's goods and services with a minimal amount of effort and at a time and place of the customer's choosing (within reasonable limits). Once customers become accustomed to a higher level of convenience, it is very difficult if not impossible to offer them anything less.

In today's society, people are under severe time pressure. This trend will likely accelerate for many years to come. Women now comprise over half the US workforce, putting additional pressure on families' scant time resources. More and more families today can be considered, in relative terms, resource rich and time poor. In such a world, marketers must strive to constantly provide customers with greater convenience, saving them time and effort. Companies that help consumers conserve time will increasingly be rewarded in the marketplace. Those that fail will soon be out of business.

Three key factors lead companies to squander customers' time; marketers aiming to deliver greater convenience must deeply understand each factor: time constraints, place constraints, and form-factor constraints.

Customers spend a great deal of time searching for product information, locating stores where products can be obtained, finding them within the store, purchasing them, transporting them, and using them. Marketers need to facilitate (and wherever possible, eliminate) each of these actions to minimize the time burden they impose on customers. They must also remove constraints on *when* customers can access their offerings. For example, banks used to operate with very limited hours (giving rise to the well-known term "bankers' hours"). Increasingly, customer-oriented banks, by closing late and remaining open on weekends, are catching up with our 24/7 world. Their ATMs are becoming increasingly sophisticated, allowing customers to engage in a wider variety of transactions quickly and conveniently.

Place constraints arise when products and services are offered at limited locations. To increase convenience, many companies now bring their products and services to the customer, rather than requiring the customer to come to the company. For example, many food companies deliver to customers' homes, a strategy that, as we've previously shown, Domino's has used to great success. Progressive Insurance sends a van directly to accident sites, expediting the claims process and often giving customers a check for repair costs on the spot. In many ways, we may be returning to a time when many products and services, such as groceries and laundry, were delivered directly to the home.

A core challenge for any retailer is deciding on the type, number, and locations of outlets. When locating bricks-and-mortar outlets, marketing has made good use of such well-established approaches as the Retail Gravitation Model, which helps determine the distance that customers are willing to travel to acquire a product. But convenience also depends on optimal placement *within* stores. For many product categories, this is not as straightforward as it sounds. For example, where should stores put a product such as Wasa's crispy, high-fiber bread—with breads or with crackers? Should salt be located in the spice section or baking section? Ideally, producers should try to get stores to place such products in both locations.

Producers and retailers are seemingly engaged in a constant battle over shelf space. All producers want as much of the shelf as possible, ideally at a height that makes it easy for customers to spot the product. Since every product cannot be placed in an optimal spot, retailers should be guided by what's best for the customer rather than by other considerations, such as charging slotting fees.

Form-factor constraints can refer to the mode in which customers receive the product. Instead of offering one "standard" size, companies must increasingly offer their products in multiple sizes, from small, single-use packages to large, institution-sized containers. Grocery chains offer customers the opportunity to purchase many products in exactly the quantity customers want through their bulk-products sections.

Another variation on form-factor: companies may increasingly offer services instead of products. For example, the carpet manufacturer Interface does not sell carpet; it sells carpet*ing*. What is the difference? The customer acquires the carpet but never actually takes ownership of it; at the end of the contracted leasing period, Interface removes the carpet and ensures that it is properly recycled.

This trend of offering services instead of products is likely to move to the consumer market. Bridgestone is experimenting with a new way of selling tires. In fact, rather than selling tires, the company is transitioning to usage-based pricing with a fixed price per kilometer. This encourages them to develop tires that last as long as possible (the longer the tire lasts, the more it earns), and ensures that the tires are properly disposed of at the end of their usable life, since the company still owns the tires.[9]

Here are four guiding principles for improving customer convenience:

- *Create convenience in acquiring and disposing as well as using the product:* Products must be easy to unpack, not require time-consuming and complicated assembly by customers, and be designed for easy and intuitive use. At the end of the life cycle, the product should be easy to dispose of. For example, Sony now offers an easy way for customers to trade in old products and receive varying amounts of credit toward new Sony purchases. It commits to customers that returned products will never end up in a landfill.
- *Reduce transaction costs by offering customers a broader range of offerings under one roof:* By creating a "one stop shopping" experience where customers can get a variety of related products and services, companies can save customers considerable time and expense, as well as spread their own costs across a broader range of offerings. For example, communications companies increasingly bundle wired and wireless telephone services, Internet access, and television service into a single bill and point of contact.
- *Reduce the time that customers expend in monitoring and managing their needs:* In our increasingly complex lives, the "cost of thinking" keeps increasing. Many of the items on our to-do lists inevitably slip through the cracks. Companies can remove some of the burden by using their extensive database technologies to assist customers in managing their lives. It is no accident that two of today's most successful companies, the Container Store and Google, are dedicated to helping people take control of their lives. The Container Store, "the original storage and organization store," helps organize people's physical lives; Google helps arrange their virtual lives, by "organizing the world's information and making it easily accessible."
- *Provide any time, any place, "any mode" access:* This should include (if possible) online access (24/7/365), home delivery, and customer premise services. Companies should automate what can be automated, starting with the "automatic replenishment" of frequently purchased items and eventually leading to

the "automation of consumption" to the degree that it adds value to customers' lives (see "Future Perfect: Assisted Living for All"?, p. 128).

Japan's Vending Machine Craze

For an interesting example of extreme convenience and how the future is all about bringing products to customers, consider the widespread use of vending machines in Japan. No country in the world uses as many vending machines for so many different types of product. The island nation has an extremely high population density, and minimal vandalism. Many citizens prefer to shop on foot or by bicycle. With about one machine for every 23 people, Japan has by far the world's highest number of vending machines per capita.

Vending machines have a long history in Japan, starting about 80 years ago with machines that sold sweets. When the 100-yen coin was introduced in 1967, the use of vending machines mushroomed. Today, Japan's vending machines have gone digital. Increasingly, cell phones are now used to pay for items purchased in vending machines; smart cards are used to prevent underage buyers from purchasing cigarettes.

While the most common products sold through vending machines are not unusual (soft drinks, coffee, tea, vitamin drinks), there are many that are. Other products sold through vending machines include batteries, cigarettes, beer, sake and other liquors, CDs, cup noodles, hot meals, disposable cameras, fortunes, milk, newspapers (offering a choice of up to 16 different papers), pornographic magazines, comics, videos, sex toys, tampons, rice, toilet paper, umbrellas, neckties, sneakers, ice, fried food, underwear, iPods, sexual lubricants, fresh meat, eggs, flowers, fresh vegetables, and potted plants.

Some of the more unusual vending machines are Coca-Cola's giant robot vending machines that walk around Tokyo; SMART Car Vending Machines that dispense a branded tube containing pamphlets on various models, dealer information, and SMART Car stickers; and live lobster vending machines that feature a "Sub Marine Catcher" arcade game for buyers to try their hand at nabbing the creatures.

Other countries can learn from Japan's example, especially in densely populated urban areas. Drive-through vending systems could work in a city like Los Angeles, where many people drive, and additional security precautions have to be taken in places where vandalism is a danger.

DELIVERING ACCESSIBILITY BY LEVERAGING ALL RESOURCES

As with the other P's and A's, it is a mistake to assume that only "Place" impacts Accessibility. That is, a product or service is accessible when it's in the right location—end of story. In fact, leveraging many of the resources available to companies can enhance availability and convenience. Just consider the following examples:

Product: A product's size and design impacts its availability. Three decades ago, computers were so large, they could only be located in sprawling commercial spaces. But as computers shrank their ubiquity increased, as it became far easier to purchase, transport, and use them. Likewise, since flat panel TVs are much thinner and lighter than standard television sets, it's far more convenient for people to purchase and transport them home.

Price: A lower price point often means that products are more widely available than their higher-priced competitors. For example, digital cameras used to come with a big price tag and were available only at specialty electronics stores. As their prices dropped, consumers could buy digital cameras conveniently at drug stores and other retailers.

Promotion: When ex-heavyweight boxing champ George Foreman began to pitch his grill on QVC television, the ads gave people an up-close look at what the grill could do. Though the product was initially available only through phone orders, it soon became very popular and could be found in numerous retail stores. Foreman demonstrated that true convenience is just a phone call away.

People: Employees are a vital part of a company's overall service. Experienced, well-trained employees make the purchase a hassle-free experience for customers. Companies such as Starbucks are renowned for treating even their part-time employees so well that they can staff locations with relative ease, which in turn makes Starbucks' primary product—its service—widely available. Nordstrom is famous for its customer service orientation embedded in its sales force.

Processes: Innovative processes can make products and services more conveniently available to customers. For example, a Wisconsin company named Super Fast Pizza makes pizza in the van while driving to make a home delivery.

Sales: Mortgage lenders, financial planners and insurance sales reps often come to a prospective customer's home to discuss their products, providing availability as well as convenience.

R&D: A great many R&D efforts attempt to devise ways to increase convenience for customers. For example, Lysol developed pre-wetted disinfecting wipes that are very convenient to use. Similar products are Pledge furniture polish wipes and Windex window cleaner wipes. A service that greatly increases convenience and access is the "on-demand" feature now offered by cable companies and other video service providers.

Customer service: Easy access to clear, reliable information about products can be as important as the products themselves. Providing customers with accurate information about products before the sale and timely, effective customer service after the sale are keys to success. Consider Linksys, one of the world's largest router and switch producers. For most people, setting up a router is not an easy task. Linksys has a well-designed website that guides users through the installation process. It also offers live, phone-based support that is easy to access.

Then there's Lexus, which provides customers with free loaner cars, so they can get on with their day while their car is being serviced. If they would rather wait for their car, Lexus equips their waiting rooms with computers with Internet connections, newspapers and magazines, a television, a playroom for children, and plenty of free coffee, tea, juices, and sandwiches, all of which makes the service experience at Lexus not only convenient, but tolerable.

IT: IT has made many information-based products and services easily available. For example, many radio stations now feature streaming audio on their websites, which extends the stations' global reach and also allows local listeners to tune in on mobile devices. IT also enables customers to have access to a large volume of information, making it easier for them to pick their purchase. This is the "long tail" effect, whereby online companies such as Amazon.com can offer a vastly greater selection than can their bricks-and-mortar counterparts.[10] IT departments have also deployed cutting-edge technology (such as the wireless handheld computers/printers used by roving rental car return agents) for customer-facing employees as well as for direct access by customers.

To appreciate IT's capacity to increase Accessibility, recall the days before the web's emergence, when music could only be purchased at retail stores or by mail order. Now, whether your tastes run to Lady Gaga or Lady Day, it's all just a click away. The success of Apple's iPod has largely been due to its iTunes music store, which makes buying music a cinch. An additional benefit is that people select the songs they like, rather than having to buy an entire CD just to get to a few favorite tracks.

Retailers: Retailers can make products dramatically more accessible by placing them in special displays near the front of the store or at the end of aisles.

Government: Federal and state agencies can have a great impact on the availability and convenience of products and services. The government invests in infrastructures of various kinds, including roads and bridges and tunnels, as well as information infrastructures such as satellites. For example, GPS systems run on satellites originally launched by the government for Defense Department applications. Through its food rating system, the federal government provides a convenient way for consumers to gauge the quality of many food products. Through its agriculture extension service, the government has helped greatly increase the availability of food by educating farmers about better ways to practice agriculture. Through the Americans with Disabilities Act, the US government has made numerous public and commercial buildings accessible to those who would not otherwise be able to enter them. The government is also a key investor in many countries in creating high-speed online networks.

Industry: There is great potential for cooperation with competitors within an industry to increase efficiencies for all. For example, cellular companies have come together to create a shared infrastructure of cell phone towers so that they don't have to incur additional costs and face regulatory hurdles in setting up their own towers. Similarly, cable companies have worked together at the industry level to develop high-speed networks, which lets them offer people access to high-definition television and high-speed Internet connections.

Partners: Partnerships work well in increasing Accessibility when there are synergies between different product lines. For example, a local bakery can stock the jams and spreads made by other local producers, thus enhancing their Accessibility.

Operations: Streamlined operations combined with fast delivery increases customer convenience. For example, most furniture companies routinely take more than 12 weeks to deliver customized sofas to customers. Companies such as England Inc. in Tennessee have reorganized their production systems to deliver sofas and chairs within three weeks. By enhancing Accessibility to its sofas, England Inc. has become a magnet for consumers. Similarly, the Vermont Teddy Bear Company has implemented a system that allows customers to order a customized bear one day and have it delivered the next.

We hope the examples above provide a sense of the rich possibilities available to companies in looking to maximize Accessibility for their customers.

THE INTERNET'S IMPACT ON ACCESSIBILITY

Technology has clearly enabled companies to make their products and services increasingly more accessible. It has also catalyzed customers' expectation that their favorite brands should always be near at hand. Now more than ever, we live in a convenience-first economy. All of which means it's going to get harder for companies to make it easier for consumers. That said, the transformation from bricks-and-mortar to online marketing is still in its early stages.

For many products, the Internet has provided a great boost to Accessibility; even if a physical outlet is not conveniently available, consumers can still access the product. For online retailing, Accessibility includes the website's usability and aesthetics—that is, the ease and pleasure with which the customer can navigate, research, and purchase the product online.

To appreciate the Internet's impact on Accessibility, it is useful to distinguish between the notion of access to information from access to goods and services.

Clearly, the Internet's greatest impact has been the nearly instantaneous, usually free and unfettered access to the world's information and knowledge. Increasingly, this worldwide access is coming to mobile devices, which are growing at a much faster rate than computers and already reach a high percentage of the planet's population.

For non-information-based products (i.e. those that have some physical form), the Internet enables the acquisition of information about the products, as well as the ability to order the products online. As illustrated in the case of Zappos, web-based ordering means that a company can better match inventory with demand. Customers are shown only those products that are readily available, ensuring 100 percent Accessibility to all the items they are exposed to. Likewise, Netflix filters its recommendations for additional DVDs to those that are in stock.

Moving forward, companies must continually explore how they can best leverage the Internet to make their products/services more accessible. With the explosive growth of "smart phones" and the hundreds of thousands of apps that are available for those phones, there is no dearth of creative ideas that enable companies to provide ever greater convenience to their customers. For example, customers of Chase Bank and USAA can deposit a check by signing the back, taking pictures of the front and back, entering the amount, and tapping send. They can then rip up the check if they want.[11]

Future Perfect: Assisted Living for All?

The following fictional scenario illustrates what could result if marketers were to fully leverage technologies that are already available today in service of improving customers' quality of life, and if customers were to have strong relationships and a very high degree of trust in their providers. Neither assumption is all that outlandish, though the resulting scenario may strike some as Orwellian and others as utopian!

On the morning of October 23, 2020, John A. Consumer awoke to the sound and smell of his automatic coffeemaker. After he stumbled into the kitchen, John poured himself a cup of coffee, thinking to himself that some of the oldest conveniences were still the best. Of course, this was no 1990s Mr. Coffee machine; this machine had a large canister of gourmet coffee beans on top, a built-in grinder, and it was connected to the filtered water supply. It automatically discarded its coffee grounds into the sink disposal, which in turn fed into a composting pit in the back yard. It was, in short, the perfect appliance—effortless, unobtrusive, reliable, and eco-friendly.

As he opened the fridge, John marveled anew at how it was always well stocked and had just about everything he could want. The thrice-weekly delivery from Fresh & Natural had replenished his fridge and pantry with fresh bread, organic milk, local organic produce, and other items the previous day. They had picked up his laundry and delivered his shirts from the previous trip. They had also left some new firewood by the fireplace, and returned his repaired (and polished) shoes.

It had two years since John had been inside a supermarket. At first, he thought he would miss it (squeezing the tomatoes and all that). But now he never gave it a second thought. Besides, he had never been very good at picking the sweetest honeydew melons or cantaloupes. Now they were just right every time. And he was actually paying less for his groceries now than he had before. Guess those huge, well-lit, air-conditioned super-markets cost a lot to run.

In the beginning, John had spent about 20 minutes a week placing his online order. As he got more comfortable, though, and as his buying patterns became more discernable to the computer at Fresh & Natural, he found that the shopping list offered to him when he first logged on was actually more appealing than what he would have created himself.

Gradually, John had found himself making fewer and fewer changes to the list. About a year after he started using the service, John decided to let it go solo. Now he looked forward to the deliveries, knowing that each one always contained two or three "surprises" that were guaranteed to delight him (if not, he would get his money back, of course). John found that, as a result, he had tried new foods that he never would have thought to try earlier—and liked most of them a lot. Sometimes, it was an exotic fruit, sometimes an unusual kind of cheese, even some new imported beer. Once a month, they even replenished his coffee machine with some great new beans, leaving a little pamphlet about it next to the machine. They did this with all of their "Just for You" selections.

Best of all were the fully prepared meals. John had invited a few friends to come to dinner that night, and he had asked for a meal for six. As he looked at the neatly packed containers and the two bottles of Italian wine, he saw the printed menu that had been sent with the meal. "Rustic Tuscany," it said across the top. John was tempted to open a couple of boxes and take a peek (and perhaps a taste), but he resisted. The price was great—just a little more than it would have cost him just to buy the ingredients. He could have tried to make the meal himself, but the cost of his time (very high) and the value of his cooking expertise (very low) made that an unappetizing proposition.

John took his croissant and coffee into his study and turned on his computer. As was his habit, he started by checking his e-mail. There was an e-mail from Paul Frederick & Co. informing him that they had selected four new shirts they thought he would like. John looked at the high-resolution images on his screen and liked what he saw. If he did nothing, the shirts would show up in his SmartBox in a couple of days, monogrammed and in his size, of course.

The next e-mail was from Jaguar. John's current Jag was coming off lease in a couple of months. The e-mail offered him a great lease rate on the hot new hybrid fuel cell XJ-class that he knew had a long waiting list. But that was only for first-time buyers. If he wanted the car, they would bring it to his house and take away the old one on the day the lease ended. John was tempted to say "Yes!" on the spot, but he reluctantly decided to think it over a bit. Not that he expected to change his mind ...

The third e-mail was from Scott Burbank over at Sleep Tight Home Services. This was John's favorite service of all. John had never been much of a handyman or a gardener, though he liked living in a big house and enjoyed looking at a well-tended garden as much as anyone else. For a ridiculously low $250 a year, Sleep Tight completely took over everything to do with the house and the yard. When he had signed up, Scott had done a complete inspection of the house, noting down all the makes, models, and condition of his appliances, heating and air conditioning systems, the condition of his carpets, hardwood floors, roof, outside and inside paint, and a dozen other things John did not even know you were supposed to worry about. Sleep Tight then set up a web page with all of this information and updated it every time any work was done on the house. John rarely felt the need to go to this other "home page." Still, he had it in his bookmarks, and it was sure nice to know that it was there. Once every couple of months, using his own key, Scott came through and did a quick inspection. He sent service people to the house to take care of problems before John even knew he had them. Best of all, he didn't have to wait around for them to show up.

John got a monthly e-mail from Scott updating him on what had been done and what was coming, and the money was paid automatically. The rates were as good as or better than those John would have paid had he dealt directly with the service contractors. In return for steady business, Scott had negotiated lower rates with them. If there was ever a problem, Scott handled it with the service technicians. Scott had also arranged for a cleaning service, and he was now looking into offering a bundled cleaning/home mainte-nance/insurance package that would be like an HMO for the home. John thought that was a great idea and fully expected to sign up when the service was offered. John had raved so often about Sleep Tight's comprehensive services that literally a dozen of his friends were now customers of Sleep Tight's, or were on a waiting list.

The next message was from John's Personal Financial Manager, with a full report on the previous month's activities in his account. John was starting to feel like one of those mega-rich athletes whose financial affairs are completely handled by a management company, and who simply receive a monthly "allowance" for incidental expenses—except there was no chance that John's money could get sunk into some fly-by-night scam. John was not mega-rich, by any means, though each monthly e-mail provided a gratifying report on his steady progress toward his goals. For a guy who had never quite mastered the art of balancing his checkbook, it was certainly comforting for John to know that all his bills were checked and paid on time.

The only time John needed to think about them was when there was something unusual, in which case the item was automatically flagged for his attention. All of his spending was automatically categorized and entered into his Quicken register, and his monthly reports would on occasion point out that he had exceeded his budget in some category or another. Even his tax return was prepared and filed automatically. The "Financial Engines Investment Advisor," a very popular computerized service developed by a Stanford professor who was an economics Nobel laureate, automatically routed John's savings into appropriate investments. As with every one of John's automated services, he had been assigned a personal advisor who could answer all his questions. As he grew familiar with the services, John found himself calling less frequently, though all his advisors always sent his personal-ized greetings on his birthday and other occasions.

The last e-mail was from his car. When he bought the car, John knew that it was equipped with a GPS device as well as the ability to send data and e-mail wirelessly, but didn't think much of it. Not anymore. The car had saved him from some sticky situations more than once. John still found it hard to get used to these e-mails, though.

The e-mails came infrequently, only when the car had something on its mind. Today, it had several things to convey. First, it reminded him (somewhat plaintively, he thought) that his lease was about to expire, and what it would cost him to buy the car if he wanted to. Second, it reminded him that it was due for an oil change, and that it had already scheduled several possible times with the dealership. John selected the one that worked for him. Finally, the car pointed out that it needed new tires within the next 1000 miles, and offered a direct link to Costco with the recommended tire size information already incorporated. With a few clicks, John purchased the tires and set up an installation time to coincide with the oil change.

The holiday season was approaching and John was starting to feel a little tense about all the gifts he still had to buy. But he was trying out a new system that he thought would make life a little easier. A nifty new website (giftoflife.com) reminded him of upcoming occasions for giving gifts, and also suggested some alternative ideas for each one. John had gone through a somewhat lengthy "interview" process when he signed up, and his "agent" knew what he expected to spend on each individual and on a given occasion. It also knew which of the recipients were personal friends, relatives, or professional contacts. So far, it had worked well; John had been able to send gifts with a single click, selecting from the offered choices and quickly personalizing a message for each. The company used John's personal font to create "handwritten" messages.

With Christmas looming, John thought he would also try out "wishlist.com," a universal gift registry that he had been subtly promoting to his nieces, nephews, siblings, and others for several months. Wishlist.com was a universal registry; it allowed all people, not just those getting married, to create their own equivalent of a bridal registry.

Sure enough, John found that about a dozen of his friends and relatives had in fact signed up. John quickly scanned each person's wish list; he smiled to himself at some of the entries ("Yeah, sure, George, someone's going to buy you a 96-inch HDTV," he thought to himself), but was able to quickly select items that were in his budget range.

John glanced up at the clock. It was only 8:30; he still had an hour before he had to make that video conference call to Bucharest. Glancing out the window, John saw a delivery truck pulling away from his driveway—an increasingly familiar sight nowadays. This particular truck was marked "FedEx," but John knew that all the major delivery companies now used each other's trucks to deliver packages, so that the FedEx truck contained many packages that had originated with UPS, the US Postal Service, or a variety of other smaller players. It was like completing a long-distance phone call; the receiver did not have to be a subscriber of the same company that the sender used.

Putting on his slippers, John went into the garage. A small door in one of the side walls opened directly into his SmartBox, which sat unobtrusively next to his garage (it was even painted a matching color).

Punching in his code, he opened the door and entered the small shed. The light went on, and he could see that he had received several packages the previous day, left there by delivery people using a code to enter the SmartBox from the outside. One was from Amazon.com. John had joined their "Must Read" club, though he now downloaded most of his books electronically into his fifth generation color Kindle. The difference between this and the old "Book of the Month" club was that the book was specifically chosen for him, rather than the same book going out to everyone.

In the one year he had been a member, John had yet to get a book that he hadn't liked a great deal. He didn't know how they did it, but it sure worked. John also saw a package from drugstore.com, containing some toiletries (they always knew when his blades and shaving cream were running low), a couple of prescription refills (he never had to remember to fill those anymore) and a 60-day supply of a customized multivitamin his doctor had e-mailed in.

As John shaved and showered, he mused about how his life had become so much less crazed and stressful in the last few years. Gone were the weekly grocery shopping trips, the long lines, handling the products a dozen times before he used then, the midnight milk runs. No more marathon bill paying sessions on the last day of the month; John hadn't written a check in years. No more worrying about balancing the checkbook. No more need to keep track of when the car needed an oil change or new tires. (Most of all, no more nagging worries about the house: "Do I need to change the air conditioning filter? Is it time to service the furnace? Do the gutters need cleaning? Does the lawn need fertilizing? Is that insect damage in the shrubs?" Good old Scott was there to take care of all that.)

Thinking back, John found it hard to imagine what life had been like in 2010; it seemed eons ago, a primitive, harried time. Now he had plenty of time to work out, socialize with his friends, even do volunteer work. And yet, he was working as much as or more than before, making a lot more money and enjoying it more as well ...

Just then, the alarm went off, and John was jolted back into his real reality. He was back in 2010, and as he lay in bed thinking about his day, John groaned to himself.

The house was a mess, he needed to do a huge grocery shopping trip, the lawn was overgrown, it was the last day of the month, he had no clean shirts, and several friends were supposed to come to dinner that evening. How was he going to finish that project at work? Shuddering, John pulled the sheet back over his face and shut his eyes tight, hoping to get back to that beautiful dream.

CONCLUSION

Inadequate Accessibility is often a key bottleneck that prevents a product from fully realizing its market potential. Recall the phrase used by Coca-Cola, which we referred to in Chapter 2: making a product available "within arm's reach of desire." Companies must determine how best they can approach this ideal in a cost-effective way, by creatively leveraging today's extraordinary technological resources, through forging win-win partnerships with other companies, and by never losing sight of the critical goal of making the lives of their customers richer, easier, and more enjoyable.

Chapter 6

Managing Awareness

INTRODUCTION

In this chapter, we discuss how companies can create and sustain high levels of Awareness for their offerings. This, of course, is essential to delivering robust sales. Although advertising is the most commonly used method for achieving Awareness, it is not always the best. Among many other companies, Google, Facebook, and Starbucks deliver very high levels of Awareness with hardly any advertising at all.

Of the 4A's, Awareness is the area where there's the greatest opportunity for improvement, since many companies' current practices are generally ineffective and inefficient. Most companies do not advertise effectively, nor do they adequately take advantage of other ways of creating Awareness. An exception is Motel 6, the brand that promises to "leave the light on" for road-weary travelers.

MOTEL 6: "WE'LL LEAVE THE LIGHT ON FOR YOU"

Paul Greene and William Becker founded the low-priced American motel chain with the nondescript name "Motel 6" in 1962 in Santa Barbara, California. Greene's vision was to create a chain of inexpensive motels that parents on a tight budget could afford while showing their children the country. He calculated that he could price his rooms at $6.00 a night (hence the name) and still score a profit. This marked the birth of the first budget motel for "no-frills" travelers—a Southwest Airlines of the lodging industry. (On second thought, it would be more accurate to say that Southwest Airlines is the Motel 6 of the airline industry.)[1]

By 1985, Motel 6 still had the lowest room rates of any national chain. However, the chain's performance had steadily deteriorated for several years. That year, the buyout firm KKR acquired the company and rolled out a plan to turn it around. Motel 6's new CEO, Joseph McCarthy, hired the Richards Group, an advertising agency, to help meet his major objectives: reverse declining occupancy; attract new categories of guests; and use customer input to improve the facilities.

The Richards Group conducted market research that revealed the need for three changes:

- First, the agency strongly recommended that Motel 6 break with its previous practice of offering only payphones to customers and instead install telephones in all of its rooms. Travelers complained that the lack of in-room phones left them feeling isolated. In response, Motel 6 soon signed a $40 million contract with AT&T to install telephones in all of its 45,000 rooms at 425 locations.
- Second, Motel 6 immediately discontinued its practice of charging guests an extra $1.49 to activate the in-room television. Though 80 percent of the guests paid the fee, research revealed that most thought of it as "nickel-and-diming" and a nuisance, and worse, led them to fear that they would be charged for other amenities such as towels.
- Third, instead of requiring that each property manage its own reservations, Motel 6 developed a centralized reservation system. This change especially appealed to infrequent customers who did not know where the motels were located.

Once Motel 6 had been improved in this manner (that is, made its offering more acceptable), the company set about raising its profile and brand recognition through a national advertising campaign. Though many hotel chains use television and print ads, the Richards Group recommended that Motel 6 use radio instead. Their reason: most of Motel 6's potential customers did not plan ahead, but instead made their lodging decisions while driving. Radio ads, the ad agency reasoned, would be more effective in reaching on-the-road customers when they were looking for lodging.

The Richards Group also recommended a contractor-turned-author named Tom Bodett to serve as Motel 6's spokesman. Bodett's down-to-earth, humorous commentaries for National Public Radio had attracted the agency's attention. Though he was relatively unknown, the agency believed that the folksy Bodett would have more credibility promoting the homey Motel 6 than some Hollywood star. The campaign was dubbed "Smart Choice" and featured the tagline "We'll leave the light on for you." (Bodett actually ad-libbed the now-famous phrase when a spot ran short.) The campaign was intended to convey, in a distinctive and humorous way, that choosing Motel 6 was a smart choice, not a cheap thing to do.

Smart Choice was an immediate hit. The first radio ad ran in November 1986, and more than 100 variations were used over the next five years. Awareness and recall of the Motel 6 name increased dramatically; the occupancy rate soon followed, rising six points in 1987 and three more points by 1989. Revenue jumped by more than 60 percent over three years. The industry had rarely seen such dramatic increases. In 2000, *Adweek* cited Smart Choice as one of the top advertising campaigns of the previous 100 years.

One of the Richards Group's most clever tactics was to create a series of public service announcement (PSA) for drivers using Tom Bodett's voice and the background music from Motel 6 ads. The agency sent the PSA to all the radio stations on which Motel 6 advertised, along with a letter from Tom Bodett asking them to air the announcement for the benefit of drivers. Nearly 30 percent of the radio stations complied. Each airing served to subtly remind drivers that the light still glowed at Motel 6. Over the next few years, the company reaped millions of dollars worth of free exposure.

KKR sold Motel 6 to the French company Accor in 1990. In 1993, Accor embarked on a $600 million renovation campaign. Today, the chain retains its lead among value motel chains. With room rates ranging from 20 percent to 30 percent below other economy chains and 50 percent below the national average, Motel 6 has maintained its low price position through strict cost controls and a high degree of standardization. Room rates, which were once uniform across the country, now vary based on the cost of living in individual markets. The "no-frills" chain also offers many extras: children under 17 stay free; pets are welcome; customers get free HBO and ESPN.

Motel 6 exemplifies a sound and thrifty approach to marketing, paying savvy and frugal attention to each of the A's, delivering great value to customers, and sustaining high profitability over time. It leverages Awareness by maintaining a high degree of brand recognition and recall in an extremely crowded marketplace, and does so in a cost-effective way that entertains while it informs.

WHAT IS AWARENESS?

Before customers can buy a product, they must first come to know it. It's not enough to simply learn that a product is available; customers must viscerally connect with the company's offering.

Of course, customers must be able to recognize and remember the brand, its key features and its overall "positioning"—that is, what it stands for. However, these minimal requirements, by themselves, are not enough to entice consumers and more importantly, keep them satisfied after the purchase. Customers must know the product as well as the brand. They must understand what the product does (and cannot do) and which of their needs and wants it fulfills.

Creating Awareness is all about awakening a latent need and triggering the process by which the customer acquires the product. When it's done effectively, creating Awareness starts to convert non-buyers into buyers and buyers into satisfied repeat customers who in turn help create Awareness with other potential customers.

"Awareness," as we define it, is about knowing and understanding the brand and the product. Both dimensions are important, although as we pointed out briefly in Chapter 2, most marketers pay short shrift to product knowledge and instead concentrate the bulk of their efforts (and virtually all of their marketing dollars) on creating and sustaining high levels of brand awareness.

"Awareness" does not include an assessment of the customer's attitude towards the offering; that's the job of Acceptability. Customers can be highly aware of a company's offering and yet remain convinced that it is not something they want or need. Note also that the goal of advertising is to not only increase Awareness, but also to positively impact people's attitudes toward the offering. We measure the latter through the "Psychological Acceptability" construct.

Most consumers do not have a high level of Awareness about product offerings. More often than not, their purchases are not truly informed. While they may recognize brand names and perhaps recall a brand's advertising jingle, they are not especially knowledgeable about the product's details. This is not surprising, since many companies would be hurt rather than helped if customers became better educated about their products. However, a basic premise of this book, and we believe the foundation of all good marketing, is that long-term success comes only when companies offer a value proposition that's demonstrably superior to competitors' alternatives for its chosen customers.

The creation of customer Awareness about products starts with early socialization. Children learn about popular brands through their families, but they gain little objective knowledge about products. They form habits, becoming accustomed to consuming certain brands. Brand awareness also comes from interactions with peer groups, and from direct experience in the marketplace.

We can distinguish between deep awareness and shallow awareness:

Deep awareness: Customers *actively* seek out reviews and educational sources of information about the product because they are highly interested in the product category. Customers acquire brand awareness and product knowledge through advertising, press coverage, store displays, events, and customer word-of-mouth. Each channel enriches the customer's store of knowledge and satisfied customers who already use the product are often evangelists for it.

Shallow awareness: Customers *passively* acquire brand awareness and product knowledge largely through advertising. Knowledge about the brand exists only in customers' short-term memory, and must be continually reinforced through additional advertising. Otherwise, Awareness soon drifts into amnesia.

The Aflac Duck

Few marketing programs in recent memory have been as successful as Aflac's "talking duck" campaign, which has made a household name out of a previously obscure company. Aflac, which sells supplemental health insurance, had advertised for ten years before launching the campaign. But its ads were largely indistinguishable from those of other insurance companies and had little impact.

The company understood that its primary problem was that most people simply did not recognize or remember its name. The talking duck campaign was, therefore, intended to make Aflac memorable. The campaign's ads shared a common theme: an irascible duck that, frustrated at being ignored, repeatedly shouted "Aflac" instead of "Quack" when passers-by discussed supplemental health insurance.

From the beginning, the campaign was highly successful. The first ad, known as the park bench commercial, scored an unprecedented 27 on Audiences Surveys Incorporated's scale, compared to a normal score of 12. (The previous highest score for any commercial was 17.) Subsequent Aflac commercials scored between 35 and 49. The company's brand recognition rose from 10 percent to 92 percent as a direct result of the campaign.[2] In an industry with little overall growth, Aflac sales rose 28 percent in 2001, the first year of the campaign, and another 29 percent in 2002.

Researchers discovered that 90 percent of people in the market found the ads fun and entertaining, and 73 percent said they "love the duck." In fact, the company has sold nearly 43,000 of its "ducks with an attitude" to consumers from its website, raising money for the Aflac Cancer Center. In 2005, the Aflac's iconic duck was enshrined in the Madison Avenue Advertising Walk of Fame. The campaign has become a part of pop culture and has featured celebrities such as Chevy Chase, Wayne Newton, and Yogi Berra.

But even with a successful campaign, there's no guarantee that profits will follow. Having achieved a remarkably high level of brand awareness and recognition, Aflac had to confront its next challenge: though 92 percent of Americans were familiar with the brand, only 10 percent actually understood what the company's services and products were, and less than 6 percent had become customers. This despite the fact that the duck exclaimed in every ad that Aflac was the answer to the characters' problems. The company has added the tagline "Ask about it at work" to get customers to follow up and learn more about Aflac. Note that Aflac's sales had risen despite the fact that most people did not understand the company's products/services. Once the company succeeds in educating customers about its products, the potential for sales to rise further is significant.

ADVERTISING AND AWARENESS

Given the amount of informational clutter that exists today, the challenges facing advertising, in terms of creating Awareness for market offerings, are greater than ever. Done right, advertising can be spectacularly successful. Done poorly, advertising can be a huge drain on a company's resources. The chances for success increase dramatically when marketers craft the right message for the right medium.

Higher Awareness should translate into higher sales, but only if: a) the level of Awareness is relatively low to begin with; and b) marketers are leveraging each of the other A's. If sales do not respond to increased advertising, the explanation is one of two things: the ad campaign is not effective at raising Awareness and stimulating interest; or the problem resides in one of the other A's. Most studies of advertising success (or lack thereof) fail to take this into account.

Marketers and advertising agencies predicate most advertising campaigns largely on faith, which results in a tremendous amount of advertising clutter, especially in the American market. Each day, the average American consumer is exposed to 3000–5000 (estimates vary) advertising-related messages. Of these, only a small fraction penetrates the average consumer's consciousness. Of those messages that do make it through, only a few are actually accorded any degree of interest or involvement, and fewer still change the consumer's perception of the offering.

Too many companies start out saying, "We need an advertising campaign." They should instead start by saying, "We need to increase consumers' Awareness and interest in our product." A campaign that seeks to increase Awareness is very different from one that simply sets out to promote a product. An advertising mindset is all about selling. An Awareness mindset is all about educating—informing consumers about the product and letting them decide if they want to buy. If the company has created high levels of each of the other A's, there should be no need for a hard sell.

As we noted in the first chapter, the "hard-sell" mindset frequently leads the marketing function to misuse resources. When we analyze the amount of money that companies spend on marketing, we find that a large proportion is devoted to advertising and promotion activities, which are primarily intended to create Awareness and trial for the offering. However, there are many ways in which companies can achieve high levels of Awareness without the use of advertising.

Consider Trader Joe's, a highly successful retailer of specialty and gourmet food products in the United States. The stores are so popular that the company regularly receives phone calls at its headquarters in Monrovia, California from customers who are moving and want to find homes that are near its store locations.

Trader Joe's has achieved this nearly unprecedented level of customer loyalty despite doing very little advertising. Instead, the company relies on a newsletter, *The Fearless Flyer*, to tell customers about its products in a humorous and informative way. This low-key approach works beautifully, since the Trader Joe's brand is all about consistently delivering a compelling customer experience.

"No amount of advertising can create what we want to create with our customers," says Trader Joe's vice president of marketing Pat St. John. "Advertising can remind people, but it can't create an experience. It's the personal relationship with these people that builds loyalty."[3]

How Well Does Advertising Work?

This question is sure to evoke a strong reaction from any group of marketing practitioners and analysts. On the one hand, you have those who swear that no marketing campaign can succeed without a heavy dose of advertising. Most advertising agencies, not surprisingly, hold this view. On the other hand, many argue that most advertising is inauthentic and uninspiring, and that customers are inherently suspicious of companies that advertise too much. Such critics of the status quo maintain that advertising is less effective precisely because there is so much of it. (See box "Advertising and the Tragedy of the Commons," this page)

Our view is straightforward: when it's done right, advertising can work spectacularly well, as Motel 6 and Aflac so powerfully demonstrate. But remember that advertising is simply one of the means available to marketers to achieve such intermediate ends as high Awareness and high psychological acceptability. Advertising that accomplishes neither of these in a cost-effective manner is a waste and should be jettisoned. Advertising that accomplishes high Awareness without high psychological acceptability is also largely a waste. As Sergio Zyman points out in his book, *The End of Advertising as We Know It*, Enron had extraordinarily high Awareness, but to what end?[4] Psychological acceptability cannot and should not be faked; marketers must create the *reality* of psychological acceptability, not the illusion of it.

Advertising and the Tragedy of the Commons

Advertising's fundamental dilemma is analogous to what economists describe as the "tragedy of the commons." When many people use a common resource without being required to pay for it, the resource gets overused and may ultimately be destroyed. (Really? What about Google or Wikipedia?) For example, consider the case of herdsmen grazing cattle on common land. Each herdsman is a profit-maximizing individual who has the choice of adding animals onto the common. The benefit to the farmer is that he gets the full profit from each additional animal. The downside is that an additional stress is placed on the common resource, a burden shared by all. But the incentives encourage every farmer to expand his herd, resulting in extreme overgrazing and the commons' eventual destruction.

The analogy with advertising is clear. The concept of the "commons" is akin to consumers' limited attention span. Collectively, marketers vastly "overgraze" this commons, with the net result that even highly relevant messages have a difficult time piercing the thicket of irrelevant information.

The famed economist Herbert Simon once said, "What information consumes is obvious: it consumes the attention of its recipients. So, a wealth of information creates a poverty of attention and the need to allocate that attention efficiently."

Since consumers face a "wealth" of marketing information, they cannot pay attention to even the information that they might benefit from, simply because there's too much to filter through. A contributing factor is that the costs are artificially low. The US Postal Service subsidizes "junk" mail by keeping first-class postage rates higher. Likewise, e-mail "marketing" is so cheap that companies can send 10 million e-mails for a few hundred dollars. As a result, there is a strong tendency to overuse and thus abuse this medium.

The impact of overmarketing is that people become indifferent. It is similar to overusing an antibiotic; the condition being treated ultimately develops resistance, and the treatment no longer works for anyone.

Even if an advertising campaign achieves both high Awareness and high psychological acceptability, it could still be a waste of valuable resources, if the offering is extremely deficient in terms of functional acceptability, affordability, and/or accessibility. This was clearly the case with the many "dotcom" era companies that achieved high levels of name recognition and notoriety for a brief spell of time, but then dramatically disappeared when the Internet bubble collapsed in 2000. Many of these companies invested half or more of their venture capital on huge advertising campaigns (recall the famous sock puppet that was briefly made famous by Pets.com), but failed to offer a strong value proposition to customers.

So the key question to ask is, "How can a company most effectively and efficiently achieve high Awareness and psychological acceptability for an offering that is functionally acceptable, affordable, and accessible?" The answer often requires the use of advertising. However, this should not be an automatic assumption.

Advertising should always be viewed as just one component of the overall mix of methods for creating and sustaining Awareness and psychological acceptability. Research shows this to be a wise approach. For example, Bailey's, the purveyors of the famous Irish Cream, looked at how people first heard about the liqueur: 48 percent learned from friends, 17 percent from relatives, 30 percent from other sources and only 5 percent from advertising.[5]

There is an old saying about advertising attributed to John Wanamaker, who pioneered New York and Philadelphia department stores in the early twentieth century: "Half of my advertising is wasted, I just don't know which half."[6] Most probably, Mr. Wanamaker was overly optimistic. Research shows that just a third of all ad campaigns result in increased sales in the short term, while fewer than 25 percent result in sustained sales increases.[7] A large-scale study of advertising spending concluded that higher levels of advertising increased the sales of established brands in only 33 percent of cases overall and in 55 percent of cases for new brands.[8] In mature markets for packaged goods, returns to advertising diminish rapidly over time.

In a recent survey of published research on advertising effectiveness, Gerard Tellis of the University of Southern California summarizes the findings as follows (with our comments in parentheses): "Research on over 260 estimates of advertising elasticity leads to the following important generalization. If advertising changes by 1 percent, sales or market share will change by about 0.1 percent—that is, advertising elasticity is 0.1. The advertising elasticity is higher in Europe relative to the United States (due to lower levels of advertising saturation in Europe), for durables relative to nondurables (because there is usually more product differentiation in durables), in early relative to late stages of the product life cycle (because Awareness is lower earlier in the life cycle), and in print over TV (because the informational content in print media can be higher)."[9]

IMPROVING BRAND AWARENESS

The three commonly used measures of brand awareness are "top of mind;" "spontaneous (or unaided) recall;" and "aided recall." Top of mind refers to the first brand that consumers recall when they're given a product category cue. Examples include Campbell's for soups, Kodak for film, and Xerox for copying; it's a strong predictor of consumer choice. Spontaneous awareness refers to consumers' unprompted recall of the brand name. Aided awareness means that consumers only recognize the brand name when prompted.[10]

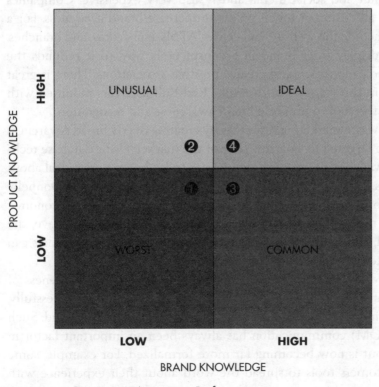

FIGURE 6.1 Diagnosing Awareness Performance

Research suggests that each of these measures is appropriate in different situations. When the consumer is presented with multiple options at the time of purchase (e.g. multiple brands on a supermarket shelf), aided awareness ("aiding the consumer's Awareness"?) is most appropriate. When multiple options are not presented, it is better to aim for spontaneous awareness. When a choice between competing brands is made quickly, top of mind awareness is more relevant. This typically occurs in low involvement impulse purchase situations such as chewing gum and candy.

Ultimately, researchers have concluded that all of these measures tap into the same underlying construct, which is "salience." Simply put, salience is the likelihood that in a purchase situation, the brand will come to the consumer's mind. All the measures cited above are highly correlated, and it is therefore not that important to distinguish between the three. What is important, however, is to measure and enhance a brand's overall salience to consumers.[11] (How so?)

To achieve and sustain high brand awareness, companies must have a clear and consistent brand identity (or "positioning") in the marketplace. If a brand is not well positioned, the message to potential customers will fail to result in a high level of salience.

In seeking to increase brand awareness, companies should reduce their traditional emphasis on television advertising, which is losing effectiveness due to the growth of the Internet and social media and is also very expensive. Companies should strive to use all customer touch points to increase brand awareness. For a bank, touch points include the website, call center, ATMs, bank cards, and branches. Companies should display their brand in a conspicuous way, so it reminds the customer of its value proposition and creates positive associations. There is great scope for creativity in this regard. For example, Red Bull uses cars mounted with an oversized can on the roof to promote brand awareness and recognition.

Some companies waste marketing resources by creating overly broad Awareness for products that are targeted to a narrow slice of the market. Using database technology and widely available information, companies today know a great deal about individual customers, consumers as well as businesses. Companies such as Donnelly Marketing have information on every US household, including socio-economic factors, the type of neighborhood they live in, the kind of house they have, the magazines they read, and the television programs they watch, etc. Companies can use this knowledge to do target marketing or database marketing.

Companies should leverage existing customers to create greater Awareness of their brand and their offering among potential customers. To do this successfully, they must convince influential customers to become advocates for the brand. Such word-of-mouth (WOM) communication has always been an important factor in marketing success, but is now becoming far more formalized. For example, some companies give customers tools to spread the word about their experience with the brand.

It is critical that marketers use word-of-mouth in a legitimate way and not abuse it. Damaging the credibility of advocates drastically reduces the level of trust that other customers place in them. Any endorsement by a customer to a potential customer must be genuine and heartfelt, never purchased.

The box below provides further details on word-of-mouth marketing.

Word-of-Mouth Marketing

The Word of Mouth Marketing Association defines "word of mouth" as "consumers providing information to other consumers." All word-of-mouth marketing techniques are based on the concepts of customer satisfaction, two-way dialog, and transparent communications. The basic elements are:

- Educating people about your products and services.
- Identifying people most likely to share their opinions.
- Providing tools that make it easier to share information.
- Studying how, where, and when opinions are being shared.
- Listening and responding to supporters, detractors, and neutrals.

Common types of word-of-mouth marketing are:

- Buzz marketing: using high-profile entertainment or news to get people to talk about your brand.
- Viral marketing: creating entertaining or informative messages that are designed to be passed along in an exponential fashion, often electronically or by e-mail.
- Community marketing: forming or supporting niche communities that are likely to share interests about the brand (such as user groups, fan clubs, and discussion forums); providing tools, content, and information to support those communities.
- Grassroots marketing: organizing and motivating volunteers to engage in personal or local outreach.
- Evangelist marketing: cultivating evangelists, advocates, or volunteers who are encouraged to take a leadership role in actively spreading the word on your behalf.
- Product seeding: placing the right product into the right hands at the right time, providing information or samples to influential individuals.
- Influencer marketing: identifying key communities and opinion leaders who are likely to talk about products and have the ability to influence the opinions of others.
- Cause marketing: supporting social causes to earn respect and support from people who feel strongly about the cause.
- Conversation creation: interesting or fun advertising, e-mails, catch phrases, entertainment, or promotions designed to start word-of-mouth activity.
- Brand blogging: creating blogs and participating in the blogosphere, in the spirit of open, transparent communications; sharing information of value that the blog community may talk about.
- Referral programs: creating tools that enable satisfied customers to refer their friends.

The power of word-of-mouth marketing can be found in companies that inspire such fanatical loyalty that customers create clubs around their products. A well-known example is Harley Davidson's HOG (Harley Owners Group) clubs. Other companies with cult-like customer bonding and loyalty include Apple and Starbucks.

Many companies spend enormous resources creating too many brands. After all, it's difficult for new brands to achieve the level of recognition and recall necessary for long-term success. Companies should thus try to reuse their existing brands whenever possible. One tactic is to develop sub-brands under strong umbrella brands. For example, the Apple brand name was a big reason for the success of the iPod, a powerful sub-brand.

Ideally, the umbrella brand should be named after the company. Companies can then use corporate advertising to improve overall marketing productivity. General Electric, for example, was very effective for many years using a single corporate advertising campaign called "We bring good things to life." This campaign firmly established corporate brand awareness for General Electric; the company capitalized by using the GE name on virtually all of its products.

Another cost-effective way to increase brand awareness is through "co-marketing" efforts. Companies can leverage their business partners to raise Awareness for their own brand name and their own offerings. For example, the Apple iPod was co-marketed with Pepsi and with Volkswagen; all three brands targeted similar customers.

An important element in increasing brand awareness in a cost-effective manner is for companies to change the way in which they deal with their advertising agencies. Rather than overpromising in order to attract customers, agencies should be encouraged to manage customer expectations so that customer satisfaction is high. Advertising agencies should be compensated according to how they cost-effectively achieve brand awareness goals, rather than the traditional practice of paying agencies a fixed percentage of media billings (usually 15 percent). Research has clearly shown that higher quality advertising requires far fewer exposures (and thus less spending) to achieve a given level of effect than average or poor quality advertising.[12]

IMPROVING PRODUCT KNOWLEDGE

The second dimension of Awareness is product knowledge, which refers to the amount of information and understanding that customers have of both the specific product and the product category as a whole. Achieving high product knowledge is especially important for innovative products that are of high significance to customers. It is not much of an issue with mature products or low involvement products.

Becoming knowledgeable about a product is easier if the product is not overly complicated. Marketers must strive to reduce product complexity and thereby simplify life for customers. Many products are overengineered and have too many features, making them difficult to understand and operate. Apple has long been known for creating products that are simple and intuitive to use. On the other hand, BMW and Mercedes-Benz have recently been criticized for the extremely complicated electronic control systems in their high-end cars. These systems require the driver to navigate through several menus to achieve simple tasks such as raising or lowering interior temperature or switching radio stations.

Many marketing setbacks can be blamed on failing to properly educate customers about the product. For example, when Sony quietly launched the MiniDisc (MD) player in 1992, customers were presented with a brand new product category that they did not understand. This problem was especially acute since Sony was the only company marketing MD players. Particularly with innovative products, it is useful if several companies jointly educate customers about their functionality and benefits. Within a few years of the launch of the MD, CD recorders became common accessories in PCs, further reducing demand for MDs in the marketplace. Rather than becoming a mass-market success (as it was in Japan), the MD was relegated to a small niche market.

In 2001, Kimberly Clark Corp. announced, with much fanfare, "the most significant category innovation since toilet paper first appeared in roll form in 1890." The announcement was deemed so newsworthy, it was covered by all the major television networks and newspapers. Kimberly Clark confidently predicted that the product would achieve $150 million in sales in its first year and $500 million annually within five years.

The "revolutionary" new product was called Cottonelle Fresh Rollwipes—essentially a roll of moist wipes in a special dispenser that clipped onto a toilet-paper holder. Since research showed that 63 percent of American adults habitually wet their toilet paper or use wet wipes, Kimberly Clark's optimism seemed well founded. The company spent approximately $100 million on research and protected the product and dispenser with 30 patents.

So why aren't we all using Rollwipes today? Kimberly Clark made several marketing mistakes:

■ First, it created a high level of brand awareness through its advertising but neglected to educate consumers about the product. Ads showed people frolicking in the water with the tagline, "Sometimes, wetter is better," leaving customers confused about what the product actually did.

■ Second, the company did not make Rollwipes available as free samples, so consumers couldn't give the product a trial.

■ Third, Kimberly Clark announced the product six months before it was actually launched. By the time the product was widely available, most consumers had forgotten what they had heard about it earlier.

■   Finally, the early publicity enabled rival Procter & Gamble to roll out its own product, dubbed Charmin Fresh Mates. Procter & Gamble's simpler product (essentially, baby wipes on a roll) was quite successful, while Kimberly Clark's was a major failure.[13]

Both Sony and Kimberly Clark could have done a better job of educating customers about the real benefits of their product compared to alternatives. Another example is a company historically known for its sure-footed approach to marketing. IBM suffered a colossal failure in the late 1980s and early 1990s with its OS/2 operating system. Though widely regarded as technologically superior, OS/2 failed to make any headway in the marketplace against Microsoft's dominant Windows operating system. While the reasons for this failure were many and complex, including numerous strategic blunders by IBM and savvy maneuvering by Microsoft, one of the more important reasons was the way in which IBM went about creating Awareness for the product in the marketplace. IBM did extensive promotions at retail stores and sponsored numerous events. In addition, it spent $40 million on a huge television advertising campaign aimed at consumers who used Microsoft Windows. However, according to industry experts, the ads only appealed to large corporate customers, most of whom already knew about OS/2. Among consumers, the ads aroused some curiosity but did not clearly explain what the product was or why they should switch to it. Indeed, the case for switching operating systems for consumers who already owned a Windows-equipped computer was dubious at best. In addition to the complexity inherent in attempting to switch operating systems, consumers were also deterred by jargon such as "preemptive multitasking" and "true 32-bit operating system." IBM also failed to make much headway in convincing computer manufacturers to preinstall OS/2 in their machines instead of Windows. Not surprisingly, OS/2 became one of the biggest failures of the PC era.

The Value of Educating Customers

Product knowledge can become obsolete, especially in the case of fast-evolving technology-based products. It's not enough to inform consumers; marketers must continue to educate them on an ongoing basis. Good companies with strong offerings that deliver real value know that "An educated consumer is our best customer," as a well-known commercial for apparel retailer Syms puts it.

Smart marketers everywhere subscribe to Syms' philosophy. For example, automobile retailers CarMax and Edmunds.com both provide a wealth of resources for consumers to become more educated and informed about car buying. Edmunds sent a professional writer to work undercover for several months as a car salesman and describe the "tricks of the trade" in great detail.[14] CarMax offers a detailed section on its website that "unmasks traditional dealer pricing games."[15] Jordan's Furniture, one of the most successful furniture retailers in the US, provides extensive information about how to buy the right mattress and exposes the deceptive games that most mattress retailers play.[16]

In today's fast changing and technologically advanced society, customers can easily get confused about many product categories. Many products today offer a great deal more functionality than the vast majority of customers are able to understand and access. Most consumers find that product manuals are difficult to navigate and largely ignore them. As a result, most customers do not take full advantage of the capabilities that are engineered into many products and therefore do not assign them a high level of value.

Companies need to educate their customers in multiple ways. For example, many financial services companies offer free retirement workshops for customers. This can be a very effective customer acquisition tool, but the primary motivating factor should be customer education. Companies should become involved with schools and colleges to encourage greater Awareness and knowledge about their products. For example, some companies provide schools with guest speakers who help students become more educated buyers in a particular product category. Companies should also offer classes. Many home improvements chains, for example, offer a variety of "how to" workshops so customers can learn how to complete various home improvement projects on their own.

A company that excels at educating its customers is Apple. Through its chain of company owned retail stores, Apple does an excellent job of helping its customers fully understand its products. Apple's venture into stores is now considered one of the most successful new retail start-ups in history. The head of its store operations has described each store as "a gift to the community," not just as a place to sell products. Employees are trained to help and educate customers first, not to sell. It offers free regularly scheduled classes in all of its stores to existing and prospective customers alike. For a fee of $99 a year, customers can also avail themselves of one-on-one training (up to one appointment a week). Such customer support goes a long way in cementing the very high level of loyalty that Apple customers have for the company and its products. These great practices have helped Apple achieve tremendous success in recent years with its retail stores, which are now considered destination sites and tourist attractions. The opening of a store in Manhattan in 2006, for example, drew extensive media coverage over several days.

DELIVERING AWARENESS BY LEVERAGING ALL RESOURCES

As with all the A's, a multitude of resources can be tapped to increase brand awareness and product knowledge. Here are some examples of how various internal and external, marketing and non-marketing resources can be harnessed to increase Awareness:

Product: When all of the products that share a brand name stand for similar things or same values, both brand awareness and product knowledge tend to be high. For example, the Disney brand is found on a wide variety of products, and has remained consistent over many decades. When people see a Disney branded product, they know it's high quality and kid friendly. Disney's consistent message makes the brand ever-present in the minds of consumers.

When a company is a serial innovator, it keeps its customers coming back for more. For many years, Apple has been a master at sustaining customers' interest. Customers are highly involved in Apple's offerings, and often seek out information on upcoming products from any sources they can find, with the expectation that a new and spectacular i-centered creation may be just around the corner.

Even when a single product line is seen as particularly innovative, it can generate Awareness through media coverage and word-of-mouth. When the Japanese watch manufacturer Seiko launched the Kinetic series (a quartz watch powered by human movement), it fueled worldwide Awareness of the Seiko brand.

Price: The price tag tells customers what they can expect from a product, and thus contributes to Awareness. Bentley, the luxury carmaker, is synonymous with quality, class, and price. It can be argued that the price alone has contributed to the car's brand awareness.

The brand name itself can contain pricing information, which in turn guides the customer's expectations. Customers who patronize Dollar Stores know exactly what to expect.

When a price is newsworthy, it can generate significant Awareness through the media. When Southwest Airlines offered $9 fares between Dallas and Houston, it generated considerable publicity and thus brand awareness for the airline.

Place: The proper placement of products aids in creating higher visibility, which increases Awareness. This is a bit of a circular proposition, as well-known brands tend to receive superior placement within stores. Many retailers leverage their power by allocating extra shelf space to their store brands, and thus creating high Awareness and higher sales for them.

Products that achieve a high level of Accessibility also attain higher levels of Awareness. Starbucks outlets are so ubiquitous now that the company's brand name has become extremely well recognized and so is the case with McDonalds and Subway. Apple's highly successful stores are located in high visibility, high traffic areas. Their sales per square foot are far higher than any other consumer electronics retailer, surpassing some of the best in luxury retail stores. In the first few years alone, Apple stores created brand awareness equivalent to about $60 million of advertising, according to analysts.

Promotion: Of course, all advertising and other forms of promotional activity have a direct impact on Awareness. But promotions vary widely in their effectiveness. Unique, memorable promotions that are strongly linked to a specific marketing objective tend to be far more effective than other types of promotions. Case in point: to improve product knowledge among its dealers, Caterpillar designed a quiz about Caterpillar products; players could win prizes based on how well they scored. The campaign was seen as a good way to increase motivation and morale, while building deeper knowledge among its dealers.

Creating a brand icon is an effective way to raise Awareness. Like the Aflac duck, Geico's gecko has become a familiar TV character and was voted "America's favorite advertising icon in 2005." The gecko even has a blog on the company's website!

People: People help create the customer experience, which aids in brand awareness. For example, Raytheon communicates plans, goals, and strategies to employees via several different methods. This ensures that all employees are on board with the company's goals and understand how their individual efforts align to the overall mission. Instead of promoting its products through celebrities, New Balance uses people and employees to market its products. Employees act as evangelists for the company's values and product offerings. New Balance also partners with lesser known athletes or "true stars," as the company calls them. Instead of endorsing New Balance's products, these top runners and race walkers educate the customer on fit and performance. The fashion retailer, The Limited, recruits its sales clerks who are similar to their target customers and provides employees discounts if they agree to wear the retailer's clothing while working.

Processes/operations: Processes can increase brand awareness through their visibility to the public. Many restaurants deliberately make their kitchens visible to customers. For example, in many Krispy Kreme stores, one can see the process used for making donuts. This increases brand awareness and product knowledge, as well as overall customer involvement.

Exposing enthusiastic customers to the operational process can enhance product knowledge and brand awareness. When a customer buys a Maybach, the luxury carmaker provides a free trip to Germany. Customers can choose options and watch the customization process for a couple of days in the factory. This experience generates significant bonding between the company and its customers, and also leads to high word-of-mouth brand awareness.

Sales: A well-trained sales staff can educate current as well as potential customers. The sales staff for the Boston Beer Company routinely go to liquor stores and sports bars that sell beer, and provide free samples and explain to prospective customers the different ingredients and brewing techniques that go into the beers. Such visits promote both brand awareness and product knowledge. In the mortgage industry, Countrywide has instituted policies and procedures to help individual loan officers educate potential customers about the terms, conditions, and consequences of different loans.

R&D: Some companies involve customers in their R&D efforts by inviting them to make suggestions and become beta testers. Six Flags theme park has expanded its R&D operation to post developments online in design, materials, and safety for new rides that are under construction. Customers can see the new roller coasters being built online. R&D that is geared towards creating products that are easier to use can help in facilitating greater product knowledge. HP has become the world's largest IT company in part by designing products that users can easily learn how to operate. It uses so-called "archetype" designs for each of its product segments, which ensure that it takes less time to learn new product features. This is often referred to as co-creation.

Customer service: Customer service can deepen consumers' knowledge of products and awaken their Awareness of new offerings. Almost all major companies operate toll-free customer service lines. When customers call in, they are introduced to new offerings. Verizon Wireless has its customer service representatives educate customers on various service options. The reps look at customers' actual usage and only promote products that make sense for the customer, which builds trust. At Pillsbury, experienced users provide free advice to consumers on how to make innovative uses of Bisquick.

IT: IT can be tremendously helpful in creating both brand awareness and product knowledge. Interactive websites enable marketers to provide recommendations for products that fit customers' requirements. For example, Amazon.com offers a "similar products" feature, where it recommends items based on the customer's interests. Savvy firms can use search engine optimization tools for popular web search engines in order to create greater Awareness among customers who are searching in their product category. IT also enables greater customization of products; because it involves the customer, customization can increase product knowledge.

Retailers: Retailers can help create Awareness in multiple ways. They can facilitate brand awareness and product knowledge through sampling programs. For example, Costco continually provides freshly heated, warm samples of food that's sold in the same aisle. Game console makers such as Nintendo and Sony work with retailers such as Best Buy and GameStop to demonstrate their new products and encourage customers to try them. Retailers can impart product knowledge to customers. When they were introducing Samuel Adams beer to the market, the founders of the Boston Beer Company used a personal approach by encouraging bartenders to sample their product and explaining why Samuel Adams was a higher quality brew. The bartenders in turn educated their patrons about the new beer.

Partners: Co-marketing with other brands can enhance the Awareness of both brands. For example, Disney often partners with fast-food restaurants to put toys in children's meals to promote their movies. This synergistic relationship builds demand for the food as well as for the movie. Companies can work with their suppliers on co-branding initiatives as well. Such "ingredient" branding can often be very successful for both parties, as was the case with the "Intel inside" campaign.

In keeping with the theme of partnering with others, companies should involve their suppliers, retailers, and other business partners in their efforts to educate customers about their product category. For example, retailers should be encouraged and supported to provide product demonstrations and other forms of assistance to customers. Experts from supplier organizations should be brought in to provide detailed information on their offerings. Companies should also cooperate with their industry peers to address common issues as well as to stimulate primary demand for their products.

Government: Companies should also leverage governmental resources where available. Many consumers turn to governmental agencies to educate themselves about different products and services. Companies should ensure that such information is readily available as well as accurate and comprehensive. They should also help customers find this information, since it is perceived to be more credible than information that comes from a company source. Again, the underlying philosophy is that the more knowledge about the product a customer has, the better for the company as well as for the customer. The government can be an important ally in helping to educate citizens about certain products in a factual, unbiased manner. For example, the Federal Trade Commission provides a great deal of detailed information on its website for consumers in industries such as automobiles, computers, financial services and many others.

Industry: Cooperative advertising campaigns such as "Pork—the other white meat" and "Got Milk?" create greater Awareness and knowledge about an industry's products. Industry trade associations can also be helpful in creating better knowledge and understanding of an industry's products and issues among regulators and the public at large.

Public/media: Public campaigns and community programs help to increase brand awareness. For example, Wal-Mart sponsors a "Teacher of the Year" program to recognize outstanding teachers in the community. This improves Wal-Mart's brand awareness and enhances its reputation. Media can be used to create both brand awareness and product knowledge. For example, the Mayo Clinic's reputation is based heavily on its research, which is published in top medical journals. Mayo also publishes the *Mayo Clinic Health Letter* and the *Mayo Clinic Family Health Box* as a way to disseminate health information to the public and enhance its own brand recognition in the process. The Oprah Winfrey show has become extremely influential in creating brand awareness and product knowledge about a variety of products, most notably books, which immediately become bestsellers upon being featured.

THE INTERNET AND AWARENESS

The Internet can have a great impact on both dimensions of Awareness. It can help a company create brand awareness through carefully placed messages that are delivered to the right customers. The Internet can serve as a virtually limitless source of deep product knowledge, especially via a company's own website as well as through third party sources.

The web is an enormously powerful medium for imparting product knowledge. For example, about 70 percent of car buyers first get information from the web. Marketers must ensure that customers can access accurate and comprehensive information about their products directly from their websites.

More and more companies use their websites to not only provide product specific information, but also to educate customers about the product category and the buying process. For example, CarMax, a company that is revolutionizing the way that new and particularly used cars are bought and sold in the United States, provides extensive information on its website about how many traditional car dealers routinely mislead and attempt to take advantage of customers. Websites can also serve as repositories for useful and objective information in the form of "white papers." Providing such information positions a company as a thought leader in its field. Toyota and Honda have staked out leadership positions in building and marketing hybrid automobiles; their websites have become useful resources for anyone seeking to learn about hybrid technology.

Websites should also serve as a platform for users to engage and interact with one another. Companies should provide the necessary infrastructure for customers to post comments, ask questions, offer "tips and tricks," and otherwise contribute to forming and running a thriving user community. It is very important that companies not attempt to bias such forums in their favor. Rather, they should participate in these forums as equals, providing the company's perspective when appropriate. Smart companies view the forums as listening posts to gather useful information that is then communicated to the right people within the company, so that they can improve the company's offerings.

In addition to facilitating customer-to-customer interactions, companies should also help expert customers "monetize" their expertise. When product knowledge evolves into expertise, marketers should take an active role in recognizing (offering psychic income) and leveraging this expertise. Amazon's top rated reviewers of books and movies are well recognized in their own right, and many are able to land paying jobs in the field. Cisco Systems has a program, called "Cisco Certified System Engineers," to certify users it deems to be experts. Such recognition not only enhances their resumes; it transforms users into evangelizers for the brand. Similarly, SAP certifies IT professionals.

Companies should take advantage of the web's tremendous flexibility and provide users with information in different forms, to accommodate different learning styles. Some users learn best by reading a document, while others prefer to listen to an audio podcast. Visually inclined customers may prefer to see a video or a slide presentation that illustrates how the product can be used.

The Internet offers marketers a cost-effective and targeted way to reach the right customers at the right time with the right message. Used intelligently, it can improve the efficiency and effectiveness of marketing, particularly in the Awareness arena.

However, the Internet is a two-edged sword for marketers. It can be highly beneficial to smart companies with good products that are targeted at the right customers. But it can be a highly effective reputation destroyer for companies that attempt to cut corners, mislead customers, or offer shoddy customer service. No longer can companies hide their real or perceived misdeeds; they must confront and deal with them head-on or see their market position erode in short order.

The Internet provides consumers with instant access to information about competing products and other consumers' experiences with products. As a result, the role of "Awareness" is changing. Now more than ever, a company's communication efforts, including its advertising, must do more informing and less persuading. In the modern, information-intensive marketplace, once they become aware of a product or service, consumers increasingly persuade themselves to make the purchase, based on factors such as perceived Acceptability and Affordability.

CONCLUSION

We have now looked at how marketing managers can optimize each of the 4A's. In the next chapter, we will examine some other aspects of applying 4A analysis.

Chapter 7

Applying 4A Analysis

INTRODUCTION

In the book's first two chapters, we introduced the 4A framework and described it in some detail. In the subsequent four chapters, we looked at each of the A's in turn, focusing primarily on how companies can creatively and efficiently increase the two dimensions of each. In this chapter, we delve into some applications of the 4A framework, show how the 4A's framework can be applied and extended, and address important implementation issues.

A POWERFUL RESOURCE ALLOCATION AND OPTIMIZATION TOOL

In too many companies, marketing groups are plagued by senior management's inability to properly allocate marketing resources. Because executives often fail to clearly define what constitutes marketing success, marketing spending decisions are often made in an *ad hoc*, even arbitrary manner. Marketing budgets (and those for subsets of marketing activities, such as advertising) are often based on past performance and the current balance sheet, and are routinely subject to pressures from finance executives who have different priorities and a poor understanding of marketing.[1] The result is all too predictable: marketing managers come up with the usual alibis to explain why so many marketing programs fail to deliver bottom-line results.

Another problem is that marketing dollars are viewed as expenses instead of investments, which is really how they should be treated. Companies that focus on the short term can justify this approach, since most of their marketing actions, such as sales promotions, have no long-term benefit. However, this is a formula for low marketing productivity and poor long-term financial performance.

When the 4A framework is properly leveraged, it takes much of the guesswork out of marketing spending decisions. It allows managers to readily see the dangers of misallocating resources. If a product is very low on one A, raising another can actually hurt. For example, just consider the dangers of extremely high Awareness with little or no Accessibility. Using the 4A's framework to align corporate resources with consumer value drivers can help companies and managers avoid what has been called the "Knee Deep in the Big Muddy" syndrome, characterized by escalating commitments to a losing cause.[2]

The 4A framework shows where a marketing program's strengths and weaknesses reside; it focuses managers' attention on where it is needed within the 4P's of the marketing mix and other aspects of the business. When a product captures just a small share of the market, the typical response is to lower the price or throw more advertising dollars at it, neither of which is generally the right response. Because the 4A's framework highlights a marketing effort's strengths and weaknesses, the company can reevaluate and redistribute its resources to deliver the best returns from its target market.

The 4A framework provides a clear means by which managers can direct resources to the marketing program's weakest link. For example, if the target market isn't sufficiently *aware* of the product, more resources (both people and money) can be made available to increase the advertising effort, as well as make adjustments to the myriad other factors that contribute to raising Awareness. And yet, when a product is ignored or undiscovered, the underlying problem might have less to do with the amount of resources dedicated to raising Awareness, and more to do with the manner in which they are being deployed. By shifting resources into more cost-effective vehicles for creating Awareness, a manager might well increase Awareness while using fewer resources—a tactic that's been vividly illustrated through systematic marketing experiments carried out at two major consumer product companies.

In the 1970s, Anheuser-Busch (A-B) conducted a series of experiments to determine whether it was spending too much or too little on advertising. The results were startling. The experiments clearly showed that A-B was overspending on advertising, and that sales would go up significantly (and profits even more so) if the amount of spending on advertising was reduced. That's because A-B's advertising had saturated its target markets and no longer informed and entertained; it had crossed the line into alienating many of its customers with excessive advertising. Over time, the company was able to reduce its advertising spending by about 50 percent per barrel, while significantly increasing its market share.[3]

Experiments at Campbell's Soup in the 1980s also found that advertising spending can often be reduced for established brands, and added other insights as well. Campbell found that increasing advertising intensity had no positive effect on sales, while it clearly had a negative effect on profits. The most important finding was that the quality elasticity of advertising was 18 times greater for Campbell than the quantity elasticity. Elasticity is a measure of the amount of change in an outcome variable for a change of one unit in an input variable. Campbell found that its advertising spending could be greatly reduced if the quality of its advertising could be increased by even a small amount.[4]

In attempting to "fix" marketing problems, companies often seem to throw good money after bad. For example, instead of addressing its Affordability problem, a product-centric company may focus on improving the product's quality. Or a consumer packaged goods company, facing declining sales, may increase advertising instead of trying to make its offering more distinctive.

Unfortunately, unbalanced resource allocation tends to be the rule rather than the exception. For example, in our experience, engineering-dominated firms tend to devote excessive resources to increasing Acceptability, at the expense of the other A's. On the other hand, firms driven by a "sales and promotions" approach tend to overallocate resources to advertising, while underfunding product development and improvement. Too many companies fail to appreciate that additional spending beyond a particular level generally generates diminishing returns.

Maximizing Bang for the Buck

For a marketing effort to succeed, it must fully leverage all of the A's. However, deficiencies in some A's are easier to remedy than others. For instance, it may be a lot easier to increase Affordability (e.g. by offering attractive financing terms) than it is to raise Acceptability. This suggests the elasticity of response of each A to additional (or reduced) spending can vary greatly across the A's. Managers seeking to maximize the productivity of their spending should allocate resources on this basis.

As an illustration, suppose $1 million of additional spending could raise Acceptability by 20 percent and Awareness by 5 percent. Even if Acceptability is already higher than Awareness, this would argue for spending the resources on further raising Acceptability, since the impact on the resulting Market Value Coverage would be greater.

A simple 4A analysis can indicate where the next marketing dollar should come from and where it should go, based on where the product is on each A, the estimated cost of increasing each A by 1 percent, and the estimated savings from allowing each A to drop by 1 percent.

In Figure 7.1, it appears that resources can be harvested from activities contributing to Awareness and invested in increasing Accessibility and Affordability, in that order.

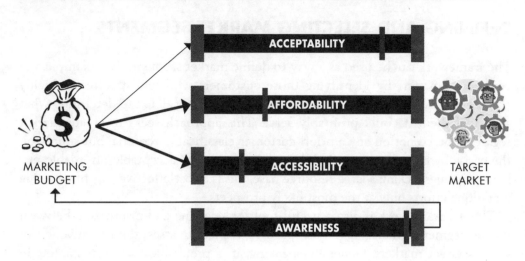

FIGURE 7.1 Resource Allocation across the A's

The Importance of Balancing the A's

For any given average level across the A's, Market Value Coverage is maximized when the 4A's are equal. Thus, instead of a distribution of 100 percent, 50 percent, 100 percent and 50 percent, which delivers a Market Value Coverage (MVC) of 25 percent, a company would be better off with all four scores at 75 percent, which yields an MVC of 31.6 percent.

We offer the following guidelines:

- Managers should try to achieve equally high scores on all A's.
- If the scores are skewed, and if lowering the highest scores can save resources, they should take out resources from the highest scoring A, and invest them in raising the score of the lowest scoring A.
- If the scores are skewed, and if lowering the highest scores *cannot* save resources, then managers should look for resource-efficient ways to increase the lowest scores.
- If managers are given additional resources, they should not automatically divide them equally among the A's. They should invest in the A's with the lowest scores first. When the scores are roughly equal, additional resources should then be invested in such a way that they result in equal increases across the A's.
- The only time it makes sense to invest first in an A that is already high is if it can be done in a far more resource-efficient manner than is the case with a lower scoring A.
- The best rule of thumb for resource allocation is to invest money where you can achieve the highest gain in the product's overall Market Value Coverage.

DEFINING AND SELECTING MARKET SEGMENTS

The framework can be used as a way to define market segments. For example, the company can start by identifying those customers who find its offering highly acceptable. It can then study these customers in greater detail to determine what subset of them it could profitably serve. This approach seeks to create market segments based not on any a priori customer classification criteria, but simply on the basis of which customers find the proposed offering acceptable, affordable, etc. For companies lacking a large resource base, this is a cost-effective way of targeting marketing efforts only at the most likely prospects.

The 4A framework is also a useful tool for selecting and prioritizing between market segments. Managers can use the 4A's as a lens to assess the attractiveness of various target markets. Generally speaking, it is preferable to target markets in which the offering can start with a relatively high market value coverage, even if they represent smaller opportunities than other markets. As the figure shows, each potential market segment should be evaluated in terms of: (1) the company's initial Market Value Coverage (MVC) score, without any additional investment; and (2) the size of the market opportunity. In general, it is preferable for a company to target a smaller segment against which it has a high MVC rather than a large market segment for which its MVC is very low. In Figure 7.2, this would be the first target market on the left. By targeting this market instead of a much larger alternative (the market shown in the middle), the company can start generating revenues almost immediately. It can then, over time, use a portion of these revenues to start increasing the attractiveness of its offering for the larger market.

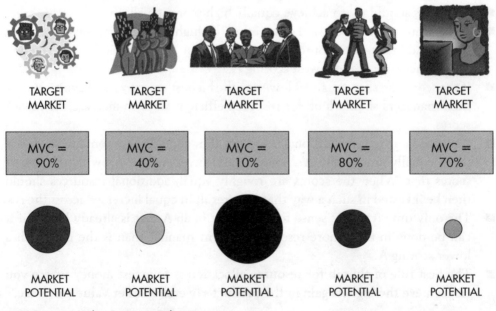

TARGET MARKET	TARGET MARKET	TARGET MARKET	TARGET MARKET	TARGET MARKET
MVC = 90%	MVC = 40%	MVC = 10%	MVC = 80%	MVC = 70%
MARKET POTENTIAL	MARKET POTENTIAL	MARKET POTENTIAL	MARKET POTENTIAL	MARKET POTENTIAL

FIGURE 7.2 Market Segment Selection

DIAGNOSING AND TROUBLESHOOTING EXISTING MARKETING PROGRAMS

For existing products, especially those that are struggling in the marketplace, the framework is a powerful diagnostic tool, allowing marketing managers to pinpoint the weakest link or links. This allows the company to direct monetary and managerial resources directly to the area in which they would have maximum impact. Managers can use the framework to understand exactly why a product is underperforming in the marketplace. They can even use it to turn outright failures into successes.

The framework also enables managers to quickly evaluate proposed changes in the offering. For example, when managers wonder whether it's worthwhile to lower the price by x to achieve y Affordability, they can use the framework to predict the impact on sales, market share, and profitability. In this way, the company's strategic leverage, which is defined as those "maneuvers that promise the highest returns," can be identified and used.

The 4A's represent a starting point from which to attempt to quantify and measure marketing performance, and help to focus efforts on the specific variable(s) that are underperforming. By so doing, the framework helps companies avoid the kind of uninformed decision-making that once plagued Levi Strauss.

In the mid-1980s, Levi Strauss & Company attempted to grow its business by expanding into a sector of the apparel industry it had heretofore ignored: traditional, three-piece and two-piece men's suits. Through an extensive segmentation study, the country's foremost purveyor of blue-jeans had discovered a demographic of men that it barely served—essentially, the so-called "yuppies" who largely defined that decade. After uncovering virtually everything it needed to know about these young, upwardly mobile professionals—including what kind of clothing they liked to buy, where they liked to buy it, and how they felt about the Levi's brand—the company designed a marketing program that systematically went against much of what it had uncovered.

Functionally, the product was fine; it was a basic wool or wool-blended suit in traditional colors and cuts. The only twist was that the suits were to be sold as separates; the customer could buy the jacket, trousers, and vest individually but not collectively. The suits were priced in the middle of the range for such products.

Nonetheless, the launch of "Levi's Tailored Classics" failed miserably. What went wrong? Consider each of the A's:

- *Acceptability:* Target customers made it clear in focus groups that they would be uncomfortable buying a Levi's branded suit.
- *Affordability:* Potential customers bought into the price, but department stores thought it was too high. As a result, many did not stock the line.
- *Accessibility:* The product was sold only in department stores, as Levi's lacked a

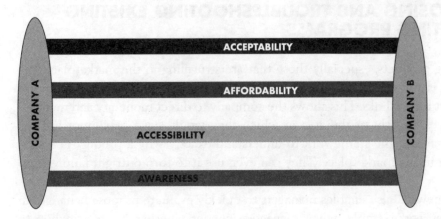

FIGURE 7.3 Fit between Potential Partners

system for distributing to men's specialty apparel shops, where targeted customers preferred to buy their suits.

■ *Awareness:* Only one advertisement ever ran for the product, in the *New York Times* Sunday magazine.

When sales failed to materialize, the company took action—but failed to address the crux of the matter. Instead of improving Acceptability by changing the brand name and Accessibility by selling through specialty stores, Levi's acted all too predictably: it rolled back prices. Had it tacked to the 4A's, Levi's probably would have had a substantial success on its hands. Instead, it failed miserably, and soon had to shut the initiative down.[5]

The 4A framework provides a very useful basis for assessing the potential advantages of alliances and partnerships. For example, if company A is strong on Acceptability and Affordability, and Company B is strong on Accessibility and Awareness, the two companies together could realize major synergies.

Too often, companies enter into partnerships or even mergers with firms whose capabilities fail to complement their own. The 4A framework can help assess the degree of potential fit. For example, companies that excel at engineering and manufacturing are generally quite capable of producing products that are highly acceptable and affordable. They should look to partner with companies that have strong brand names and established distribution channels.

Managing Distribution Channels

The 4A framework can be applied to channel relationships as well as to end-users. Firms employing intermediaries to reach the final customer should therefore use the 4A framework twice, once in their dealings with channel members and once in relation to end-users. The reason for this is that companies must treat intermediaries as customers. Managers can use 4A analysis to determine which distribution channels will result in the highest Market Value Coverage for their target markets. For example, some stores may have a downscale image that is not compatible with a premium product; selling through them would result in a lower level of Acceptability. Other retail chains may have a low degree of overlap with the target market.

In the 1990s, "big box" retailers changed the landscape of appliance retailing in the US. With broad selections, national economies of scale, aggressive pricing, and quick delivery, chains such as Best Buy became a huge threat to the thousands of small appliance stores that were located in small towns. These family-owned stores could not compete with the big chains in terms of Accessibility (they couldn't offer as broad an assortment of products or as quick a delivery) or Affordability (their prices were higher since they lacked economies of scale).

Instead of letting such retailers perish, GE came up with an ingenious, win-win proposition. Its Direct Connect program offered participating retailers two huge advantages: they could jettison their own inventory and take advantage of all the inventory available in GE's regional warehouses (creating a kind of "virtual inventory" for the stores), and GE would drop ship appliances directly to consumers' homes, with the same kind of speed the big chains offered. Thus, GE broke the trade-off that smaller retailers faced: if they carried a high inventory, their cost structure could not sustain competitive pricing with the large chains.

Thanks to Direct Connect, the small stores were competitive once again, especially since they could leverage their superior customer relationships and closer

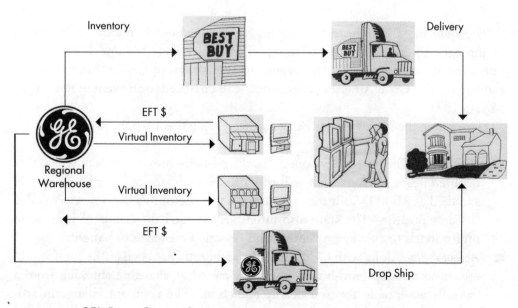

FIGURE 7.4 GE's Direct Connect Program

proximity to the customer. In exchange for being allowed to participate in Direct Connect, the stores had to guarantee that GE would account for at least 50 percent of their appliance sales. This resulted in a net gain in market share for GE, more satisfied consumers, and thousands of happy and loyal, GE-focused retailers.

MANAGING DEMAND

The 4A framework is a very useful way to think about not just increasing demand (the traditional concern of marketing), but also about how to control it. More broadly, we can use the 4A framework to shape the "level, timing, and composition of demand."[6] In other words, the framework can help determine who buys, when they buy, and how much they buy. Demand management is especially important in cases where the supply is fixed but demand varies seasonally (as with airlines and hotels).

Consider the demand for tobacco, which society would like to greatly reduce. The state of Massachusetts has become a worldwide leader in the battle against tobacco addiction, particularly among teenagers. According to Terry Pechacek, associate director for science in the CDC's Office on Smoking and Health,

> The experience of Massachusetts is being used around the world as an exemplary model of what is possible. Massachusetts has shown we can turn the corner, we can stop the epidemic, and what is being learned from Massachusetts will lead potentially to millions of lives being saved around the world.

The state has a long history of aggressive involvement in public health issues dating back to the eighteenth century, when Paul Revere became Boston's first public health commissioner. The origins of the American Cancer Society iconic campaign, "The Great American Smokeout," can be traced to an event in Randolph, MA, in 1971.

Here's how the state's efforts can be viewed using the 4A framework:

- *Awareness:* The state developed "stark, no-nonsense" television spots that featured heavy smokers such as Pam Laffin, who developed emphysema at 24 and died at 31. MTV put the commercials together into a documentary called "I Can't Breathe." The state also intensively trained thousands of healthcare professionals to convey prevention and cessation messages to patients.
- *Acceptability:* Along with California, Massachusetts has been at the forefront of efforts to develop hard-hitting messages aimed at changing smoking from a "socially acceptable act to a deadly addiction." The resultant change in atti- tudes towards smoking has been so substantial, even the state's most dogged

adversaries, such as the Tobacco Institute and Philip Morris, have largely surren-
dered to public opinion and now state that they agree with many of the
Massachusetts Tobacco Control Program's objectives.

- *Affordability:* In November 1992, despite $6.8 million in advertising by the
tobacco industry, Massachusetts voters approved a 25 cents a pack tax hike;
some of the tax revenue was earmarked for antismoking initiatives.
- *Accessibility:* The state aggressively restricted the locations where cigarettes
could be purchased as well as used. Restrictions were placed on smoking in
workplaces, restaurants, courthouses, schools, colleges, museums, transit
stations, healthcare facilities, and childcare centers. Restrictions on sales to
minors were stringently enforced.

According to Matt Myers, president of the Campaign for Tobacco Free Kids,
"The combination of mass media, community-based funding, and school programs
in Massachusetts has set the standard for what makes these programs successful.
People forget, but ten years ago, there were a lot of experts who said there was
nothing we could do to reduce tobacco use among teenagers. Massachusetts proved
them wrong."

Massachusetts' effort to reduce smoking is an unequivocal success, as underlined
by the following indicators:

- Cigarette consumption fell by close to 40 percent between 1992 and 2000.
- The number of adults who smoke each day declined by 18 percent from 1993
to 2000.
- Youth smoking rates declined 26 percent from 1994 to 2000.
- Successful underage buying attempts dropped from 39 percent to 10 percent.
- The number of women who smoked during pregnancy declined 58 percent
from 1990 to 1999.
- Exposure to environmental tobacco smoke in the workplace, restaurants, and
private homes was significantly reduced.

Massachusetts' example shows how the levers of the 4A's can be used to impact
demand in a socially desirable direction.

4A'S THROUGH THE PRODUCT LIFE CYCLE

4A analysis can be applied at every stage of a product's life cycle, from birth through
maturity and decline. Products, technologies, and distribution channels undergo a
life cycle. The cost of production declines as volumes increase and producers gain
experience and scale advantages. Customer expectations and perceptions also
change. For example, customers are likely to be willing to pay less as a product

category matures. Look at what people are willing to pay for cell phones today compared with a few years ago.

At the beginning of the product life cycle, when concepts are on the drawing board, the 4A's can be a valuable starting point for evolving concepts with regard to the target market, distribution channels, product features, and pricing. Similarly, 4A analysis can be applied following a launch, to determine why a product is succeeding or stumbling. Once a product's position in the market is understood, decisions can be made to shift the marketing effort to a particular customer segment, or change the product, its pricing, or the way it's delivered to the customer. At the end of a product life cycle, an evaluation of the 4A's can yield lessons about how to develop future product concepts.

For a well-established product in a mature market, high Acceptability and Awareness may have already been achieved. To increase market share, a good strategy to consider is to put more of an emphasis on Affordability and Accessibility. A case in point is McDonald's US operations. McDonald's has an extremely high level of Awareness among the American public and a large percentage of American consumers already consider Mickey D's products to be acceptable. So over the past few years, the company has attempted to build market share by expanding availability at new sites within Wal-Mart stores and other non-traditional locations. McDonald's has also packaged several "combo" meals, which are designed to increase consumers' perception that the servings are affordable and offer good value. However, the company's effort to raise Acceptability (consider its unsuccessful McLean Deluxe and the Arch Deluxe offerings) have not fared as well.

GROWING THE MARKET

Marketing resources can be directed toward one of two goals: steal market share or grow the market. The search for growth is perhaps the greatest preoccupation of companies and their managers. Too often, this search is focused on growing market share, rather than on growing the overall market. While growing market share is certainly a legitimate objective, it is potentially dangerous (as it invites a heightened level of immediate retaliation) and far less valuable than a strategy that's based on growing the overall market.

Marketers can dramatically grow the total market by creating a high level of Affordability. Such a strategy pays off most dramatically in product categories with low variable costs, such as electronics, software, and airlines. For example, Japanese manufacturing techniques increased the market for many electronic products dramatically, just as Henry Ford did for cars.

Then there's Southwest Airlines, whose ability to survive and even prosper in the shadow of much larger airlines is based on its relentless focus on growing the market rather than grabbing market share. In its early years, Southwest dramatically expanded the total airline traffic on sectors that it entered. Typically, the total number of passengers flying a particular route rose by as much as 300 percent when Southwest entered the picture. Southwest's approach was to target customers whose primary reason for not flying was a lack of Affordability.

While Southwest was an upstart, its strategy works for industry leaders. Typically, such companies have 40 percent or higher market share. Incremental share gains are difficult to attain, and often lower profits by bringing in customers who generate less revenue and cost more to serve. Instead, such companies would be better advised to use the 4A framework to identify the most profitable growth vector. For example, they could leverage their broadest strengths via extensions. Thus, a company that is very strong on Accessibility could add new products and services for the same customer base. One that is especially strong on Acceptability could leverage that strength into other markets.

Overall, market growth is constrained by the company with the highest Market Value Coverage (MVC). If any one company achieves 100 percent MVC, the potential for market growth has been exhausted. If the highest MVC among all competitors is 60 percent, the formula suggests that 40 percent of the market remains untapped.

What happens to the 4A's when a marketing program's reach is expanded (i.e. its target market is broadened) is a critical indicator of a product's growth potential. If companies find that they still have reasonably high levels of MVC, they should immediately broaden their market focus. Just consider Campbell's Soup's "Soup is Good Food" advertising campaign, which targeted all consumers, not just those who enjoyed soup. (Campbell's already had a market share of more than 60 percent among soup lovers.) This campaign was highly successful, since it focused on growing the market rather than on capturing more market share.

Then there's Coke's highly successful launch of Diet Coke, which was likewise aimed at all those who consumed soft drinks, not just at dieting women, as its previous product (Tab) had been. Diet Coke's advertising campaign ("Just for the taste of it") made no mention of calories, and the ads featured men as well as women. The results: Diet Coke rapidly became the third highest selling soft drink (behind Coke and Pepsi), and was the most successful new soda launch since the original big two (Coke and Pepsi).

The right marketing approach can grow markets dramatically. Consider the substantial changes that have come to three product categories: radios, watches, and eyeglasses. Not too long ago, consumers perceived each of these products primarily in terms of their functional utility. But that has changed, as consumers now think of these products in terms of their aesthetic value and social value, as well as their functionality.

There was a time when every American family owned one big radio, which occupied a central place in the family home. Fast forward to today, when the average American household has at least a dozen radios, from bedside tables to the kitchen, the garage, and of course, the car. Why has the market for radios expanded so dramatically? It's not that people are listening to more radio programming than ever before (in fact, they're probably listening to a lot less). It's because radios have become so affordable and compact, purchases have exploded.

Watches have enjoyed a similar growth curve. People used to own one watch at most, repair it when it broke, and finally replace it with a new one when it could not work anymore. Today, it is not uncommon for people to own five to ten watches. The watch has evolved from being a functional time-telling device to a full-fledged fashion accessory. It has even become a collectable, thanks in large measure to the efforts of Swatch, the Swiss company that introduced the notions of affordable fashion and rapid introductions of new designs to the watch market.

Likewise, eyewear has become a fashion accessory as well as a functional purchase. It is not uncommon for individuals to own several pairs of glasses, to match the mood and occasion.

Each of these markets grew because of marketers' specific actions, not because of consumer demand. Peter Drucker advised marketers to look very closely at those consumers who don't purchase the company's products. Even for leading companies, 70 percent or more of potential buyers aren't customers. If marketers focused more on growing the market than on grabbing market share, they might convert more of those prospects into customers.

THE 4A'S AND PROFITABILITY

In utilizing the 4A framework as the basis for managing a company's marketing programs, there is a potential for "overkill." Naturally, every company or product manager will want to score as highly as possible on each of the A's. But an all-out pursuit of the 4A's could lead some managers to needlessly overspend on advertising or to distribute too widely. This highlights the need for managers to adopt a bottom-line orientation when applying the framework. That is, investments in improving the A's should be made only if the benefits exceed the cost.

It's important to understand that an MVC of 100 percent does not automatically translate to optimum profitability but to maximizing unit sales, since it means that everyone in the market is aware of the product and finds it Acceptable,

TABLE 7.1

To Maximize	MVC Should Be
Unit Sales	100%
Revenue	<100%
Profit	<<100%

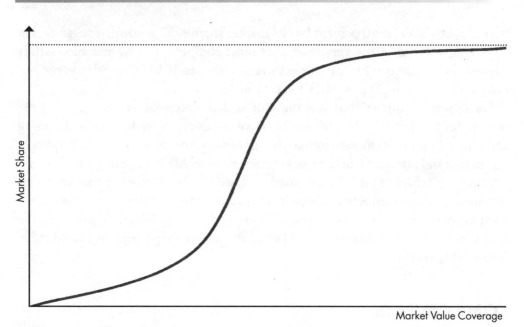

FIGURE 7.5 Diminishing Returns

Affordable, and Accessible. To achieve this, the product is probably priced very aggressively and may incur very high distribution costs to make it ubiquitously available. Financially, this may not be an acceptable position to be in. Revenue is actually maximized when MVC is somewhat less than 100 percent. In such cases, the A's are close to 100 percent, except for Affordability. The idea is to leave out the most extremely price sensitive customers in the market, if serving them means lowering the price to all.

Ultimately, revenue maximization is not the goal of a business; profit maximization is. This generally occurs with an MVC that is throttled back even further below 100 percent. The reason: for each A, there is a saturation point, beyond which additional spending does not yield positive results from a profit standpoint. This is because at some point, the additional spending required to increase the level of an A is not offset by the benefits derived from doing so.

Market Value Coverage and Market Share

Market share is correlated with but not equal to MVC. It can be greater or less than MVC, depending on the market's competitive conditions. If only one company targets a market but has a low MVC, it still will attain a 100 percent market share. The relationship between a product's MVC and its market share provides a proxy measure of the level of competitive intensity (CI) in a market, as well as the degree to which the offerings in the market are aligned with customer needs. For example, if a product's MVC is 40 percent but its market share is 50 percent, it suggests that CI is very low—or, at the very least, that most competitors have not successfully aligned their actions with the market's requirements. If MVC is 80 percent but market share is only 20 percent, CI is very high.

For example, Apple's iPad was the only touch screen tablet computer on the market for a while. While it is an attractive product, its high price and lack of certain features (e.g. camera, external storage options) made it less than 100 percent acceptable and affordable in the marketplace, with an MVC of perhaps 60 percent. However, it achieved an effective market share of 100 percent within its niche, lacking any direct competitors. Now that several other companies have launched competing products, the iPad's market share is dropping. When version 2 of the iPad was launched, it increased its MVC, but market share remains considerably below 100 percent.

SOME CAVEATS

Before we conclude this chapter, we should clear up some commonly held misperceptions about the 4A framework.

- First and foremost, it is essential to understand that the 4A's are not the 4P's. As we have pointed out, actions undertaken for each of the P's can impact all of the A's. We've also discussed the fact that many actions taken in areas beyond the purview of the 4P's can influence the A's.
- Second, maximizing Acceptability does not require "gold-plating"—that is, overengineering a product. The most acceptable offering best meets the customer's needs; it doesn't simply deliver the highest possible quality. Many companies, especially those with an engineering and manufacturing mindset, make the mistake of gold-plating their products, while paying insufficient attention to other elements. Gold-plating, even when it may be a positive factor for customers, inevitably raises costs to such a level that making the offering affordable is next to impossible.
- Third, maximizing Affordability is not the same as offering the lowest price. Rather, it's all about delivering the right value-exchange proposition. It is entirely possible for a product with a higher price to rate higher on Affordability than one with a lower price, if the latter delivers a significantly lower level of value to the customer. For example, many consumers would consider a used Volvo at $10,000 to be more affordable than a lesser brand at $9,000.
- Fourth, and in a similar vein, achieving high Accessibility does not mean that a product must be available everywhere in the market. Products can be distributed too widely, which leads to higher costs and greater channel conflict, while failing to deliver real benefits to customers.

■ Finally, achieving high Awareness does not mean that the product should prompt "top-of-mind" recall. It's enough that customers know about a product and consider it when making a choice.

Seek Synergistic Marketing Actions

Using the 4A framework requires that marketing managers adopt a customer-oriented view of all company actions that impact customers. Since the objective is to increase each of the A's to the highest level possible in a cost-effective manner, every marketing action should be assessed in terms of its cost and its impact on each of the A's.

Figure 7.6 depicts three types of marketing actions. In the first, the marketing action has a direct impact on one of the A's, and does not impact any other. For example, when a software application is modified in response to a customer complaint about certain "bugs," its Acceptability is improved, but nothing else is changed. In such cases, the cost of making the change should be assessed directly against the amount of improvement in the relevant A and its impact on overall Market Value Coverage.

The second type of marketing action has a "trade-off" impact. In this case, one A increases and another decreases. The most common instance of this is when a product is significantly upgraded and its price is raised. This will likely improve its Acceptability while lowering its Affordability.

The most powerful, and thus most desirable, types of marketing action are those that simultaneously raise two or more of the A's. These actions have a

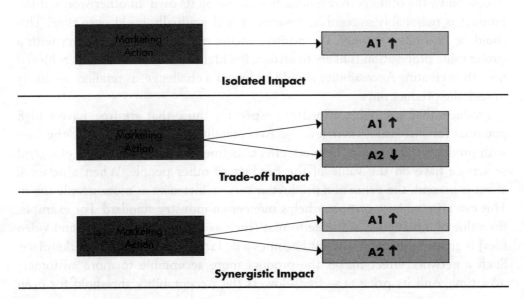

FIGURE 7.6 Impact of Marketing Action

synergistic impact on Market Value Coverage, and can therefore be enormously profitable. For example, a company may redesign a product to simultaneously improve its functionality, make it more reliable and less prone to malfunctions, and lower the cost of production. If the changes are dramatic enough, they could generate some free publicity. Such an action thus simultaneously increases Acceptability, Affordability, and Awareness; it even has the potential to improve Accessibility, as more retailers may become interested in carrying the product.

HOW THE A'S CAN IMPACT EACH OTHER

Over time, the A's can be mutually reinforcing. In other words, achieving a high level on one A can help improve performance in regard to the other A's. For example, a highly acceptable product will sell a certain number of units even when it is underperforming in terms of the three other attributes. Such incremental success will gradually lead to positive word-of-mouth communications, which should enhance Awareness. And as the product sells more units, the per-unit production costs should gradually decline, which will in turn make the product more affordable. Greater Awareness and Affordability also facilitate greater Accessibility over time. As more customers ask retailers for a particular product, retailers are more likely to start carrying it.

This "domino effect" is most pronounced when a product is highly acceptable, but may be less noticeable in terms of Awareness and Accessibility. If a product has a fundamentally strong value proposition (which is based on its Acceptability and Affordability), and if it can generate a reasonable level of either Awareness or Accessibility, the other A may gradually increase on its own. In other words, if the product is reasonably accessible, Awareness will gradually build over time. This could be facilitated through the positive media exposure that a product with a strong value proposition is likely to attract. If a high level of Awareness is achieved first, then creating Accessibility should be less of a challenge, as retailers are likely to seek the product out.

Products that are highly affordable, especially those that are free, have a high potential for increasing their level of Acceptability. This is particularly the case with products that enjoy a "network effect," defined as the impact users of a good or service have on the value of the product to other people. When a network effect is present, the value of a product or service increases as more people use it. This can arise when a company helps pioneer an industry standard. For example, the value of a particular software format (such as RealAudio for music and video files) is greatly enhanced when it becomes a de facto standard in the marketplace. Such a network effect makes the product more acceptable to more customers over time. And its price tag—free—lowers the Acceptability threshold for even more customers.

IMPLEMENTATION AND CONTROL

While the 4A framework addresses all of the major aspects of a successful marketing program, we discuss below some additional points to consider.

We start with the notion of alignment, by which we mean coordinating the long-term interests of the company, its customers, and other stakeholders. Marketers must also ensure that the product benefits society as well as customers. They must then see to it that all the A's are properly positioned for the target market. This is where companies create their Market Value Coverage.

However, alignment is not the whole picture. A critical next step is activation. Sometimes, customers need a little nudge—a small incentive—to get them to act. The product may be perfectly acceptable and affordable; the customer knows about it and it is within arm's reach. And yet, the customer is unmoved. This is because most customers exist in a state of inertia, as though they are subject to Newton's First Law of Motion (also known as the Law of Inertia): "An object at rest tends to stay at rest and an object in motion tends to stay in motion with the same speed and in the same direction unless acted upon by an external force."

Think of an object sitting on a table that is inclined in one direction. The object does not move because of static friction (resistance to movement when an object is stationary), which is much higher than kinetic friction (the resistance to movement when an object is already in motion). All it takes is a small push to get the object moving. And once the object moves, it accelerates.

A big part of the marketer's job is to get the *customer* moving. A marketing effort must provide enough oomph to convert prospects into customers, customers into advocates, and advocates into partners. Marketers can trigger such a chain reaction by offering small incentives that make a big difference in the customer's thinking, and ultimately get the ball rolling in the right direction.

Consider the following scenario. A potential customer gets an e-mail from a Lexus dealer saying "If you come in and test drive one of our cars, we will give you a $100 coupon for dinner for two at a well-known gourmet restaurant." A $100 incentive to consider purchasing a $40,000 car is less than 0.25 percent of the price. And yet, it might well be big enough to get the customer into the showroom. Once there, the customer discovers what is, for him, the perfect car at the perfect price, coupled with a fair value for the customer's trade-in. Everything is just right, and much to his own amazement, the customer drives home in a brand new Lexus.

Trouble is, companies often engage in what we call "premature activation." Companies should only attempt to overcome customer inertia if all the 4A's are right for that customer. More often than not, marketers overwhelm the customer with coupons, discounts, and other inducements before ensuring that the value proposition amounts to a good fit. Although it may be possible to get customers to act if they're offered enough inducements, the purchase might not be right for them. The result: customers act, but then regret having acted. They're unhappy

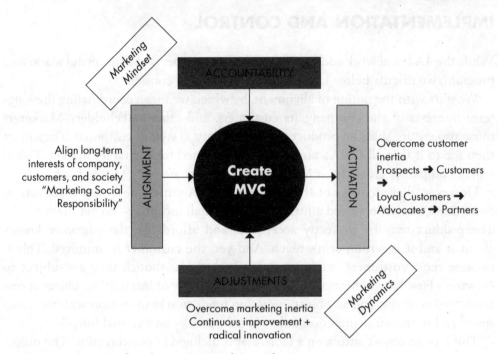

FIGURE 7.7 The 4A's of Implementation and Control

with the purchase, speak badly of it to friends, and are far less likely to return to the brand in the future.

Premature activation builds customer resistance, which puts marketers in a vicious cycle: they have to offer ever more extreme inducements to get customers to buy their products. US automakers know this cycle all too well. Lacking cars that customers truly desired, they offered manufacturer rebates that grew exponentially, and then moved on to unsustainable gimmicks such as "employee pricing for everyone." Soon, they found it difficult to sell without massive incentives.

Even after marketers have created alignment, crafted a strong value proposition, and activated customers, they must be held accountable for the results. As we noted at the book's outset, marketers too often haven't had to own up to their comparatively massive expenditures and paltry achievements. The result: increasing levels of marketing waste, low returns on marketing investments, and growing customer resistance to marketing initiatives.

Marketing's overall goal must always be to create value for customers, the company, and society. When judging a marketing effort, we must look at its full impact, and not just at market share or revenue growth. We must consider long-term wealth creation for the corporation; customers' physical and emotional well-being; and the effort's broader impact on society. In addition to financial wealth, we must assess a marketing campaign's capacity to create intellectual, social, cultural, environmental, and spiritual wealth.

Activation is about overcoming customer inertia. The next step, adjustment, is about overcoming *marketing* inertia.

Marketers, like just about everyone else in business, too often try to repeat past successes. They take the view that what worked yesterday should work again today. Such myopia causes marketers to fail to adapt to the world's changes. To guard against a blinkered world-view, marketers must continually fine-tune their efforts and look for opportunities to introduce radical innovations to targeted customers. When there are disruptive changes in technology, market structure, or customer behavior, marketers must dare to rethink their assumptions about what it will take to seize the future.

In the framework depicted in Figure 7.7, the upper left part depicts the right marketing mindset, while the lower right part traces marketing dynamics in terms of customer and marketing inertia. The marketing mindset is about having the right philosophy about marketing, which considers the marketing triple bottom line and the stakeholder's perspective, while marketing dynamics is about overcoming customer and marketer inertia. Deploying this comprehensive approach ensures that marketing will add value to customers, companies, and the wider community.

To summarize, the four additional A's consist of:

- *Alignment:* Ensures that the true long-term interests of customers, the company and society are in harmony. It highlights marketing's *social responsibility* dimension.
- *Activation:* Helps to overcome customer inertia and triggers purchasing behavior. We can think of Activation as a logical progression over time: Prospects → Customers → Loyal customers → Advocates → Partners.
- *Accountability:* Elicits the productivity dimension, as well as reemphasizes the importance of social responsibility. Think of Accountability in terms of a "triple bottom line"—financial, social, and environmental—for marketing.
- *Adjustments:* Recognizes that customers and markets are dynamic; that what works today may not work tomorrow. To stay relevant, marketers must continually refine their value proposition. They must also understand when to make incremental improvements and when to offer radical innovations.

Taken together, this additional set of 4A's makes for a *more comprehensive framework* that addresses areas that are crucial to long-term marketing and business success.

We can cluster the original 4A and the additional A's listed above into four groups, each of which includes two interdependent constructs:

1. The value proposition: Acceptability and Affordability
These two marketing attributes can and often do move in tandem. Customers for whom the offering has a high level of Acceptability are likely to exhibit a higher willingness to pay.

2. Facilitating factors: Awareness and Accessibility

These two factors also often move in tandem. Accessibility plays a role in creating Awareness. Clearly, prominently displaying a product makes customers aware of it, which in turn makes it easier for a company to acquire prime shelf space.

3. Marketing mindset: Alignment and Accountability

These two factors are important in ensuring that the marketing division generates value for customers, companies, and communities that exceed its costs, and that stakeholders' interests are continually served.

4. Marketing dynamics: Activation and Adjustments

Activation and Adjustments relate to overcoming customer and marketing inertia. They are about getting customers to act once marketers have crafted a value proposition that they know to be in customers' best interests, and ensuring that success does not lead to complacency.

The original 4A's reside at the heart of this expanded framework, and remain quantifiable. The additional A's are essentially qualitative in nature.

ORGANIZATIONAL ISSUES

No doubt, organizational questions arise for companies looking to implement the 4A framework. In essence, the 4A's represent a set of generic marketing objectives. Which begs the question: Who is responsible for measuring and managing the company's performance in regard to each of the A's? The answer is not always clear. Some activities are product-specific (those contributing to Acceptability and Affordability), while others often leverage corporate assets (those impacting Availability and Awareness). Perhaps brand managers should be responsible for the former, while general managers or the CMO handles the latter.

Regardless of who takes ultimate responsibility for leveraging the 4A's framework, companies should require *all* functional managers to do an "impact assessment" of their decisions and actions on *each* of the A's, not just the one that is most closely aligned with their functional domain. Thus, product managers would be asked to assess the impact of their actions on Affordability, Accessibility, and Awareness, in addition to Acceptability.

Ideally, companies should appoint individuals whose job it is to monitor the levels of the 4A's and ensure consistency and coordination across the various functional areas impacting each A.

CONCLUSION

Of all the business functions, marketing needs to be the most dynamic, as it deals with multiple changes on a continual basis. Marketing must keep pace with demographic changes, cultural shifts, new economic realities, and the impact of new technologies. A marketing team that isn't adapting is probably failing.

Unfortunately, the marketing function has remained far too static over time. Most businesses have not adequately adjusted to the changing requirements for business success and for customer loyalty. They have continued to focus excessively on internal goals and constraints, and not enough on what it truly takes to succeed with customers.

Equally important, the marketing function has consumed a large and growing proportion of society's resources without producing sufficient benefits for customers, companies, and society. Being able to spend marketing resources in a more effective way is a classic case of "less is more." Lower spending can be accompanied by better results all around. What's not to like?

As we have tried to show, the 4A framework presents a deceptively simple but powerful way to think about marketing. It is a framework that forces companies to continually see the world through the customer's eyes, no matter what the issue. Do this, and more likely than not, the company will anticipate and better satisfy the customer's needs, and the customer will reward the company.

The "Market Value Coverage" (MVC) Audit

The 4A's measure marketing actions from the perspective of the customer. Initially, we are not interested in the actions that marketing managers take, only in the effects that those actions have on customers. Therefore, it is important to try to gauge customer perceptions of the components of Market Value Coverage, rather than ask them for input on specific marketing actions. For example, rather than ask customers how often they have seen an ad for a product, we should determine the level of Awareness about the product that the customer has, regardless of whether that Awareness was achieved through advertising, word-of-mouth, or simple exposure to retail displays of the product. Once a marketing manager determines that the level of Awareness is unacceptably low, he or she may then deploy one or more marketing levers in order to raise it.

A second important point is that marketers should not impose a priori constraints on how the customer defines each element of MVC. Clearly, all four components must be present for a customer to make a purchase or continue a relationship. However, the elements that constitute each element may differ considerably across customers. For example, some customers may focus solely on functional attributes when considering Acceptability, while another may almost entirely disregard those and focus instead on experiential factors. By asking summary questions (such as those below) as well as detailed questions, we should be able to determine the extent to which this is the case.

FIGURE A.1 Overall Assessment of Each of the 4A's

Acceptability: This product exceeds my expectations for what I am looking for in a product in this category, in terms of its overall quality and its capabilities. The brand has an image that makes it attractive for me. I am also pleased with the experience of purchasing and using the product.	Strongly Disagree 1 2 3 4 5 6 7 Strongly Agree
Affordability: Given my income and wealth resources, I am well able to afford to purchase this product. The price of the product is well within my budget. I also feel that it is priced fairly and represents good value. The price is in line with what I would expect for the product, given its characteristics.	Strongly Disagree 1 2 3 4 5 6 7 Strongly Agree
Accessibility: I am able to acquire the product with a reasonable amount of effort—I don't have to drive too far or wait too long before I can start using it. I also generally find that there is enough inventory of the product on hand, so that I do not have to go to different stores or get a rain check.	Strongly Disagree 1 2 3 4 5 6 7 Strongly Agree
Awareness: I know a great deal about this brand—about its characteristics, strengths, and shortcomings. I also have a strong interest in this product category, and have a high level of familiarity with several products in the category. The category has a high level of personal relevance for me.	Strongly Disagree 1 2 3 4 5 6 7 Strongly Agree

ACCEPTABILITY		
Functional	The product gives me all the features and functionality I need.	Agree—Disagree
	I believe that this product will prove to be durable and reliable.	Agree—Disagree
	This product is aesthetically appealing.	Agree—Disagree
	This product fills a need that I have.	Agree—Disagree
	This product is packaged in an attractive and convenient way.	Agree—Disagree
Psychological	The brand has an image that makes it attractive for me.	Agree—Disagree
	I am pleased with the experience of using the product.	Agree—Disagree
	I received excellent customer service with this product.	Agree—Disagree
	The product is a delight—fun and easy to use.	Agree—Disagree
	I don't feel there is any real risk in using this product.	Agree—Disagree
AFFORDABILITY		
Ability to Pay	Given my resources, I am well able to afford to purchase this product.	Agree—Disagree
	The price of the product is well within my budget.	Agree—Disagree
	I can afford this product with the right financing.	Agree—Disagree
	My net worth is sufficient to afford this product.	Agree—Disagree
	My income will rise rapidly enough to afford this product now.	Agree—Disagree
Willingness to Pay	The price of this product is in line with what I would expect.	Agree—Disagree
	This product is priced fairly.	Agree—Disagree
	This product represents great value ("bang for the buck").	Agree—Disagree
	I would be more likely to buy this product if the price were lower.	Agree—Disagree
	I have better uses for my money right now.	Agree—Disagree

Continued Overleaf

FIGURE A.1 *Continued*

		ACCESSIBILITY	
Availability		This product is usually in stock at my favorite store.	Agree—Disagree
		There is a wide choice of functions and features.	Agree—Disagree
		I am able to find related products and services in the same place.	Agree—Disagree
		I am able to use the product when I want to (capacity at peak usage).	Agree—Disagree
		There is no shortage of this product in the market.	Agree—Disagree
Convenience		I am able to acquire the product with a reasonable amount of effort.	Agree—Disagree
		I don't have to drive too far or wait too long before I can start using it.	Agree—Disagree
		I can get all the help I need (delivery, installation, training, etc.).	Agree—Disagree
		The product is easy to find in the store.	Agree—Disagree
		Store personnel are knowledgeable about the product.	Agree—Disagree
		AWARENESS	
Brand Awareness		I am very familiar with this brand.	Agree—Disagree
		I know what this brand and the company behind it stand for.	Agree—Disagree
		I can describe several characteristics of this brand.	Agree—Disagree
		I can tell you the "tagline" used for this brand.	Agree—Disagree
		I have discussed this brand with my friends.	Agree—Disagree
Product Knowledge		I have a strong interest in this product category.	Agree—Disagree
		I am very familiar with several products and brands in the category.	Agree—Disagree
		The category has a high level of personal relevance for me.	Agree—Disagree
		I read everything I can about this product category.	Agree—Disagree
		My friends often ask me for advice about products in this category.	Agree—Disagree

Mini Cases

AMAZON KINDLE AND SONY PRS 500 READER

Books have occupied a central place in the development of human civilization. Since ancient times, they have been the containers that housed human knowledge. However, they remain expensive to produce and cumbersome to distribute. The economics of the book business are such that most of the revenues generated are absorbed by overhead and intermediaries, with authors getting only 10–15 percent. Just as music and movies are rapidly moving toward digitization, many expect that books too will become more of a pure content business, disaggregated from their physical form. However, all attempts at launching e-book readers thus far have been considered failures, and e-books still account for only a tiny fraction of books sold. E-book readers were first introduced around 1999. For example, Sony launched its $900 Bookman around that time—a device that weighed two pounds, measured 7 inches × 2 inches × 6 inches and was designed to read books from CDs. Not surprisingly, the product was a total failure.[1]

Amazon.com has already revolutionized the sale and distribution of books and countless other products. Now, Jeff Bezos, the company's founder and CEO, wants to fundamentally transform the book business. He wants to make the distribution of books far more efficient and effective than it currently is. From the reader's perspective, he wants to make books more acceptable (through value added features), affordable (through significantly lower prices), and accessible (readers can instantly download books to their reader as soon as they want them). The Kindle took three years to develop and was launched in late 2007.

Acceptability: The Kindle did well on functional acceptability, but suffered (at least initially) in terms of psychological acceptability. Functionally, the Kindle offers readers a large capacity (initially 200 books, now up to 3500), a clear and sharp e-ink display that requires no backlight and consumes very little power, and access to a wireless network that permits instant downloading of a large and growing number of titles. Text can be displayed in multiple sizes, and the battery lasts for weeks and can be recharged in a couple of hours. The Kindle could play MP3 files, and also "read" the text of a book to the listener. The device was lightweight and slim, and did not require users to synch with a computer to download and manage their books. On the psychological/emotional side, the device did have some drawbacks. It lacked a color screen, and was thus not suitable for viewing illustrated books. Most significantly, it required readers to break a habit that is by now deeply engrained in our psyches—the act of physically holding a book and reading from paper.

Affordability: The Kindle was launched with a price of $399; the second generation device sold for $189. The price for the content is generally low ($10 for most books, including bestsellers, and $0.99 to $1.99 for blogs and magazines). There is no cost associated with the wireless network, which gives users direct access to Wikipedia and other sites. Given the lower price of books, the typical reader can expect to break even in about two years. One measure of value: as of February 2008, the going rate for a Kindle on eBay was $700, indicating a high willingness to pay.

Accessibility: Amazon struggled to keep up with demand for the Kindle after it was launched, constrained in part by the availability of the e-ink screens. With the launch of the Kindle 2 in February 2009, demand continued to outstrip supply. In terms of access to content, readers have instant access to a rapidly growing catalog of books, magazines, newspapers, and blogs.

Awareness: Amazon promoted the Kindle heavily on its website, and the product received significant publicity in the media (for example, Jeff Bezos and the Kindle were featured on the cover of *Newsweek* in the November 26, 2007 issue). There have been a huge number of blogs, reviews, discussion boards, and YouTube videos about the Kindle. The lack of retail distribution initially meant that most buyers had to purchase the device without actually experiencing it first—a significant drawback for many potential buyers.

Overall, the Kindle's prospects look fairly bright, especially in comparison to its primary competitor, Sony's PRS 500 Reader. That device was a little cheaper than the Kindle ($299) and was available at physical retail outlets such as Best Buy and Costco. However, the Kindle shines when it comes to access to titles and its wireless network.

APPLE IPOD VS. MICROSOFT ZUNE VS. CREATIVE NOMAD JUKEBOX ZEN

This is a tale of three products from three companies—a pioneer, a fast follower, and a late follower. The pioneer was Creative Labs, the fast follower Apple, and the late follower Microsoft. The category: portable music players. Of the three, only Apple's iPod has been an unqualified success, with over 70 percent market share.

Microsoft and Creative Labs each have market shares in the low single digits. How did this happen? In a nutshell, the early entrant Creative Labs focused heavily on functional acceptability but not adequately on psychological acceptability. The late entrant Microsoft Zune failed to offer superior value over the incumbent iPod, and also failed by comparison on psychological acceptability.[2]

Music formats have evolved rapidly over the past 50 years, from spool tapes to vinyl records to cassette tapes to CDs. With the growth of computing and networking technologies since the 1990s, the medium of music has shifted rapidly away from tangible "records" purchased in music stores to electronic formats that can be purchased and downloaded instantaneously over the web. These formats have given birth to a new type of music device: a portable player that could hold vast quantities of music and thus allow music lovers to carry their entire collection with them at all times.

The pioneer in this business was a little known player known as "MPMan," which was launched in 1997. This was soon supplanted by the Creative Nomad line of players, offered by a company that had established itself as a leader in sound card technology for personal computers. Creative dominated the small but growing market until 2001, when Apple launched its first iPod. The greatest difference between the offerings was in their psychological acceptability. Simply put, Creative had a clunky looking product that was functionally superior but had a very weak uncool image. The product was primarily advertised in computer magazines and seemed to be aimed at so-called computer geeks—not heavy consumers of cutting edge music. Apple, on the other hand, capitalized on its already hip image to position the iPod as the must have music accessory for the in crowd. It leveraged its great strengths in industrial design to create a product that was incredibly sleek (especially compared to Creative's bulky hard drive-based Jukebox player) and very easy to use (adapting an interface that Creative itself had developed). Functionally, Creative managed to stay a couple of steps ahead of Apple, with better sound quality, larger storage capacities, and features such as recording capability and an FM tuner—but all to no avail. Apple's mastery of design, and its ability to generate buzz, hype, and anticipation have few equals in the world, and the company's dominance has continued to grow. By 2002, the iPod and Creative Jukebox each had about 15 percent market share; by 2004, Apple's share had shot up to 90 percent. In November 2004, Creative renamed its product Zen and launched a $100 million advertising campaign to go after the iPod's "cool" status—but to little avail. By this time, Creative had come to be seen as "me too" player—a cheap imitator in a market that it had created. By 2008, Creative's market share was down to 2 percent.

As it has done in many product categories, Microsoft sought to make a successful late entry into the portable music business with its Zune player, launched in 2007. However, it too failed against the Apple juggernaut of coolness and continuous improvement. Microsoft launched what was essentially a parity product with no price advantage over the iPod. While the Zune was functionally quite acceptable (despite some glitches in its online store), it came nowhere close to matching Apple on psychological acceptability. In contrast with Apple's iconically hip and memorable advertising, Microsoft used a campaign that featured claymation blobs with one eyeball. The ads did not feature any music and failed to illustrate what the Zune actually is.

Apple's tremendous strengths in creating a very high level of psychological acceptability and high willingness to pay have been supplanted in recent years by the tremendous success of its new retail stores. These have helped to strengthen Apple's Accessibility and its Awareness among prospective customers. Microsoft has announced its intention to also open retail stores; however, they are highly unlikely to have the same impact on the business that Apple's stores have had.

CA$HÉ

Cottage Software (subsequently known as Business Matters) introduced a new financial analysis and modeling tool named Ca$hé in 1995. The advantage of Ca$hé over existing tools such as Ronstadt's Financials was that it was to be built on top of the newly popular Windows operating system, employing a Graphical User Interface and offering highly detailed modeling and reporting capabilities.[3]

Ca$hé was built using Visual Basic 3 (VB3), at the time a relatively new programming language developed by Microsoft. VB3 enabled software developers to generate user interface screens relatively quickly. Ca$hé enabled users to readily model every facet of a business: sales, operating expenses, non-operating expenses, salaries, benefits, cost of goods sold, and so on. It incorporated "Assumption Editors" which enabled users to drill down into specific areas. While VB3 was a good choice for screen design, it suffered from poor execution speed and had problems recognizing other Microsoft applications on a user's machine. These problems proved to be serious obstacles to the product's success.

Ca$hé Version 1 was launched in 1995 for $995. Over the next year, the company introduced incremental improvements with bug fixes, and tested a range of prices, with the lowest being $495. The product was initially available only from Business Matters, with a small number of third party distributors added in 1996. The product was promoted using "mail drops" and cold calls by the sales department. Some advertisements were run in *Inc.* magazine and in airline in-flight magazines.

The product was a complete failure in the market; only a few hundred copies were ever sold. By early 1997, the company was out of business. The offering suffered from problems with each of the A's.

Acceptability: Positioned as "Quicken for Executives," Ca$hé offered very sophisticated functionality that far exceeded that offered by Ronstadt's Financials.

However, despite its GUI, the program was too complicated and bewildering for small companies with very small financial staffs. For medium and large companies, the program was woefully underpowered. Ca$hé was not expandable or customizable in any way. It had no macros, no internal database system, and not much capability to import or export data. Many small customers were content with using Microsoft Excel models that they customized in ways they found useful. Given that Ca$hé failed to hit the sweet spot for small, medium, or large businesses, its Acceptability rated very low—perhaps only 1 percent of all potential customers.

Affordability: The price was seen as too high by small companies (which typically had IT budgets of $2500 or less per year) and too low for medium and large companies. These companies preferred to buy larger, customizable packages that included consulting. Business Matters did not offer any consulting or other ancillary services. Affordability can thus be rated as only about 10 percent.

Accessibility: Ca$hé was initially available only directly from Business Matters. The company made no attempt to sell directly to small businesses at retail stores such as CompUSA. The World Wide Web boom was just getting underway in 1995–1996. The company eventually produced a four screen home page. This exposure was simultaneously too early (there were very few Internet users) and too late (the company was close to collapse by then). The company's sales department also did a mail drop of tens of thousands of postcards and letters using mailing lists purchased from third party vendors. However, the response rate was extremely low, with only one customer query for every 200–300 mailed items. Since only a small minority of inquiries resulted in sales orders, this channel proved highly ineffective.

Awareness: The company did very little advertising in then-popular computer and industry magazines, and also did not receive much publicity. Most potential customers did not know what the product was, what it could do and how they could use it.

Ca$hé was thus a product that had no customers, no market, and no future. It was too feature-rich, complex, and costly for small businesses. It was too feature-poor, lacking in interoperability, and had no consulting service component for medium and large companies. It could not be customized for users in different industries (e.g. tire manufacturers have very different financial models from fast-food companies). Despite venture capital investments of $10 million, only $500,000 or less of sales ever ensued, and the company had to close its doors by 1997.

EXUBERA

Diabetics have been using insulin as a critical therapy to manage their blood sugar levels for over 80 years. While insulin production and treatment options have advanced over these years, the fundamental mode of delivery has not. Diabetics must administer subcutaneous or "under the skin" injections for the insulin to take effect.[4]

In January 2006, the US Food and Drug Administration and the European Medicines Agency approved the first inhalable insulin product. Exubera Inhalation Powder, developed by Nektar and marketed by Pfizer, allows diabetics to do without syringes, needles, pens, and insulin pumps. Instead, Exubera is delivered and absorbed through the lungs. Analysts predicted that Pfizer would generate billions in revenue from Exubera, primarily from newly diagnosed sufferers and patients who were uncomfortable with injections. However, the product was discontinued after little over a year having generated sales of only $12 million, and Pfizer had to take an enormous charge of $2.8 billion because of the failure. The failure also cost Pfizer in terms of damaged external relationships and loss of reputation. The reasons why such a seemingly promising treatment option failed can be clearly understood by using 4A analysis.[5]

Acceptability: There are many tried and true methods of insulin delivery. Needle size had dropped dramatically over the years, so that patients experience little or no pain. The development of insulin pens had made injecting insulin even less painful. Patients as well as physicians thus had many issues with Exubera's functional value. Because it was absorbed through the lungs, it excluded patients suffering from any kind of lung disease. Furthermore, even for users with healthy lungs, there was a risk of decreased lung capacity and other complications. Users were required to undergo regular pulmonary testing, which was an added expense and inconvenience. Another functional issue was the dosing: Exubera was available in dosages of 3 or 9 milligrams, which is not what doctors were used to. Inserting packets of powder into the device was difficult to do, especially for elderly patients who represented a large proportion of the target market. The inhaler itself was huge—the size of a can of tennis balls—and using it did not provide the level of discreet treatment that patients might have responded to. It was too bulky to carry around readily, especially for men who do not carry purses. Contrast this with a traditional asthma inhaler, which is small and discrete.

Affordability: Exubera was priced at a 30 percent premium, or about $2–3 a day more than injectable insulin. This additional $60–90 monthly cost was a lot to bear, especially since users have to use it for the rest of their lives. Given its higher price and lack of therapeutic advantage, many insurers refused to cover it, or if they did, imposed a higher co-payment for it.

Accessibility: While the product was readily available, it did require a prescription, and most doctors were very reluctant to prescribe it to their patients for all the reasons cited in the Acceptability analysis above.

Awareness: Pfizer initially focused all of its marketing efforts toward physicians, with the result that nearly 90 percent of doctors had a medium to high Awareness of the drug. Physicians were not enthusiastic about the product, viewing it as "old wine in new bottles." This was because Exubera did not provide any therapeutic benefits to users. Pfizer failed to educate other healthcare professionals such as nurses and certified diabetes educators, who have a great deal of face time with patients and could spread Awareness with them. Exubera did receive a great deal of industry and Wall Street buzz, but Pfizer did not do much to directly educate patients. In June 2007, a year after the product was introduced, Pfizer launched a Direct to Consumer (DTC) marketing campaign. However, this was a case of too little, too late. The campaign did not accurately depict the product; it did not show the actual size of the unit, and did not emphasize its needle-free aspect.

Nektar Therapeutics partnered with Pfizer largely because of its superior marketing abilities, which would be able to take a niche product and make it a mainstream blockbuster success. However, Pfizer apparently made its own assumptions about what the market wanted, rather than trying to truly understand the needs and priorities of patients.

NINTENDO WII

Approximately 25 years after it launched the breakthrough Nintendo Entertainment System, Nintendo created another sensation when it launched the peculiarly named Nintendo Wii game system in late 2006. Unlike rival offerings from its two main competitors, Sony and Microsoft, the Wii proved to be an immediate and spectacular success. The reasons for this are not hard to understand, given a 4A analysis.[5]

With the launch of Microsoft's Xbox 360 in Fall 2005, the fifth "next generation console battle" was on. Market leader Sony launched its long anticipated PS3 on November 11, 2006, and Nintendo followed with the Wii eight days later. The PS3 was a technological wonder, studded with cutting edge technology such as highly sophisticated processors and a Blue-Ray high definition disk drive.

Acceptability: The Acceptability of an offering includes its functional acceptability, which examines how well and consistently a product serves its principal function, and psychological acceptability, which refers to sensory enjoyment, attainment of desired mode states, achievement of social goals, and self-concept fulfillment. Nintendo made a brilliant decision in designing the Wii so that it would appeal to a much broader audience than game systems typically do. As the CEO of the company stated, "We are not competing against Sony or Microsoft. We are battling the indifference of people who have no interest in video games." In addition to appealing to gaming diehards waiting to play the latest Super Mario Brothers or Legend of Zelda games, the console is designed to appeal to many first-time players such as women and older customers who do not typically play video games. Because of its unique interface design, the Wii allows for far more active and natural involvement by players, and has proven to have many positive health benefits. It has even been used to help injured patients regain their range of motion. Clearly, the Wii has succeeded in achieving one of the key objectives Nintendo had for it: to expand the market for video games. They did so by focusing on functional appeal over raw processing or display power. The most innovative aspect of the Wii is its unique wireless controller, which uses an infrared motion sensor that adds a physical dimension to gaming. The console itself is small, quiet, and quick and easy to operate. It is backward compatible with GameCube games, and can connect wirelessly with Nintendo's popular DS handheld gaming system. Its wireless capabilities include the "WiiConnect24" online network that downloads updates while in sleep mode, and includes channels for news, weather, shopping, social networking, and game play with remote users. The network also enables players to create a Virtual Console; for a low price, users can download classic games going back to the original NES system of the 1980s.

Affordability: The Wii is far more affordable to users as well as the company than the Xbox 360 or the PS3. In the US, the Wii retailed for $249, compared with $299–399 for Xbox 360 and $499–599 for the PS3. Not only was the Wii cheaper to buy, it was also much cheaper to make. It was estimated that Microsoft was losing $126 on each unit it sold, while Sony was losing $300 per unit. Nintendo, by contrast, was making a $92 profit on each unit sold! Games for the Wii cost $2 million–5 million to develop and are sold at $49, while games for the other systems cost $10 million–30 million to develop and sold for $59. The Wii offered a better "out of the box" experience, including a Wii Sports game and a WiiMote with fresh batteries.

Accessibility: Nintendo was caught off guard by the intense demand for its new console, and there were long lines to buy the unit even seven months after it was launched. By the end of 2007, Nintendo had sold 20.13 million units, and had to pull its ads in Europe because of continued supply shortages.

Awareness: Nintendo announced the Revolution (as it was known then) at the E3 conference in 2005, without providing many details. At E3 in 2006, Nintendo began to demonstrate the WiiMote playing style, and received the critics' awards for "Best in Show" and "Best Hardware." The company built on the huge buzz that had already been created around its new console by launching a $200 million North American ad campaign with the theme of "Experience a New Way to Play."

Nintendo's ability to think outside the box has paid rich dividends for the company. By getting all the A's right, the company has created tremendous value for itself as well as for its customers.

SLINGBOX

Many of the most successful products in history have been created as a direct result of customer frustration. Products that are able to address the source of this frustration have a built-in advantage of high Acceptability. One such product is the

Slingbox by Sling Media. In this case, the cause of customer frustration was an inability to access local programming while being out of the home. The founders are avid sports fans, and came up with the idea of "place shifting" technology when they were trying to follow their hometown San Francisco Giants as they made a run for the baseball post season.

Acceptability: The simple but compelling value proposition for the Slingbox is the ability to access locally subscribed to content from anywhere with a high speed Internet connection. In addition to allowing live access to all the channels available at home, various versions of the device also give access to content stored on a user's DVR. In essence, it is like having access to your living room TV from anywhere in the world. Content can be viewed on a computer monitor or on a mobile phone. The device is simple to set up and easy to use. Its unique brick-like shape and size make it distinctive and unobtrusive at the same time.

Affordability: Slingbox offers three distinct products, ranging in list price from $129 to $229. There are no recurring fees associated with using the device. The device is thus highly affordable to most potential customers, costing little more than a month's cable bill. For customers who travel a great deal, the value proposition is very strong; by having access to their own programming in their hotel room, they save time (hunting for a bar that carries their game), energy (finding a place to sit/stand and watch), and money (transportation plus food and drinks).

Accessibility: Slingbox is available online as well as through a wide range of retailers such as Best Buy, Sears, Wal-Mart, and Office Depot. Within stores, the device is usually displayed next to networking hardware, rather than with television sets. The company has managed to keep up with consumer demand, and setting up the device does not require much technical knowledge or expertise.

Awareness: Slingbox created a new category of offering, and it has taken potential customers some time to understand the value proposition. Within a short amount of time, both the product concept and the brand name have become well known.

THE MOTOROLA ROKR

In the summer of 2004, Motorola and Apple made a much anticipated announcement: the launch of the first cell phone that would be compatible with Apple's wildly successful iTunes music store. This was to be Apple's first foray into cell phones, and was meant to head off competition from a new generation of music-enabled cell phones. The product was released amid much hype and high expectations in September 2005. However, it was roundly panned by customers and critics alike, and sales were very disappointing. The reasons for the failure become evident through the lens of 4A analysis.[6]

Acceptability: The functional acceptability of the ROKR was very low, especially with regard to its music capabilities. The phone had a storage limit of 100 songs, which was well below what most customers wanted; a study by the Diffusion Group found that users between the ages of 15 and 24 wanted an average of 335 songs on their music-enabled cell phones. Customers could not download songs directly onto the phone; they had to download to a computer and then synch the phone with the computer. Download speed was extremely slow: 0.12 MB per second, compared to 1.38 MB for the iPod Shuffle and 7.49 MB for the iPod Photo. The ROKR's psychological acceptability was low as well. Both companies were known for their product design, embodied in Apple's distinctive and diminutive iPods and Motorola's smash hit ultra-thin RAZR phones. However, the ROKR was a bulky, brick-like device based on an earlier Motorola phone, and its music performance was criticized for being slow and counter-intuitive.

Affordability: The ROKR debuted at $249 with a minimum two-year contract, which was high in comparison to other offerings. Because of its limited song capacity, the ROKR could not replace an iPod; customers would need to own both devices, making the ROKR economically unaffordable. Another factor contributing to this was that buyers would have to break existing contracts and pay early termination fees to purchase the ROKR right away. The psychological affordability of the ROKR was also low. Most potential customers already owned a cell phone and a portable music device. The high price for a hybrid device that was inferior in both respects made most buyers unwilling to pay the price.

Accessibility: The ROKR was released exclusively through Cingular, thus limiting its availability to a small segment of cell phone users.

Awareness: The ROKR garnered extensive publicity and breathless anticipation before its release. Most potential customers were familiar with the category as well as with both brands. However, Apple provided only a lukewarm introduction to the product when it was launched. The ROKR was introduced at an invitation-only event hosted by Steve Jobs, the iconic CEO of Apple. At the event, Jobs focused more on the redesigned iPod Nano (describing it as the "biggest revolution since the original iPod") while referring to the ROKR as "pretty cool."

In retrospect, it appears that Apple withheld its design "crown jewels" from the ROKR effort, saving them for the iPhone, which would launch to tremendous hoopla and sales success a couple of years later. Had Apple been truly committed to the success of the ROKR, it would not have crippled it in the ways that it did. Given the limitations of the product, it was doomed to fail from the beginning.

THE SWIFFER

In developing new products, most companies look to create something completely new and innovative. However, there are many opportunities to take existing "mature" products and rejuvenate or "demature" them through rethinking their value proposition to customers. One such product is the lowly mop.[7]

Procter & Gamble (P&G) is one of the world's leading producers of consumer products, with a broad range of offerings that includes numerous billion dollar brands such as Always, Bounty, Charmin, Crest, Dawn, Duracell, Gillette, Olay, Pampers, and Tide. In the mid-1990s, P&G made a decision to develop a new billion dollar brand in its Fabric Care/Home Care business segment. The result of this effort was a unique new cleaning tool, a specialty mop that did not require a bucket or a dust pan: the Swiffer.

More than a standalone mop, the Swiffer is a cleaning system that includes a versatile, lightweight sweeper and dry, disposable cleaning cloths that are attached to the sweeper and can be used to clean floors, ceilings, furniture, electronics—any dry surface that needs cleaning. The uniqueness of the system comes in part from the fibers in the Swiffer cloth, which create an electrostatic charge when wiped across surfaces. The charge attracts dirt, dust, and crumbs into the cloth, where Lift and Lock Pockets™ trap and hold it. The Swiffer WetJet for wet mopping is a variation that required bringing together technologies from several different business units: absorbency technology from the diaper business, top sheet and one-way liquid transfer technology from the feminine care business, and surfactants and hard surface cleaners from the chemistry business. The result of all this sophisticated technology applied to a humdrum household cleaning utensil: a wildly successful product that has customers gushing with praise. The Swiffer is one of the few cleaning products in the world that actually inspires love on the part if its users!

Acceptability: The Swiffer provides great functionality and handily exceeds customer expectations. Customers have been "blown away" by its ease of use and its cleaning performance ever since the product was launched. The buzz started even before the product was launched; market testing results were so positive that people started calling P&G to find out how and when they could buy a Swiffer. In addition to basic cleaning, the Swiffer allowed people to clean ceiling fans, support beams, under the refrigerator, window blinds—all without leaving behind a residue of dirt like traditional mops do.

Affordability: The Swiffer's superior cleaning performance combined with the psychosocial effects of saving time and eliminating many other cleaning tools demonstrated a clear value proposition to users. It allows people to throw away their feather dusters, brooms, mops, and buckets. The Swiffer Sweeper Complete Kit retails for $20, and a 32 pack of Swiffer cleaning cloths costs about $23. The value proposition relies heavily on convenience and time saving, which makes people not only willing but happy to pay the price.

Accessibility: P&G enjoys a tremendous reputation and long-standing relationships with its distribution partners. It was able to leverage this to obtain ideal shelf placement for the Swiffer, in stores ranging from discount merchandisers, hardware stores, home improvement stores, grocery stores, and even drug chains. It is also available online through Amazon and other outlets. The mop is collapsible and fits in a small box. The cloth refill packaging is compact and fits easily under the sink, and the coloring of the refill packages matches the color of the core product, making refill purchases easier.

Awareness: P&G is the biggest and in many ways the savviest advertiser in the US. With the Swiffer, it did not need to advertise as much as it does for other new product launches because of the great word-of-mouth that the product generated. The Swiffer almost instantly became a "cult" brand, with celebrities such as Jessica Simpson posing with the product on the covers of magazines. The product received the ultimate badge of cultural mainstreaming when it was spoofed on *Saturday Night Live*.

The Swiffer line of products has been broadened to include the Sweeper+Vac, Swiffer Dusters, and Swiffer WetJet. The Swiffer brand now generates between $500 million and $1 billion in annual revenues, and has created a new and highly successful category for the company.

Notes

Introduction

1 Kevin J. Clancy and Randy L. Stone (2005), "Don't Blame the Metrics," *Harvard Business Review*, June.

2 Frederick E. Webster, Jr., Alan J. Malter, and Shankar Ganesan (2003), "Can Marketing Regain a Seat at the Table?," MSI Report No. 03-003, Cambridge, MA: Marketing Science Institute, pp. 29–49.

3 A fifth role is that of "evangelizers." Companies don't simply want customers to use the product—they want them to recommend it to others. As we will discuss, this helps spread awareness and fits in with the "seeker" role played by other potential customers.

Chapter 1

1 Research paper by Elizabeth Papp, Bentley University, October 18, 2010.

2 Research paper by Elizabeth Naughton, Bentley University, October 18, 2010.

3 Jagdish N. Sheth and Rajendra S. Sisodia (1995), "Feeling the Heat," *Marketing Management*.

4 J.C. Larreche (2008), *The Momentum Effect: How to Ignite Exceptional Growth*, Wharton School Publishing.

5 Nearly 70 percent of Americans agree with the statement, "I don't know whom to trust anymore," according to a February 2002 Golin/Harris Poll.

6 J.N. Sheth, R.S Sisodia, and A. Barbulescu (2006), "The Image of Marketing With Consumers and Business Professionals," in J.N. Sheth and R.S. Sisodia (eds.), *Does Marketing Need Reform?*, M.E. Sharpe, Inc., p. 360.

7 John Philip Jones (2000), "The Mismanagement of Advertising," *Harvard Business Review*, January–February.

8 www.copernicusmarketing.com/about/six_sigma_branding.shtml

9 www.nytimes.com/2007/01/15/business/media/15everywhere.html

10 For example, see Magid M. Abraham and Leonard M. Lodish (1990), "Getting the Most Out of Advertising and Promotion," *Harvard Business Review*, May–June, Vol. 68, No. 3, 50–1, 53, 56.

11 Frederick E. Webster, Jr. (1992), "The Changing Role of Marketing in the Corporation," *Journal of Marketing*, Vol. 56, No. 4 (Oct.), pp. 1–17.

12 For a thorough review of the empirical evidence on this, see Bernard J. Jaworski and Ajay K. Kohli, "Market Orientation: Antecedents and Consequences," *Journal of Marketing*, 1993 Summer, Vol. 57, No. 3, p. 53.

13 Papers by Bentley University students Nikki Parness, Hua Ye, and Jens Kullmann, March 2005. Additional sources: www.everydayrobots.com/index.php?option=content&task=view&id=2; www.roombareview.com/roomba/roomba-review.shtml; www.onrobo.com/reviews/At_Home/Vacuum_Cleaners/on00rc3000rokac/index.htm; www.everydayrobots.com/index.php?option=content&task=view&id=5;l; Tom Harris, "How Segways Work," www.howstuffworks.com; "Milestones In Our History," www.segway.com; Dawn Kawamoto, "Human Transporter Sales Move Slowly," CNET News, March 31, 2003, www.CNET.com; "Creating Empowered Pedestrians with ANSYS Multiphysics," February 2004, www.ansys.com; Early Adopters Pick: The Segway, November 2002, www.amazon.com; Edward B. Driscoll, "Defying Gravity: The Segway in Action," *Lite Wheels Magazine*, April 2002.

14 www.itu.int/ITU-D/ict/material/FactsFigures2010.pdf

Chapter 2

1 Alan Mitchell, "Pepsi Still Losing the Cola Wars," *Marketing Week*, Apr. 12, 1996, Vol. 19, No. 3, pp. 26–27.

2 www.coca-colahbc.com/aboutus/mission.php

3 brandcoolmarketing.com/brand-misc.html#a

4 Nicole L. Mead, Roy F. Baumeister, Tyler F. Stillman, Catherine D. Rawn, and Kathleen D. Vohs. "Social Exclusion Causes People to Spend and Consume in the Service of Affiliation," *Journal of Consumer Research*, April 2011 (officially published online September 9, 2010).

5 Unfortunately, as the housing bubble also shows, people do buy things they can't "economically afford." According to the Federal Reserve and Fitch Ratings, total US consumer debt is $2.42 trillion and US credit card default rate is 13.01 percent. While marketers cannot force customers to be responsible, they must at a minimum not knowingly sell people products they clearly cannot afford. Products should be targeted toward people who can purchase them without accumulating excessive debt; in the long run, such a strategy adds to a company's reputation capital.

6 sramanamitra.com/articles/159/

7 www.jamieandersononline.com/uploads/ANDERSON_MARKIDES_SI_at_Base_of_Economic_Pyramid_FINAL.pdf; in.redhat.com/casestudies/Eveready.php3

8 Mohan Sawhney talk at Bentley College Symposium on "Does Marketing Need Reform?," August 9, 2004.

9 Mohan Sawhney, op. cit.

10 Al Ries and Laura Ries (2002), *The Fall of Advertising and the Rise of PR*, HarperCollins.

Chapter 3

1 www.automobilemag.com/reviews/convertibles/0503_ikigai_man/index.html
2 *Business Week*, August 1957.
3 Eugene Jaderquist, "Why the Edsel Will Succeed: The brains behind America's newest car are not only sure they'll sell 200,000 automobiles this year—they even know who is going to buy them," *True's Automobile Yearbook* 1958, Issue 6.
4 Based on paper by Emory MBA students Scott M. Huff, Rhett Marlow, and Keith Walker, April 2000.
5 Based on a paper by Emory MBA student Claudia Blake, April 2000.
6 Peter Golder and Gerard Tellis *Will and Vision*, 2002.
7 Gary Hamel and C.K. Prahalad, "Corporate Imagination and Expeditionary Marketing," *Harvard Business Review*.
8 Based on a paper by Emory MBA student Odilia Cohen, April 2000, and www.palm.com
9 Bruce Brown and Margo Brown, "Internet Appliances Reconsidered," *PC Magazine*, February 20, 2001, p. 61.
10 Stephen Manes, "Web Appliances: Smarter, Still Dumb," *Forbes*, January 22, 2001, p. 136.
11 www.idsa.org/whatsnew/decadegallery/winners/g-sensor.html
12 Based on a paper by Emory MBA student Stephen Autera, April 1996.
13 Cheryl Lu-Lien Tan (2005), "Reducing the Cringe Factor in Sofabeds," *Wall Street Journal*, March 31, p. D1.
14 Monte Burke (2002), "Revenge of the Nerds: MIT's Brainy Jocks Try to Build a Better Ski Boot," *Forbes*, September 16, p. 88.
15 David Pringle (2005), "Softer Cell: In Mobile Phones, Older Users Say More is Less," *Wall Street Journal*, August 15, p. A1.
16 Rajendra S. Sisodia, (1992) "Competitive Advantage Through Design", *Journal of Business Strategy*, Vol. 13, No. 6, pp. 33–40.
17 www.networkworld.com/community/node/40012
18 www.dfma.com/
19 www.ncbi.nlm.nih.gov/books/NBK45345/
20 www.suite101.com/blog/mitchkaplan1
21 seekingalpha.com/article/172981-tech-sector-does-r-d-spending-matter

Chapter 4

1 wikicars.org/en/Volkswagen_Phaeton
2 www.motorauthority.com/blog/1025163_vw-analyses-phaeton-failure-reveals-new-details-about-next-gen-model
3 en.wikipedia.org/wiki/Ford_Model_T#cite_note-3
4 www.reputationinstitute.com/webinars/2010_Global_Reputation_Pulse_Webinar_23jun2010.pdf
5 For a terrific treatment of the power and value of trust in customer relationships, see Glen Urban (2005), *Don't Just Relate—Advocate!: A Blueprint for Profit in the Era of Customer Power*, Pearson Prentice Hall.

6 Benson P. Shapiro, "What the Hell is 'Market Oriented'?," *Harvard Business Review*, November 1988.

7 Hermann Simon and Robert J. Dolan, "Price Customization," *Marketing Management*, Vol. 7, No. 3, Fall 1998, pp. 10–17.

8 Shobhana Subramaniam, "The Making of Brand Nano," *The Business Standard*, March 31, 2009.

9 www.nytimes.com/2010/12/10/business/global/10tata.html

10 www/netjets.com, accessed September 29, 2006.

11 Ron Lieber, "All of 1/8 of This Could Be Yours—Fractional Ownership Moves Beyond Jets to Include Yachts, Bentleys, Even Deluxe RVs," *Wall Street Journal*, January 19, 2000, p. D1.

12 Kate Kelly, Ethan Smith, and Peter Wonacott, "Movie, Music Giants Try New Weapon Against Pirates: Price," *Wall Street Journal*, March 7, 2005, p. B1.

13 Lendol Calder (1999), *Financing the American Dream: A Cultural History of Consumer Credit*, Princeton University Press.

14 Based in part on "Culture of Debt Was Driven by GM," aired on December 25, 2009 on Marketplace radio, marketplace.publicradio.org/display/web/2009/12/25/pm-gmac/

15 Michael Arndt, "Giving Fast Food a Run for Its Money," *BusinessWeek*, April 17, 2006, pp. 62–64.

16 Melanie Trottman, "Nuts-and-Bolts Savings—To Cut Costs, Airlines Make More of Their Own Parts," *Wall Street Journal*, May 3, 2005, p. B1.

17 Pui-Wing Tam, "Fill 'er Up, With Color—Ink-Jet Cartridge Refillers Spread to Malls, Main Streets; Going After H-P's Lifeblood," *Wall Street Journal*, August 3, 2004, p. B1.

18 Charles Forelle, "Do You Really Need a Turbo Toothbrush?" *Wall Street Journal*, October 1, 2002, p. D1.

19 Since then, Proctor and Gamble has acquired Gillette at a significant premium.

20 *The Economist*, "The Price is Wrong," May 23, 2002.

21 en.wikipedia.org/wiki/King_Camp_Gillette

22 Chris Anderson (2009), *Free: The Future of a Radical Price*, Hyperion.

23 Anderson, op. cit.

24 Anderson, op. cit.

25 Banwari Mittal and Jagdish N. Sheth (2001), *Value Space: Winning the Battle for Market Leadership*, McGraw Hill.

26 Daniel Lyons, "Bang for the Buck," *Forbes*, November 25, 2002.

27 Bruce Einhorn and Nandini Lakshman, "Nokia Connects," *BusinessWeek*, March 27, 2006, pp. 44–45.

28 Peter Engardio, "Business Prophet: How C.K. Prahalad is Changing the Way CEOs Think," *BusinessWeek*, January 23, 2006, pp. 68–73.

29 Nandini Lakshman, "Linux Spreads Its Wings in India," *BusinessWeek*, October 2, 2006, pp. 40–41.

Chapter 5

1 hbswk.hbs.edu/item/5459.html

2 www.toyota.co.jp/en/environmental_rep/03/torihiki.html

3 Stanford Business School Case GS65, "Zappos.com: Developing a Supply Chain to Deliver WOW!" by Michael E Marks, Hau L. Lee, and David Hoyt, 2009.

4 Based in part on L'eggs Products, Inc., Harvard Business School Case 575–590, by Harvey Singer and F. Stewart DeBruicker.

5 Michael V. Copeland, "Reed Hastings: Leader of the Pack," *Fortune*, December 6, 2010, pp. 121–130.

6 Based in part on Netflix, Harvard Business School Case No. 9-607-138, by Willy Shih, Stephen Kaufman, and David Spinola.

7 www.businessweek.com/magazine/content/05_41/b3954102.htm

8 Marketing to Rural India: Making the Ends Meet, knowledge.wharton.upenn.edu/india/article.cfm?articleid=4172

9 C.K. Prahalad and Mayuram S. Krishnan (2008), *The New Age of Innovation: Driving Cocreated Value Through Global Networks*, McGraw Hill Professional.

10 Chris Anderson (2006), *The Long Tail: Why the Future of Business is Selling Less of More*, Hyperion.

11 David Pogue, "The Pogies: Best Tech Ideas of the Year," *The New York Times*, December 29, 2010, accessed at www.nytimes.com/2010/12/30/technology/personaltech/30 pogue.html?pagewanted=1&ref=technology&src=me

Chapter 6

1 Based on Mark W. Cunningham and Chekitan S. Dev, "Strategic Marketing: A Lodging 'End Run'," *Cornell Hotel and Restaurant Administration Quarterly*, August 1992, Vol. 33, No. 4, pp. 36–43; Michael Totty, "Motel 6 Radio Ads Credited for Rise in Occupancy Rate," *Wall Street Journal*, May 12, 1988, p. 1, www.motel6.com

2 Based on Patricia R. Olsen, "The Secret Word Was Duck—Interview with Daniel P. Amos," *The New York Times*, June 4, 2006, p. 9; Mary Daniels, "All He's Quacked up to Be: How a Web-Footed Insurance Mascot Became One of the Most Vocal Animals in Advertising," *Knight Ridder Tribune Business News*, Feb. 21, 2006, p. 1; Laura Rich, "Big in Japan, But Mostly a Duck Here," *The New York Times*, Oct. 22, 2005. p. C3; Eleanor Trickett, "Inside the Mix," *PRweek*, Feb. 14, 2005, Vol. 8, No. 7, p. 12.

3 Chris Penttila, "Wake Up! Your Brand Isn't Your Savior, and All the Goofy Ads in the World Won't Save Your Company. What Can? Well…Have You Given Good Business a Try?," *Entrepreneur Magazine*, September 2001, www.Entrepreneur.com/article/0,4621, 291888,00.html

4 Sergio Zyman and Armin Brott (2005), *The End of Advertising as We Know It*, Hoboken, NJ: John Wiley & Sons.

5 Michael Philips, Salli Rasberry, and Diana Fitzpatrick (2005), *Marketing Without Advertising: Inspire Customers to Rave About Your Business and Create Lasting Success*, NOLO.

6 adage.com/century/people006.html

7 John Philip Jones, "The Mismanagement of Advertising," *Harvard Business Review*, January–February 2000, pp. 2–3.

8 Demetrios Vakratsas and Tim Ambler (1999), "How Advertising Works: What do We Really Know?," *Journal of Marketing*, Vol. 63, No. 1, pp. 26–43.

9 Gerard J. Tellis (2009), "Generalizations about Advertising Effectiveness in Markets," *Journal of Advertising Research*, June 2009, pp. 240–245.

10 Jenni Romaniuk, Byron Sharp, Samantha Paech, and Carl Driesener (2004), "Brand and Advertising Awareness: A Replication and Extension of a Known Empirical Generalization," *Australasian Marketing Journal*, Vol.12, Issue 3, pp. 70–80.

11 Romaniuk et al., op. cit.

12 AB and Campbell's, op. cit.

13 Emily Nelson, "Is Wet TP All Dried Up?," *Wall Street Journal*, April 15, 2002, p. B1.

14 www.edmunds.com/advice/buying/articles/42962/article.html

15 carmax.com/dyn/research/dealerpricing/games.aspx

16 jordans.com/sleeplab/buyer.asp

Chapter 7

1 Rajendra K. Srivastava, Tasadduq A. Shervani, and Liam Fahey (1998), "Market-Based Assets and Shareholder Value: A Framework for Analysis," *Journal of Marketing*, Vol. 62, No. 1 (Jan.), pp. 2–18.

2 Barry M. Staw (1976), "Knee Deep in the Big Muddy: A Study of Escalating Commitment to a Chosen Course of Action," *Organizational Behavior and Human Performance*, Vol. 16, No. 1 (June), pp. 27–44.

3 Russell L. Ackoff and James R. Emshoff (1975), "Advertising Experiments at Anheuser-Busch," *Sloan Management Review*, Vol. 16, No. 2 (Winter), pp. 1–16.

4 Joseph O. Eastlack, Jr. and Ambar G. Rao. (1989), "Advertising Experiments at the Campbell Soup Company," *Marketing Science*, Vol. 8, No. 1, pp. 57–71.

5 "Levi Strauss—Not by Jeans Alone," Enterprise series video, 1985.

6 Philip Kotler has written extensively about demand management, most recently in the book *Kotler on Marketing: How to Create, Win and Dominate Markets*, The Free Press, 1999.

Appendix B

1 Based on papers by Brigid Considine and Sharat Kumar; Renee H. Callahan, "Amazon Kindle vs. Sony Reader," *Forbes.com*, January 29, 2008; Carl Howe, "The Kindle Book Reader: What Were Amazon's Marketers Thinking?" *Blackfriars*, November 20, 2007; and Stephen Levy, "Gadgets: The Constant Reader," *Newsweek*, October 23, 2006.

2 Based on papers by Matthew Karlsson and Ryan Donnelly; Eliot Van Buskirk, "Introducing the World's First MP3 Player," CNET http://reviews.cnet.com/4520-6450_7-5622055-1.html, 01/21/2005; and Leander Kahney, "Straight Dope on the iPod's Birth," *Wired Magazine*, October 17, 2006.

3 Based on a paper by Steve Paris.

4 Based on papers by Melissa Cortina, Melissa Payer and Tricia Paruti; Carl Gutierrez, "Pfizer Washes Its Hands of Exubera." *Forbes, Market Scan*, October 18, 2007; Avery Johnson, "Insulin Flop Costs Pfizer $2.8 Billion." *Wall Street Journal*, October 19, 2007; Steve Johnson, "Did Pfizer's marketing fizzle with Exubera?" *San Jose Mercury News*, August 31, 2007; John Simons, "How the Exubera debacle hurts Pfizer," *Fortune*,

October 19, 2007; Arlene Weintraub, "Pfizer's Exubera Flop." *Business Week*, October 18, 2007; and Arlene Weintraub, "Pfizer's Exuberant Ad Rollout." *Business Week*, July 24, 2007.

5   Based on papers by Jeffrey Hannigan and Ben Beaty; Kevin P. Casey, "Nintendo Hopes Wii Spells Wiinner," *USA Today*, August 15, 2006; Kenji Hall, "The Big Ideas Behind Nintendo's Wii," *Business Week*, November 16, 2006; Mariko Sanchata, "Nintendo's Wii Takes Console Lead," *Financial Times*, September 12, 2007; and Nick Wingfield and Yukari Iwatani Kane, "Wii and DS Turn Also-Ran Nintendo into Winner in Videogames Business," *Wall Street Journal*, April 19, 2007.

6   Based on a paper by Joseph Sicree; Kevin Fitchard, "Industry Sounds off about Motorola's New Music Phone" *Telephony*, September 19, 2005: 10-11; Laurie J. Flynn, "The Cellphone's Next Makeover: Affordable Jukebox on the Move" *New York Times*, August 2, 2004: C4; Peter Lewis, "Moto's ROKR is a STINKR," *Fortune*, October 3, 2005: 170–171; and Bruce Nussbaum, "Is ROKR Missing that Special "Magic"?" *Business Week*, October 20, 2005.

7   Based on a paper by Bill Kracunas; Karl Greenberg, "P&G Invites Consumer Videos in Swiffer Cross-Promo," *Media Post's Marketing Daily*, January 10, 2008; and Wendy Widmen, "A Witch's Broom Spells Big Profits," *Forbes*, August 2, 2005.

Index